協作的藝術：
領導者如何影響團體成長

The Art of Facilitation:
Discovery of the Group Growth Process

協作的藝術 The Art of Facilitation

Copyright © 2021 by Steve Haines
© 2021 史蒂夫. 海恩斯

All rights reserved. No part of this publication may be reproduced, distributed, or transmitted in any form or by any means, including photocopying, recording, or other electronic or mechanical methods, without the prior written permission of the author, except in the case of brief quotations embodied in critical reviews and certain other non-commercial uses permitted by copyright law. For permission requests, write to the author at the address below.

本書所有著作權及版權為作者所有。未經作者書面許可，本書任何內容不得以任何電子或機械形式或透過任何管道予以複製、抄襲、轉載或轉播，只除了著作權法允許，以報導評論為目的或其他非商業性使用之簡短摘錄。欲徵求書面許可，請循下方提供之通訊地址聯絡作者。

First Printed in the United States of America in 2021
ISBN (print book): 978-1-7348772-2-9
ISBN (digital book): 978-1-7348772-3-6

Steve Haines, President/CEO
Global Education and Cultural Alliance Consultants
P.O. Box 304, Jamison, Pennsylvania 18929, U.S.A.
Web: www.Advantage-USA.org
Email: Advantage-USA@comcast.net

獻給每一位曾以無私的工作提高了另一個孩子的人生的人，
我向你致敬。

To anyone who ever worked selflessly to improve the life of another child,
I salute you.

獻給每一位經意或不經意教育我的人，我讚美並感謝你。

To anyone who had to teach me, I commend and thank you.

獻給唐.馬丁代爾，你改變了我一生的方向和目的地。祝福你。

To Don Martindale, you changed the direction and destination of my life.
Bless you.

目錄
Table of Contents

引言	6
Introduction	
引導的藝術	10
The Art of Facilitation	
保持好奇心	27
Be Curious	
團隊變革的挑戰	36
The Challenges of Group Change	
It 要素	54
The "It" Factor	
我的課堂很無聊嗎？	67
Is My Classroom Boring?	
動機的魔力	88
The Magic of Motivation	
勇氣、膽量還是運氣？	104
Grit, Cuts or Luck?	
目的地 vs. 方向	116
Destination vs. Direction	
教學生面對失敗——建立情商	133
Teaching Students to Fail – Building EQ	
學校需要智商，人生需要情商	165
IQ for School, But EQ for Life	
預備，開火，瞄準	190
Ready, Fire, Aim	

你打算什麼時候挑戰自己？ When Are You Going to Challenge Yourself?	**196**
結論 Conclusion	**208**
額外材料 Bonus Material	**215**
關於作者 About the Author	**242**
附加值獎勵：耐心計劃 Added Bonus: The Patience Plan	**246**

引言
Introduction

本人在中學任教超過二十五年（教授體育、健康和美國歷史），設計和指導了許多夏令營活動，這些經歷都在團隊引導方面給了我完美的訓練。領導學生、夏令營營員和營地工作人員等多樣化的訓練讓我了解了團隊成長的過程，只要人們聚在一起，這一過程就會發生。無論是一個班級的學生、一群營員或是一群同事聚在一起制定課程或設計一套營期日程，在團隊運作的過程中，都會有一個過程發生。一位有經驗的引導者應該是這樣的領導，他能夠提高團隊的效率，並引導它朝著預期的目標或目的地前進。

Spending more than 25 years as a middle school teacher (Physical Education, Health, and U.S. History) and designing and directing summer camp programs has been a perfect training ground for group facilitation experience. Leading students, campers and camp staff members, the diverse training has taught me about the group growth process that occurs anytime people come together. Whether it involves a class of students, a group of campers, a group of colleagues creating a curriculum or designing a camp schedule, there is a process that occurs within the functioning of a group. An experienced facilitator is a leader who can improve the efficiency of the group as well as steer the direction of the group towards the desired goal or destination.

在過去的十多年裡，我多次來到中國，這又為我個人的成長提供了新的契機。我原本是為了招生而去的，結果卻變成了教師培訓之旅。每次面對四十至五十名中國英語教師，讓我有機會利用自己擔任教師和團隊引導者的經驗，去幫助他們在教師和學生之間建立聯繫的課堂體驗。我深知人際關係的價值，所以我的目標是為這些教師提出挑戰，使之成為領導者，並因此成為他們自己課堂上的引導者，並引導班級團隊的成長過程。我把教師們訓練成為領導者，而這將惠及他們的學生。

Taking many trips to China over the past 10+ years has afforded me new opportunities for personal growth. What started out as primarily student recruitment trips have turned into teacher training tours. Finding myself in front of 40-50 Chinese teachers of English has given me the opportunity to assimilate my experience as a teacher and group facilitator in helping them build a more connected classroom experience for teacher and student. Knowing the value of personal connections, my goal is to challenge teachers to be leaders and therefore facilitators of their own group growth process that will take place in their classrooms. My training of teachers to be leaders benefits the students they teach.

本書內容取自我在「趣味研討會」上向受訓教師展示的材料。在研討會上，我向教師們展示了團隊成長的過程。儘管我和每個小組共處的時間只有短短兩天，他們卻能夠在他們與學生長達十個月的關係裡看到有力的成果和潛力。我將教師們訓練成他們自己的團隊成長過程中有意識的構建者。透過培養正確的思維方式、提高引導技能、學習領導力特徵以及運用細緻的定向設計，老師們得以學會引導的藝術。

The content of this book has been taken from materials I present to teachers in my multi-day "fun-shop" seminars in which I model for them what the group growth process looks like. Although I have only 2 days with each group, they can see the powerful results and potential for their 10-month relationship with their students. I train teachers to be the intentional architects of the growth process that will happen in their group. By developing a proper mindset, sharpening facilitation skills, learning leadership characteristics and utilizing careful directional design, teachers learn the art of facilitation.

領導他人就意味著影響他人。教師之所以能成為領導者，正是因為他們能夠對學生的人生產生巨大的影響。教育所涉及的遠不只教授考試內容而已。教師應該成為學生的導師，教會他們如何度過難關並為未來的人生做好準備。教師的責任不僅僅是為全班授課，他們也承擔著教育每一個孩子的責任。要做到這一點，他們必須接受引導者的角色，並認識到他們對每一個孩子的人生會產生多麼大的影響。

To lead is to influence. Teachers are leaders because they have a tremendous opportunity to impact the life of students. Teaching involves far more than just communicating subject content to be given back on an examination. Teachers are mentors who help teach students how to navigate through and prepare for future life. Teachers bear the responsibility to teach not only the whole class but also each individual child. To do so, they must embrace the role of facilitator and recognize the impact they can have on the life of each child.

我希望本書的每一位讀者都能在書中找到有助於其個人和職業成長的元素。我感覺教師這一身份讓我成為了一位更好的父親。同時我也感覺父親這一身份，反過來也讓我成為了一位更好的教師。我的個人成長促進了職業成長，反之亦然。我們每個人都應該努力對那些與我們最親近的人和那些我們所領導的人產生最大的影響。在我作為教師、領導者和個人的幾種角色的成長和發展過程中，許多老師都做出了貢獻。我的動力來自幫助別人做到同樣的事情，來回報我的那些老師在我身上傾注的心血。

I hope each reader finds elements within this book that are helpful to both personal and professional growth. I feel I am a better father because I was a teacher. I also feel I am a better teacher because I am a father. My personal growth fed my professional growth, and vice-versa. Each of us should strive to maximize our impact for those closest to us and to those we lead. Many teachers contributed to my growth and development as a teacher, leader, and person. My motivation is to pay that investment forward by helping others do the same thing.

　　每個人的人生旅途都是獨一無二的。擁抱個人成長的過程吧。在這一過程中，我們將承受痛苦，但也享受快樂，因為成功總是建立在另一個成功基礎上的。學會慶祝所有時刻吧，因為它們對你的個人旅途有著同等的貢獻。

　　Each person's journey is unique. Embrace the process of personal growth. The process has moments of pain, but also moments of pleasure, as one success builds upon another. Learn to celebrate all the moments because they contribute equally to the story that makes up your personal journey.

——史蒂夫 Steve

引導的藝術
The Art of Facilitation

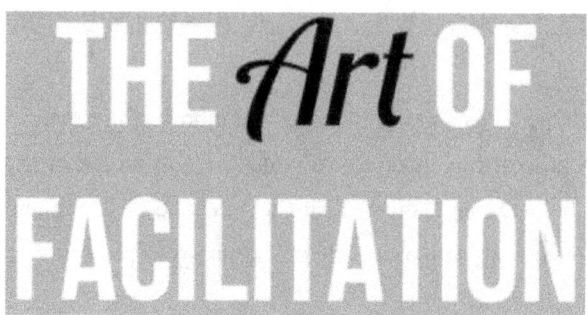

Image credit: Alexy Krivitsky

　　不知你有沒有經歷過那種無聊的研討會或者培訓呢？我指的是那種讓你眼皮發沉，忍不住要睡著的無聊。它們的吸引力確實太低了，低到你一個字也聽不進去，更不要說吸收掌握了。問題也許並不在講授內容本身，而是在授課人身上，或者說問題在於他們沒有能力靠任何個人魅力征服一個課堂或一群聽眾。與這種無聊形成對比的是音樂會歌手們的表現，無論他們的演出是在三百人的場地還是在三萬人的體育場，他們都能完全掌控，讓在場的每一個人都感覺自己融入了這場表演。在這種情況下，由於你完全沉浸在其中，想睡著壓根兒就不可能。偉大的表演家會在「舞台表現」方面下很大的功夫，因為讓觀眾感受到連結能幫助他們傳遞音樂，給聽眾帶來全面的體驗。為什麼有些人上台之後能抓住觀眾，而有些人就——客氣點說吧——讓人過目即忘呢？要製造難忘的回憶而不是遺憾的回憶，關鍵是要掌握引導的藝術。雖然引導者無法直接讓觀眾深信他們所講授的內容或訊息，但他們可以在訊息呈現的過程中創造或者破壞一種氛圍，要嘛讓觀眾聽得入迷，要嘛弄得他們恨不得立馬走人。

　　Have you ever been in a workshop or training that is painfully boring? I am talking about the type of boring where your eyes are so heavy you cannot even keep your head up and eyes open. The level of disengagement is such that you cannot listen or absorb a single spoken word. The content itself may not be as much of the problem as the person who is delivering it. Maybe it is their monotone voice, their apparent lack of personality in the delivery, or their inability to command a room or audience with any type of personal charisma. Compare this level of boredom to a concert performer who manages to entertain a room of 300, or a stadium of 30,000, where and when they seem in complete control to make each participant feel connected and involved in the show. In this scenario, you are so engaged that falling asleep would be humanly impossible. Great performers work very hard at their "stage presence" because how they make an audience feel connected helps them communicate their music and provide an overall experience for the audience members. What makes some presenters captivating while others are, let's just say, forgettable? Mastering the art of facilitation can be the key to creating unforgettable memories and avoiding regrettable ones. Whereas the facilitator cannot make the audience believe in the content or message, they can make or break the aura surrounding the presentation of information in a way that leaves the audience either wanting more or wanting to leave.

　　認識到引導的藝術是一項需要打磨的技能，這很重要。這不是觀眾的任務，而是訊息傳遞者的任務。對於表現者而言（無論他們是為一個班級授課還是發表演講或進行培訓），認識到他們所做的事情是一種表演是極具價值的。所有表演家都應該在表現技巧（包括舞台表現、聲線投射、外表、傳達等）各方面下功夫，以確保他們呈現的訊息和材料都是以一種最能被觀眾接受的方式進行傳達，從而對他們產生盡可能大的影響。所謂引導，更多指的是清楚該「如何」講，而不僅僅是「知道」要講什麼。

　　It is important to see the art of facilitation as a skill that needs to be perfected. It is not the job of the audience, but rather of the message giver. For the presenter (whether teaching a class or giving a speech or training), there is a value in seeing that what they do is a performance. All performers should work on their presentation craft (stage presence, projection voice, appearance, delivery, etc.) to ensure the message and material is given in a way it can best be received to make as strong an impact as possible. To facilitate is more than just "knowing" what it is you're are going to say - it is more about "how" you say it.

我是知名論壇「TED演說」的粉絲。我很欣賞TED演說發言者的表現，由於時間有限，他們大多數人讀的都是精心編排過的發言稿，以保證在嚴格的時間安排下完成演說。為了與觀眾迅速建立聯繫，這些「表演家」必須精心遣詞造句並運用生動的故事講述技巧。有些TED演說者能夠成功地與觀眾建立連結，而另一些人則似乎在演說中融入了他們自己的雜音。那些能吸引人的演說之所以具有吸引力，可能在於他們的聲音、他們的面部表情、故事本身或者他們用言語講述故事的方式。他們的表現力決定了到底是建立與觀眾之間的連結，還是打破這種連結。遣詞造句以及發言者講話的方式是重要的引導因素。

I am a fan of the popular forums called "Ted Talks". I appreciate that a Ted Talk speaker has a limited time allotted and so most of them read their well-worded and rehearsed script in order to stay on a very strict time schedule. These "performers" must connect quickly with an audience through careful word choice and dynamic story telling skills. Some Ted Talk performers manage to connect, while others seem to blend into the noise of their own voice. For those speakers that I find engaging, it may be in their voice, their facial expressions, the story itself or in the way they tell the story they have constructed in spoken words. The power of their performance is what can make or break the speaker's connection with the audience. The words used and the way someone delivers the spoken word are important elements of facilitation.

我聽過一個說法，說公開演講是人們能經歷的最可怕的事情之一。一想到要站在一群陌生人面前（甚至哪怕是朋友也一樣），許多人都會心生恐懼。公開演講從小學早期已經開始練習，「展示和講述」活動、讀書報告或在全班面前演講的機會等等都是練習的方式。既然有這麼多機會進行公開表演，為什麼大多數人在必須這麼做的時候還是覺得它們這麼可怕呢？

　　I have heard it said that public speaking is one of the most frightening experiences anyone can have. The thought of standing in front of strangers (or even friends) strikes fear into the hearts of many. Public presentations are practiced from early elementary school days with "show & tell," book reports, or other opportunities to speak in front of the class. If these types of public performance exposures are so readily available, why do they continue to be so frightening for most people who must do them?

　　我最棒的經歷之一，就是在我大學時期成立的搖滾樂隊擔任主唱。雖不能說舞台對我而言是最舒服的地方，但我的確有一種自我意識，在上台之前，它幫我把緊張感轉化為一種自信。我心中的「恐懼」並不一定是對失敗的恐懼，而是一種預期，即我是否能夠找到一種方式，透過我的聲樂和舞台表現，建立觀眾與我們的音樂和歌詞之間的連結。當我們作為一個樂隊走上舞台，把音樂表演好，把音符演唱和演奏控制好的時候，我（作為主唱）能否把觀眾帶到到一個情感空間來傾聽我的思想和想法呢？這一場景所展示的就是引導藝術的一種形式。對於一位表演者（或一群表演者），運用抒情的語言和舞台動作來傳遞訊息就是一種獨特的引導形式。

　　One of my best life experiences came from being the lead singer in a rock and roll band that I began back in college. I cannot say that the stage was always the most comfortable place for me to be, but I did have an ego, and that helped transform my nervous energy into a form of confidence before taking the stage. My "fear" was not necessarily the fear of failure, but rather it was the anticipation of whether or not I would be able to find a way to connect the audience to our music and lyrics through my vocal and stage performance. Could we as a band step on stage, perform the music well, singing and playing the right notes, while I (as the lead singer) tried to invite the audience into the emotional space of hearing my lyrical thoughts and ideas? This scenario exemplifies one form of the art of facilitation. For a performer (or group of performers) to use lyrical words and stage movements to project and communicate a message is a unique form of facilitation.

對我們而言，沒有兩場樂隊表演是一樣的。這也使這種引導更加讓人感到興奮。每天晚上的觀眾都不一樣，對音樂的反應也各不相同。我發現有些晚上我的表現比其他晚上好，有些晚上觀眾的活力水平也比其他晚上要高。雖然我認為我的活力水平一向都比較高，但它有時候還是會受到觀眾反應（或者是觀眾沒啥反應）的影響，甚至觀眾數量也會對此產生影響。站在舞台上，我可以對觀眾的面部進行視覺解讀，觀察他們的反應，以確定我是否與他們建立起了連結，或者我是否需要更加努力地建立起這種連結。對我而言，舞台表演是最佳的訓練，使我明白了自己作為群體引導者的角色。每天晚上都是一場表演，而我明白自己的角色，就是向觀眾傳達內容（歌詞）並影響觀眾對演出的接受方式。我學會了擁抱這種角色，而不是對它心懷恐懼。

For us, no two band performances were ever the same. This also contributed to the excitement of this type of facilitation. Each night, the audience was different and would react in a variety of ways to the music offered. I realized that some nights I was better than others, and some nights the audience had a higher energy level than others. My energy level, though I thought it was always high, at times may have been affected by the response and reaction (or lack thereof) or even size of the audience. From the stage, I could visually read the faces, see the reactions and determine whether or not I was connecting with the audience or if I needed to do more to forge a connection. For me, the performance stage was my best training to understand my role as a group facilitator. Each night was a performance, and I understood my role in delivering the content (lyrics) and in influencing how the audience would receive the show. I learned to embrace that role, instead of fear it.

如果你是一名教師或領導，站在你管理或教育的人面前可能是一種可怕的經歷。我認識一些老師，他們在自己的課堂非常出色，但一旦讓他們進行一場培訓，或者跟成年人或者甚至年齡大一些的學生說話都會讓他們一下子嚇得心驚肉跳。有些領導也有這種情況，他們需要發表演講或發佈公司新的計劃或方向時，他們連幾句通順的句子都說不出來，因為他們既缺乏自信，也不具備足夠的舞台表現力，無法有效地傳達自己需要傳達的訊息。那麼，就算這些都是一次性的表演，少數登台的時刻也可能產生日常生活中無法感受的恐懼。當我討論引導這個話題的時候，你面對的可能是認識的觀眾，環境也是讓你覺得自在的，但你也有可能需要對一群從未見過面的陌生人進行培訓。不管是哪種情況，在傳達訊息的時候，你都應該學會引導的藝術，只有這樣，你要傳達的訊息才最有可能以你希望的方式被觀眾傾聽。

If you are a teacher or a leader, getting up in front of those you manage or teach may be a frightening experience. I know teachers who are excellent teachers in their classrooms but ask them to give a training or talk to adults or even older students and they suddenly are gripped with fear. The same can be said of leaders who, when asked to deliver a speech or reveal a new company plan or direction, can barely speak a few fluid sentences because they do not have the confidence or stage presence to effectively deliver their message. Now, granted, these are more one-time performances, and it is possible that the rare moments on stage cause fear that is not felt on a daily basis. When I am talking about facilitation, it can either be with those participants you know, and in a setting in which you feel at home, or it could be the training you have to deliver to a new group of strangers whom you have never met. Whatever the case, the art of facilitation should be studied so that when you deliver your message, it has the best chance of being heard exactly has you hope it will be.

我發現許多老師僅僅把自己視為教授書本內容的人。而我認為這只是老師角色的一小部份，老師應被看作課堂的CEO。老師不僅要教學生知識，也要教會他們如何學習知識。他們透過教授必要的內容來評估和教導學生如何進行批判性思考。但同時他們也具有引導者的角色。引導者的工作就是創造學習的空間和氛圍。引導者要為參與者／學習者創造令他們身心都感到安全的場所。

I find that many teachers see themselves as simply those who teach content. I find this to be only a small part of the role of a teacher. I ascribe to the view that the teacher is a CEO of their classroom. As such, a teacher teaches students WHAT to know and HOW to know it. They teach content necessary to assess and teach students how to think critically. But they also play the role of facilitator. The facilitator creates the SPACE & ATMOSPHERE for learning. A facilitator creates an emotionally and psychologically safe place for the participant/learner.

根據定義，引導者指的是「幫助一個群體理解他們的共同目標並協助他們制定計劃以達成這些目標」的人。但定義中並沒有指出引導者該**如何「幫助」**群體理解。這是扮演引導者角色的關鍵部份，但也常常被忽視。這個部份往往沒有得到充份的練習。

By definition, a facilitator is one who *"helps a group of people to understand their common objectives and assists them to plan how to achieve these objectives."* However, what is not implied is the significance of this role related to HOW a facilitator "HELPS" a group understand. This is a crucial part of embracing the full role of facilitator, and one that is often missed or overlooked. It tends to be the part that is not practiced or rehearsed enough.

在深入探討老師／引導者的具體角色之前，讓我們先看看引導者可能會扮演哪些角色。

Before we zero in on the specific role of a teacher/facilitator, let's look at the different types of roles a facilitator may play.

1. 中立調解——在一些情況下，如幫人解決個人矛盾時，引導者的角色更像一位客觀的第三方。他們的任務就是傾聽，確保當事各方都平等地獲得被人傾聽的機會。並且在必要的時候幫他們進行澄清。在這個角色中，他們的作用不是裁判，而是確保當事人之間進行清楚的溝通。有些人專職做這件事，而所有老師和領導在管理他們的團隊時都時不時地需要這麼做。調解員／引導者的技巧至關重要，能把這件事情做得很好的人在任何組織中都會是備受重視的成員。

1. Neutral Mediation - There are situations, like helping to resolve personal conflicts, where the facilitator is more like an objective third party. Their role is to listen, ensure all sides are given fair opportunity to be heard, and to provide clarification when the need arises. In this role, they are not there to judge, but to ensure clear communication is carried out with those involved. Some do this as a profession, and certainly all teachers and leaders do this occasionally in helping to manage those they lead. The skill of mediator/facilitator is very important and those who do it very well are valued team members in any organization.

2. 群體引導者——這一角色承擔召集會議，以及會議或班級活動議程的責任。關於會議的目的，參加者可能知道，也可能不知道。在需要明確會議目的的情況下，引導者必須以恰當的方式設計和傳達這訊息，確保參加人員能明白。教師／領導力研討會就是一個例子。很多時候，與會人員並不確定他們報名研討的到底是什麼內容。我在中國舉辦的研討會，很多時候就是這個情況，與會人員只是被告知這是一個職業發展的機會，以及我是一個來自美國的教育家。作為引導者，了解這一點對我而言非常重要。同樣，對於我與他們最初的互動，我必須仔細地列出我與他們共度的時間裡我的目標是什麼。透過這樣做，我能讓他們知道我們的研討會將走向何方。一旦大家明白了「目的地」（預設目標），就可以進行（調整）「方向」這一過程，或者至少已經有了指導方向，讓大家在引導者的帶領下朝著預期的結果邁進。

2. Group facilitator - The role here is to take charge of the gathering and assume responsibility for the flow of the meeting or class. The objective for a gathering/meeting may or may not be known by the participants. In cases when the clarity of meeting purpose is required, the facilitator must design and deliver this message in such a way that the purpose can be known. An example of this may be teacher/leadership training seminars. Many times, those in attendance are not sure exactly what it is they have signed up for. Many times, as is the case with my workshops in China, they are simply told that it is a professional development opportunity and that I am an educator from the United States. Knowing this is quite important for me as the facilitator. As such, my initial interaction with them requires that I carefully lay out an overview of my objectives and goals for our time together. In doing so, I give them a sense of where we are headed. Once the "destination" (projected goal) is understood, the process of "direction" can be delivered, or at least guided, by the facilitator to help achieve the desired outcome. Most often, this is the role of a teacher, a supervisor, a trainer or someone chosen and placed in this role by position or appointment.

打磨你的引導技巧
Sharpening Your Facilitation Skills

在這一點上，你可能對於引導者的責任落到自己身上而感到戰戰兢兢，或者你可能會搖搖頭說，我已經知道這是我的職責了，但我怎麼才能在這方面做得更好呢？我想說明的是，任何人都可以引導他人（可能是這麼回事），但並不是每個人都能像其他人一樣有效地做這件事。在引導的藝術中，為什麼有些人比較高效，而其他人則不行呢？

At this point, you may be either shaking in your boots, fearing the responsibility that now rests with you as a facilitator, or possibly shaking your head saying, I already knew that was my role, but how do I get better at it? I would like to proclaim that anyone can facilitate (and that might be true) but not every facilitator is as effective as another. Why are some people effective and others are not as effective at the art of facilitation?

引導者的關鍵因素
Key Facilitator Factors

個性———一個很容易調動他人、顯得真誠、有風度、能夠與他們建立連結的引導者可以對人們形成強大的激勵作用。這些個性特質可以幫助人們更容易地團結在一起。

舉個例子，如果觀眾發現引導者具有吸引人的性格，他們就容易接近引導者，並參與對話。這可以成為引導者在傳遞訊息時的槓桿因素。

Personality - A facilitator who can easily engage others, appear genuine, personable, and able to relate to others can be a great motivator of people. These personality characteristics can help unify and bring people together more easily.

For example, audience members find it easier to approach facilitators and engage in conversation if they perceive their personalities to be inviting and engaging. This can be used as leverage by facilitators in communicating their messages.

自信———在考慮站到人群面前時，每一個引導者都應該具有一定的自信心，因為引導就是表演。雖然自信並沒有固定的表現方式，但它有助於引導者找到他們表演的「最有效點」，並努力將其做好。

例如，一位害羞、內向的引導者可能會表現得缺乏自信，而這很容易削弱訊息的正當性和完整性。

Confidence - Every facilitator needs to have a healthy dose of confidence when considering being in front of others because facilitating is performing. Whereas there is not one set way to show confidence, it is helpful for the facilitator to find their performance "sweet spot" and work at it to do it well.

For example, a shy, introverted facilitator may project a lack of self-confidence, which can easily diminish the legitimacy or integrity of the message.

高情商——引導者必須始終「解讀整個房間」，以對觀眾的反應進行衡量。出色的引導者知道什麼時候該發聲，並根據感知到的反應做出改變。有經驗的引導者心中有一個明確的目標，他們可以進行改變，而這並不會分散受眾對訊息的注意力。

舉例，有時候我發現，聽眾在午餐休息前的三十分鐘很難集中注意力。於是我改變了自己的表達方式，加入了一個簡短的互動遊戲，幫助他們重新參與進來，而不偏離既定的目標。

Strong EQ - Facilitators must always "read the room" to gauge the response. Good facilitators know when to call the audible and make a change based on the perceived reaction. When the experienced facilitator has a clear destination in mind, changes may be used without causing a distraction from the message.

For example, sometimes I find audience members struggling to keep focused 30 minutes before the scheduled lunch break. I change my method of presentation to include a short interactive game that helps bring them back to engagement without detouring from the intended destination.

謙遜——作為一個引導者，具備一些自我意識固然很好，但過多展示自我只會讓聽眾疏遠你。如果自我意識能讓你對你自己、你傳達的訊息或者你的表現能力感到自信，便是健康的自我意識。然而，如果你的自我意識暗示你比房間裡任何人都優越，那便不過是一種軟弱罷了。

舉例，引導者會在他們的「表演」中營造氣氛。如果一位引導者過多地談論自己的專業知識、經驗或成就，這種過度自信就可能讓觀眾覺得他沒有任何謙遜之心，並因此對他所傳遞的訊息失去興趣。

Humility - As much as it is good to have some ego as a facilitator, displaying too much of it can alienate you from your audience. Ego that gives you confidence in yourself, your message, or your ability to perform can be healthy. However, ego that implies you are better than anyone else in the room is a weakness.

For example, facilitators cast an aura during their performance. If one talks too much about their expertise, experience or accomplishments, the audience may perceive this over confidence as a total absence of humility and lose interest in the message.

彈性——在外國做引導時，我曾多次經歷這樣的情況：我想要的條件完全不是最優的。比如，當我需要活動空間時，我有時會被塞進一個比事先約好的小得多的空間。還有一些時候，對方明明承諾滿足我的技術需求，但實際提供給我的卻遠遠不夠。恰恰就是在這種時候，你必須牢記（團隊的）目標，根據眼前的實際情況調整方向，以確保自己仍然能按照原計劃傳達訊息。這並非易事，有時這種情況確實還會影響內容的傳達。然而這種情況很少會阻礙我產生影響或達成預期的結果。為什麼呢？因我引導方面的經驗讓我具備了全面看問題的能力，所以在我無法控制的臨時情況下，我依然可以靈活應對。面對挑戰和適應預料之外的情況會讓引導者獲得更多經驗，儘管他／她可能並沒準備好，也不希望這種情況發生，但每一次挑戰都是有益的課程。在逆境中迎接挑戰需要一種健康的心態,而靈活應變永遠是實現這一目標的一種途徑。

Flexibility – When facilitating in a foreign country, I have experienced, on many occasions, a situation where the parameters of what I wanted for optimal conditions were anything but optimal. For instance, when I needed room space for activities, I would sometimes end up squeezing into a much smaller space than was agreed upon. In other instances, the stated technology demands, though clearly promised, were under-delivered by more than just a little bit. It is during these times that you must keep the destination (of the group) in mind, but alter the direction based on the circumstances, to ensure that you are still able to deliver the planned message. It is not easy, and at times it certainly impacts the delivery of the content. However, rarely does it stop me from having an impact or from achieving desired results. Why? Because experience in facilitation provides me with the ability to see in full perspective so I can be flexible in those circumstances that I cannot control. Challenges and unforeseen adaptations can quickly provide a facilitator with more experience than he/she may be ready for or deserve, but each challenge is a lesson. Meeting challenges in the face of adversity requires a healthy mindset, and flexibility will always be a means to that end.

塑造你的經驗——提高引導技能是需要付出努力的。那到底是什麼樣的努力呢?如何邁出第一步?

Shape Your Experience – Improving facilitation skills takes effort. What does that effort look like? Where does one start?

1. 練習——為了在觀眾面前表現自如,你必須把自己置於「脆弱」的境地——這是一個擴展你舒適區的境地。這種練習很簡單,比如在陌生人面前K歌,或者邀請一群聽眾,然後在他們面前演講等。重要的是你需要透過練習來獲得經驗。認識到你的恐懼或過度自信,並勇於承認,然後直面挑戰,解決問題。勇於直面恐懼是一項技能,恐懼並不會自動神奇消失，只有靠經驗的積累來戰勝它。同樣，請他人提出建設性的批評意見也需要深刻和徹底的反省。你終將把恐懼從無能轉化為健康、急切的興奮感，就像你可以把過度自信轉化為健康的平衡一樣。這兩者都是透過經驗積累來實現的。

1. Get Practice - In order to appear comfortable in front of an audience, you must put yourself in vulnerable positions – positions that stretch your comfort zone. Getting practice could be as simple as doing Karaoke in front of strangers or presenting in front of an invited audience. The important message is that you need to GET PRACTICE in order to get experience. Identify and acknowledge any fear or over confidence and then face the challenge to fix it head on. Facing fear bravely is one skill that does not magically disappear with anything but experience. Likewise, inviting constructive criticism requires deep and thorough introspection. You can eventually turn the fear from incapacitation to a healthy, anxious excitement just like you can turn over-confidence into a healthy balance. Both are accomplished simply through gaining experience.

2. 發現你的「最有效傳遞點」——引導者必須適應自己的個性和傳遞方式。可能你天生就不具備幽默感，但幽默是使聽眾放鬆的好辦法，也能讓他們在你營造的氛圍中感覺自在。假設你實在無法在演講中融入高雅或幽默的話語，請至少確保你的演講和表達是自信、正確而鼓舞人心的。沒有什麼是比聽一個文法不通、語氣單調的人講話更糟糕的事情了。你的演講中可能會有一些讓你的聽眾聽不明白或有些反感的方言或詞語。有時候，發言者的口音就足以讓聽眾抗拒他們傳達的訊息。在提升演講風格的過程中，你應該試著找到自己最好的演講風格。一定要從公正的聽眾那裡去獲取誠實的回饋。記住，雖然肯定在某種意義上是有價值的東西，但你真正需要的其實是那些誠實的、建設性的批評意見。

2. Discover Your Delivery "Sweet Spot" - Facilitators must be comfortable with their own personality and delivery style. Maybe you are not funny by nature, but humor is a great way to put your audience at ease, and it is an inviting way for them to feel comfort in the atmosphere you create. Maybe you can find ways to add humor to your delivery approach, which may also put yourself at ease.If you cannot blend in tasteful and acceptable humor, at least make sure your speech and delivery is confident, correct and invigorating. There is nothing worse than listening to someone who uses poor grammar or speaking skills with a monotone voice delivery. Your speech may have identifiable dialects or phrases that are not understood or appreciated by your audience. Sometimes, just the accent of the speaker is enough to block the message. As you are perfecting your delivery style, you should also try to discover what your best delivery style is. Be sure to get some honest feedback from an impartial audience. Your friends, spouse, or family may not be the best source of feedback. Remember, though affirmation may be valuable in one sense, what you really need is honest, constructive criticism.

3. 獲得自信——這可能是最簡單的一項，它與第一條直接相關——經驗是沒有捷徑的。自信源自經驗的積累。糟糕的經歷可能反而大有益處。好的經歷可以建立自信。我想表達的意思很簡單——只要走出去，大膽地做，你的自信就會提升！你表達得越多，你就能變得越自信。自信源自經驗。

3. Gain Confidence - This may be the easiest one, and it is directly tied to number 1- there is no shortcut for experience. Experience breeds confidence. Bad experiences can be extremely instructive. Good experiences can build confidence. The message is simple - get out there and do it and your confidence can grow! The more you deliver, the more confidence you will gain. Experience begets confidence.

4. 尋找機會———旦你發現了自己必須傳達的訊息，你就要盡可能多找機會去傳達。要積極地尋找引導的機會。如果你想成為一名收費演說者，你有可能必須先進行免費演說，然後才能獲得報酬。如果你想領導團隊，那就去找一些團隊來進行領導。關鍵是你要積極地尋找這樣的機會，因為你的動力是成長為引導者，而這只能透過尋找機會、積累經驗來實現。

4. Seek Opportunity - Once you find out what message you must give, seek out as many opportunities as you can to deliver your message. Actively seek out opportunities to facilitate. If you want to be a paid speaker, you may have to initially speak for free before you get some that will pay you for it later. If you want to lead groups, then find groups to lead. The key is that you actively seek out these opportunities because your motivation is to improve as a facilitator, and that can only happen with experience through opportunities.

5. 簡潔的訊息——這可能是最難提升的一點。我發現，隨著經驗積累得越來越多，我所傳達的訊息變得越來越簡潔。根據我在經驗積累的過程中收獲的回饋，我對訊息進行塑造。曾經要一個小時才能說完的內容，我現在只需要三十分鐘，因為我已經找到了更好的表達方式。訊息的鞏固並不是突然獲得啟示的結果，而是來自經驗積累的機會中獲得的直接回饋。

5. Concise Message - This may be the hardest of all to develop. I found that my message became more concise with each additional experience. I shaped my message based on the feedback received through experience. What I once said in an hour, now takes me 30 minutes, because I have found better ways to say it. Consolidating my message was not the result of a sudden revelation, but rather listening to direct feedback gained over several experience-building opportunities.

尊重「引導者」職位的力量——引導者可以對任何群體產生巨大的力量和影響。如果你不小心維護的話，這種力量足以很快地沖昏你的頭腦。引導者能很輕易地建立或打斷一個群體的成長歷程。透過擁抱和提升引導技能，教師可以提高每個學生的學業表現。善於引導的商業領袖則能提高公司的生產力和利潤。在任何組織的每個層級上，訓練有素、經驗豐富的引導者都能夠成為強大的資產。

Respect the Power of the Position - There is tremendous power and influence that a facilitator can have on any group. This power can quickly go to your head if you are not carefully guarded. A facilitator can easily make or break a group process. Teachers who embrace and sharpen their facilitation skills can elevate the learning of every student. The business leader who facilitates well can improve the productivity and profit of a company. At every level, a well-trained, and seasoned facilitator can be a powerful asset to any organization.

尊重你扮演的角色以及你所能產生的影響力，因為一位扮演「引導者」角色的領導是會獲得重視的。你的團隊指望你能把這個角色做好！做好了這個角色，團隊成長過程將令人滿意，而成果也將是顯而易見。這樣你就能體會到透過影響他人而帶來的甜蜜感。偉大的引導者身上的魅力在於他們願意承擔風險，然後透過努力和經驗積累來強化他們要傳達的訊息。請抓住機會，最大程度地發揮你作為引導者的影響力吧，你可以改變許多人的人生。

Respect for the role, and influence you can have, as a facilitator leader is to be valued. Your group is counting on you to get it right! When you do, the process is satisfying, and the product is evident. That is the sweet spot of influence you want to experience. The magic in the power of a great facilitator is in the willingness to take the risk and then to sharpen the message through hard work and experience. Seize the opportunity to maximize your influence as a facilitator and you can change the lives of many.

保持好奇心
Be Curious

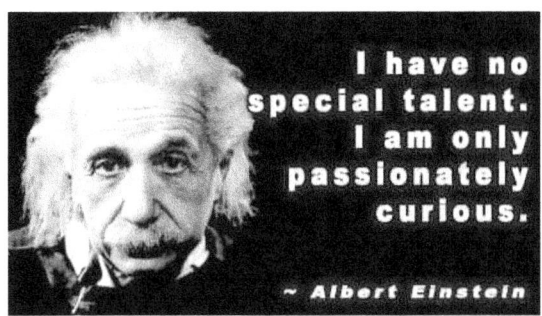

Image credit: www.thequotes.in

　　教師的影響力和工作內容遠不只向學生傳授知識內容。理想的情況是，教師應該激發學生的好奇心，讓他們去鑽研比教學內容更深入的內容。這樣做將激發學生以一種更加豐富、深入和富於參與性的方式去探索知識。如果一個老師僅僅告訴學生應試所需要知道的東西，那他就剝奪了學生懷著好奇心探索未知而獲得的樂趣。採用「應試教育」的教學方法不僅束縛了學生的學習，而且也使導師這一角色變得廉價。

　　The impact and job of a teacher extends far beyond just being the person responsible for delivering content knowledge to those who will listen. Ideally, the teacher should stimulate the curiosity of the learner so that they dig deeper than the extent of the content delivered. Doing so will invite the learner to explore learning in a rich, deep, and engaging way. A teacher who simply tells the students what they need to know for the examination robs the students of the joy that can be found through curious discovery. When a "teaching to the test" teaching method is used, it not only constricts the student learning but also cheapens the role of being a mentor.

通常，在開學的第一節課上，我會做一個開場白，大概告訴學生如下內容：「我知道對於你們中的很多人而言，在這門歷史課裡，並非所有內容都能讓你們興奮，甚至可能連興趣都勾不起來。有時你們可能會討厭這門課，但我希望在其他時候，它能激發你們保持好奇的興趣。作為學習者，投入的方式之一便是始終努力保持好奇心。如果你們能對某個話題感到好奇，這種好奇就會幫你找到有趣的視角、真相、思路或想法，並且也許會激勵你進行更深入的挖掘。如果你們能這樣做，它就能為你們開啟額外的學習，並使該話題以及學習過程與你們更加相關。」我喜歡配圖中這句愛因斯坦的名言，並且覺得我自己作為一個學習者頗為符合它的描述。（我並不是在拿自己和愛因斯坦比較！）當我自己還是一名學生的時候，我並不覺得自己有學習、記憶、解決問題或深入思考方面的過人天賦。我真正擁有的是好奇心。它促使我分析、閱讀、學習、發問，並對許多不同的話題有了更好的理解。請保持你的好奇心！

Typically, in my first class of the school year, I would give an opening message to my students that went something like this: *"I know many of you will not find all of the topics covered in this history class to be exciting or even interesting to you. At times, you may hate it, but I hope that at other times, it will pique your interest to be curious. One way to engage as a learner is to always strive to be curious. If you can be curious about the topic, it will help you look for an interesting angle, fact, thought, or idea about the topic and maybe inspire you to dig a little deeper. When you do that, it opens up additional learning and can help make the topic and the learning far more relevant to you."* I love the above Einstein quote, and felt it described me as a learner. (I am not drawing any personal comparison to Einstein!) As a student, I did not feel I had a special talent for learning, memorizing, problem-solving or deep thinking. What I did possess was an appreciation for curiosity. Curiosity has caused me to analyze, read, study, ask questions and better understand many diverse topics. Be curious!

教師如何激發學生的好奇心？
How can teachers inspire curiosity in the learner?

教師需要養成正確提問的技能。事實上，很多教師都不會正確地提問，他們只會提容易的問題。如果是在法庭上，對方律師將會對引導性問題提出「反對意見」。許多老師只提顯而易見的問題，而不是深刻的問題。知道如何構建問題將幫助你激發好奇心。

Teachers need to develop a skill for asking the right questions. In fact, many teachers do not ask the right questions, they ask the easy questions. If it were in a court of law, the "objection" outcry from the opposing attorney would be for a leading question. Many teachers simply ask the obvious question and not the deep question. Knowing how to scaffold questions can invite curiosity.

不過，並非所有問題都足以激發好奇心。有些問題屬於最簡單的那一類，只要它們能在適當的時候引出更高層次的思考，那就沒有什麼問題。最好的問題能夠引出激烈見解和角度，或者能夠促進不同意見，這些意見可以幫助闡明主題，或幫助正在傾聽或投入其中的個人、群體或班級提升他們的理解。當然，有些問題可能直接有正確或錯誤的答案，但含有許多層次的發問會導致諸多變化和選項，而這就是學生們參與的地方。教師應構建能夠激發討論、引發更深刻的思考且提升聽課人好奇心的問題。

Not every question can inspire curiosity. Some questions are of the easiest kind, and there is nothing wrong with that, provided they lead to a higher level of thinking at the appropriate time. The best questions are those that invite a provocative opinion, angle, or promote a difference of opinion which can help elucidate the topic or increase understanding for an individual, group or class who may be listening and engaged. Sure, there is content that may have a direct right or wrong answer to it, but there are many levels of questioning that invite variations and options, and this is where student engagement can occur. Teachers should scaffold questions that provoke discussion and elicit deeper consideration to pique the curiosity of the listener.

問題類型應包括在小組討論中引發思考並推動討論的問題。問題的類型可以推動小型或大型的小組討論或辯論。提出的問題或許較常屬於微觀層面（比如讓學生進行思考—結對—分享的交流），讓他們獨立思考，然後與同伴分享，再在一個更大的群體內進行討論。教師應努力成為最好的提問者，因為這是激發學生好奇心的最佳方式之一，並能讓學生更深層次地參與課堂內容，以及課堂本身。

Question styles could include those where a thought-provoking question provides fuel for small group discussions. The style of question asked can provide fuel for small or large group discussion or debate. Maybe the question asked is more at the micro-level (like having students engage in a think-pair-share exchange) to individually contemplate, then share with a partner before discussing it as a larger group. Teachers should work to become the best question askers because it is one of the best ways to inspire student curiosity and invite a deeper level of student engagement with the material, and in the class itself.

正確提問很重要，在正確的時間提問也同樣重要。根據學生（或年級）水平的差異，學生可能已經掌握某些知識基礎，也可能沒有掌握，而這些基礎知識能夠讓他／她自如地回答各種探究或拓展他／她知識基礎的問題。若向沒有足夠知識基礎的學生提困難的問題，則非但不能激發他們的好奇心，反而會讓他們心生恐懼。務必要熟悉你的學生。許多教師尚未有效地搭好舞台，就開啟了「新」的話題或章節。他們可能會先宣佈話題，然後就一頭栽進內容講解、背景閱讀或回答問題的環節。然而，在引入一個新的話題或章節時，若能提出一些正確、引人深思的問題，將會帶來全新的意義，並極大地激發學生的好奇心。這就是教師可以影響、贏得並激發學生參與、激發他們的好奇心——或者完全壓抑他們好奇心——的地方。

As important as it is to ask the right question, it is equally as important to ask a question at the right time. Depending on the learner (and maybe the grade level) a student may or may not have acquired a base of knowledge that would allow him/her to feel comfortable with answering questions that probe into, or expand, his/her knowledge base. Asking difficult questions to students without enough knowledge base may instill fear rather than pique the intended curiosity. Be sure to know your learners well. Many teachers start a "new" topic or chapter without setting the stage effectively. They may announce the topic and then proceed to dive headfirst into content, background reading or the answering of questions. However, asking the right, thought-provoking questions when introducing a new topic or chapter can take on an entirely new meaning and powerfully spike the curiosity of the student. This is where a teacher can influence, win, and inspire student engagement and pique their curiosity…or squelch it completely.

在引入一個新的單元或主題時，應考慮精心設計且具有創造性的策略。學生可以從這些方面看到教師的創造力，如果這些策略富於變化、難以預測，那麼它們就可能引發學生更深的好奇心和興趣。在引入一個需要背景知識的新話題時，教師可能要提供必要的知識訊息讓學生分類和整理。給學生一份「基礎知識一覽」可以快速有效地給學生提供基本事實或者所需的知識背景，讓他們更快地參與進來。

Carefully designed and creative strategies should be considered when a new unit or topic is introduced. This is where teacher creativity can be visible to the students and, if varied and unpredictable, may lead to deeper student curiosity and interest. When introducing a new topic where background knowledge needs to be taught, maybe the teacher provides essential knowledge information that the students categorize and organize. Giving an "essential knowledge fact sheet" can quickly and effectively give students basic facts or a needed landscape of knowledge to allow for faster engagement.

　　有時候還可以透過學生來激發其他學生的好奇心。比如，讓學生成對或者結成小組使用輪流分享的方式通常是有效的，學生們在這個過程中分享閱讀、構建內容、提供可用於活動或作業的實際結構。透過這一策略，教師還可以事先給學生分組，把有學習困難的學生和高分學生安排在一起，讓他們獲得同伴的幫助。對於同一水平分組，它也可能起到幫助，因為高分學生分到一組的話，他們可以很快將材料過完，這就讓你可以向他們提出更高的挑戰，為他們安排更高水平的練習。無論你採用什麼策略，都應該對學習者多加思考，給你教育的學生最好的管理和激勵。你對新學習內容初始階段的設定和任何單元評估測試同等重要。

　　Sometimes, students can be used to inspire the curiosity of other students. For instance, it is often effective to have students work in pairs or small groups and utilize rotating station work that involves shared reading, content building, and providing a factual fabric able to be used in activities or assignments. Using this strategy allows teachers to also design pre-selected student groupings that may put challenged students with high-achieving students for peer support. It may also lend itself to homogenous grouping because a group of high achieving learners can easily move through the material, allowing you to further challenge them by giving them additional work on a higher level. Whatever your strategy is, think about the learner and how to best manage and inspire those you teach. How you set the initial stage for new learning is as important as any end of unit assessment of knowledge.

　　我喜歡提問題，因為我喜歡認識新朋友，遊歷新地方。我發現自己最明顯的人格特質之一就是我在提出疑問方面的能力和興趣。每到一個新地方，或第一次遇見某人，我總會採取調查員進行任務的心態，先了解各項事實。我若是初來乍到，就會花時間觀察其他人的行為。我喜歡看人。我著迷於觀察別人的一舉一動，因為這能幫助我深入了解自己所在之處，以及我如何才能適應這裡。隨著觀察的進行，我可以進一步質疑自己先前的各種臆測，用各種相關問題來加以證實或否定。

My love of asking questions was born out of my interest in meeting new people or going to new places. I found that one of my prominent personality traits was my ability and interest in interrogation. When I go somewhere new, or meet someone for the first time, my mindset is more like that of an investigator on a quest to learn all the facts first. If I am in a new place, I spend a lot of time observing the behaviors of those around me. I love to people-watch. I find it fascinating to observe the behavior of others because it can help me learn more about where I am and what I should do to fit in. As I process these observations, I can then challenge my assumptions and validate or disprove them by asking pertinent questions.

我發現，當我與某人初次見面時，我會遵循類似的模式。一段寒暄之後，我會問一些簡單的引導性問題（你來自哪裡？是做什麼的？）而這只是為了激發我自己的興趣，看看雙方是否存在共同點。我鍛煉傾聽的技巧，因為通常而言，人們總是喜歡談論他們自己。我也這樣做，是為了測試我在某些領域，是否略知一二或者能給點意見。如果答案是肯定的，那麼對話的過程將變得很容易，並且，基於我了解更多的知識、興趣或好奇心，我的提問水平將變得更加深入。我希望自己的學生在學習過程中也有同樣程度的參與感。通常，好奇心可以透過簡單的提問過程達到頂點。在此過程中，學習者從純粹的興趣出發尋找訊息，以找到共同點，而不是簡單地，以必須存儲知識，以便可以用在考試中為出發點，去尋找訊息。好奇的人會提出有趣的問題，而這些問題通常源自於提問人的樂於傾聽。

I find that I follow a similar pattern when I meet someone for the first time. After exchanging pleasantries, I find myself asking simple leading questions (Where are you from? What do you do?) simply to spark my own interests and to see if there are areas of commonality. I exercise the skill of listening because people usually like talking about themselves anyway. I also do it to discover if there are areas on which I may have some knowledge or opinions. If so, conversation flow is easy, and my level of questioning will become deeper based on my knowledge, interest, or curiosity to learn more. This is the same level of engagement I would like my students to use when learning. Often, curiosity can be piqued through the simple process of question asking. In this process, the learner seeks information from a place of pure interest to find things in common, rather than from a place of simply having to store the knowledge so it can be regurgitated back on an exam. Curious people ask intriguing questions, often born out of the willingness to listen first.

　　好奇心會引起更深入的個人探索。我喜愛那些讓我充滿好奇心的年代，那時我會突然間發現自己在詢問訊息。我回想起有一次家庭旅行，那次旅程中的流行語是「**這背後是什麼故事呢？**」那時我們正在進行穿越美國西南部的長途旅行，當我們經過歷史事件或地標時，或者只是談論某個隨機話題時，我們自發地會問：「**那背後是什麼故事呢？**」如果我的學生也問這個問題，我會很樂意的，因為這個問題可能帶領他們進行深入的自我探索，進而尋求真實而有意義的知識。不幸的是，太多的教育把注意力集中在了考試成績上。教育的目的應該是激發每個人的好奇心，而不是非得規定，評估或測試應記住哪些內容。這限制了學習並扼殺了好奇心。

　　　　Curiosity can then lead to deeper personal investigation. I love those times when my curiosity is engaged, and I suddenly find myself on a quest for information. I recall a family road trip when the catch phrase on the trip became *"what's the story with that?"* We were on an extended trip through the American southwest and when we would pass a road marker about a historical event or place, or when simply talking about random topics, we found ourselves saying, *"what is the story with that*?" I would love it if my students would ask that question because it could lead them to a deep self-discovery quest for true and meaningful knowledge. Unfortunately, too much of education is focused on the exam results. The goal of education should be to inspire curiosity in each individual, and not necessarily to mandate which content should be remembered for the assessment or test. That limits learning and stifles curiosity.

我見過很多好心的老師用他們無聊的演講、糟糕的內容傳達方式、無力的提問、乏味的「舞台表演」，甚至是因為他們那缺乏個性的性格而將生命力從教室中抽走，從而壓制和破壞學生的好奇心。許多老師關注學生的成績，而非他們的好奇心。他們沒能激發學生好奇心，因為他們自己就沒有好奇心。並不是每個老師都應該成為老師的。我認為，一位老師和一位偉大的老師之間的區別在於，偉大的老師可以從學生身上喚起學生的參與度。每位老師都必須是一個堅定的終身學習者，而且還應致力於提高他們的溝通、陳述和傳達能力。他們需要樹立純粹的好奇心榜樣，以激發學生們也這樣做。

I have seen so many well-meaning teachers squelch and destroy student curiosity through boring presentations, poor content delivery methods, weak questioning, dull "stage presence", or even because of a disengaged personality that sucks the life out of a classroom. Many teachers focus on student results and not student curiosity. They fail to inspire curiosity because they themselves are not curious. Not every teacher should be a teacher. In my opinion, the difference between a teacher and a GREAT teacher is the level of student engagement that great teachers can evoke from students. Every teacher needs to be a committed lifelong learner, but also committed to sharpening their skills of communication, presentation and delivery. They need to model pure curiosity, themselves, in order to inspire their students to do the same.

團隊變革的挑戰
The Challenges of Group Change

Image credit: CyberPR

改變一個人已經不易，要試圖改變整個群體或團隊，挑戰將更大！有時，領導者需要改變的不僅僅是一個人，因為需要的是對更大的「團隊文化」的改變。許多領導者發現所需的變革之路在於他們能否影響一大批人，因而感到不安。

　　Bringing about change in just one person is difficult. The challenge becomes significantly greater when trying to change an entire group or team! Sometimes leaders need to change more than just one person because it is a change in the larger "team culture" that is required. Many leaders face trepidation when they consider that the path of change needed rests in whether or not a large group of people can be affected.

　　每個群體、階級或工作場所都會發展出自己獨特的文化。每年，我的班級都會因其內在的性格而形成獨特的群體文化。這種文化由習慣、習俗、規範和行為構成，它們在任何群體中都作為標準出現。即使對於最具影響力的領導者而言，改變任何一個團隊的文化也是一項艱鉅的任務，因為要使團隊成員在變革方面保持一致是很難的。通常，群體會因適應了常態而抵制變化。適應變化需要犧牲固有己見，需要犧牲自我權利。變革是艱難的，而看到變革需要的領導者，應該為前方的艱難道路做好準備。

Each group, class or workplace develops its own unique culture. Each year my class has a distinctly unique group culture that forms, based on the personalities within. This culture is made up of habits, customs, norms, and behaviors that emerge as standards within any group. Changing the culture of any group is a daunting task, even for the most influential leaders, because getting the members of the group on the same page, with respect to change, is difficult. Often, groups are resistant to change because they have become comfortable in their norms. Yielding to change requires a sacrifice of autonomy and self-reliance. Change is hard, and the leader who sees the need for change should be prepared for the tough road ahead.

少數人可能將變革視為令人興奮的冒險，但同時，大多數人卻將其視為對自身穩定性的攻擊。每個人對改變的想法或需求的反應和反響都不盡相同。每個人接受改變的決定更多地取決於心態，而非此種改變本身的環境。不得不接受改變通常是一個逆耳的提醒，因為這等於在告訴團隊中的成員，他們根本做不了主。他們的獨立性和自治權受到威脅，因為他們可能看不到個人或團體的改變需求。如果採取這種態度，那麼領導者的工作就困難得多。許多人會僅僅因為難以改變而抵制改變。

Where a few may see change as an exciting new adventure, most see it as an assault on their stability. Everyone reacts and responds differently to the thought or need for change. Everyone's decision to embrace change is more dependent on mindset than it is about the circumstances surrounding the change itself. Having to accept change is often a stinging reminder that individuals within the group are not in charge at all. Their independence and autonomy feel threatened because they may not see the personal or group need for change. When this is the attitude, the leader's job is significantly more difficult. Many will resist change simply because making change is hard.

為什麼有些人能夠像接受新的令人興奮的冒險旅行一樣擁抱變化，而另一些人卻將其視為對其自主性和自我導向的威脅呢？當然，變化可能會令人不舒服而不安，因為我們已知的標準正在被修改，而任何不同的內容都意味著需要做更多的工作。但是，我發現許多面對變化時刻的人，只要得知，學習新事物可能最終更有價值或者能帶來改善，他們都擁有或可以發現，忽視不適或經受不適的能力。我們必須對變革的需求和過程有一個清晰的願景，以便團隊知道、理解並能接受預期的方向。這便是成長型心態可以在變化過程起作用的地方。

Why is it that some individuals can embrace change as if it is an invitation to go on a new and exciting adventure trip, whereas others see change as a threat to their autonomy and self-direction? Granted, change can be uncomfortable and disconcerting because what we knew as standard is now being modified, and anything that is different means more work is needed. Yet, I find many people who are facing moments of change have, or can find, the ability to look past or through the discomfort, if reminded that the prospects of learning something new may ultimately be more valuable and bring about improvement. A clear vision for the need and process for change must be cast so that the group knows, understands and can embrace the intended direction. This is where a GROWTH MINDSET can help the process of change.

美國心理學家、史丹佛大學教授卡爾.德懷克撰寫了《心態》一書，透過更好地理解思維方式的力量，幫助改變了數百萬人的生活。在她的精彩著作中，她簡明扼要地展示了人們對自身才幹和能力的認識和看待方式，如何極大地影響著人類在各領域的成功。德懷克的研究表明，那些擁有**固化思維模式**的人（即認為人的能力是固定的人），相較於擁有**成長型思維模式**的人（即認為能力可以發展的人），發展起來的可能性更小。這不僅僅是樂觀和悲觀的問題。它是自我反思的鏡子，可以成為人生方向和經驗的有力燈塔。領導者需要認識到，當涉及到變化這個問題時，人們需要一種成長型思維模式，固化思維模式是有害的。對於團隊文化變革，領導者必須了解團隊成員的思維模式。

American Psychologist and Stanford Professor, Carol Dweck, wrote the book, *MINDSET*, which has helped transform millions of lives by giving a better understanding of the power of mindset. In her brilliant book, she simplistically shows how success in every area of human endeavor can be dramatically influenced by how we think and view our talents and abilities. Dweck's research shows that those people with a *fixed mindset*—those who believe that abilities are fixed—are less likely to flourish than those with a *growth mindset*—those who believe that abilities can be developed. It is more than just optimism versus pessimism. It is a lens of self-reflection that can be a powerful beacon for life's direction and experiences. Leaders need to understand that when it comes to change, a growth mindset is needed and a fixed mindset is detrimental. For a collective group culture change, the leader must understand the mindset of those in the group.

德懷克的書是我讀過的最具變革性的書之一。在我的家庭中，我有一對慈愛的父母，我是五個孩子中最小的一個。我父親是一位牧師，作為一個人，一位父親和一位丈夫，儘管他非常出色，但他不一定抱有什麼大夢想。他喜歡自己的例行工作，也喜歡那種知道自己是誰、做過什麼以及為什麼選擇這樣做的一貫性。甚至確切知道自己的收入也令他感到滿意。這種一貫性給了他安全感和放心的感覺。在我成長過程中，我發現這種心態對他似乎是有用的，因此，我認為它對我也有用。然而，我的心態被重塑了，首先是因為絕望，然後是出於自己的選擇。

I found Dweck's book to be one of the most transformational books I have ever read. I grew up the youngest of five kids to a loving mother and father. My dad was a preacher, and in all his greatness as a person, father, and husband, he did not necessarily dream big for himself. He loved his routine and the consistency of knowing who he was, what he did, and why he chose to do it. He even found comfort in knowing exactly what he would earn for his work. This consistency gave him a sense of security and a feeling of reassurance to his psyche. As I was growing up, I could see that that mentality seemed to work for him, and therefore, I thought it would also work for me. However, I think my mindset began to reshape first out of desperation and then out of choice.

當我向妻子求婚時，她已經是兩個小女孩的母親。我們之前在大學期間約會過，之後分手，後來我們重新建立了關係，唯一不同的是這次有兩個小生命要加到我們的關係中。當然，我不知道如何成為父親，那時我認為我只有和一歲和兩歲的孩子一起學習「育兒之道」，而沒法返回到她們嬰兒時開始學習。像許多新婚夫婦一樣，至少可以說我們的財務狀況十分艱難。當時我並沒有從事什麼視為「長遠職業」的工作，結婚後三個月內，我被解雇，在一家餐館當服務員謀生。但那時，我很快就發現自己（那之後很久我才讀到德懷克的書）有很強的成長型心態。

When I proposed to my wife, she was already a mother to two little girls. Having dated previously, we reconnected and picked up our relationship where we left off from our college dating days, except this time there were 2 little lives to add to the relationship mix. Granted, I had no idea how to be a father, but I assumed I would just learn the "parenting thing" with kids who were already 1 and 2 years old, versus starting out with them when they were babies. Like many newlyweds, our financial start was rocky to say the least. I did not have a "career" job at the time and, within 3 months of being married, I found myself laid off and waiting tables in a restaurant for economic survival. What I soon discovered about myself (long before I had read Dweck's book) was that my growth mindset was strong.

這些早期的經濟困難使我改變的需求變得顯而易見。要說服自己並不難，我已經有了一個四口之家，不得不迅速做出一些重要的改變。我知道我可以找到很多謀生的方法。我打零工（多謝卡爾姆巴赫太太和克雷恩太太），我的妻子也同樣努力工作，我們就這樣度過了艱難的早期歲月。透過這些奮鬥，我倆都具備了更堅強的心態，這種心態讓我們明白自己可以做到什麼。這些情況需要個人進行改變。改變很困難，但卻是必須做的事情。具有成長型心態使我們能夠接受變化帶來的不適，因為我們可以看到變化帶來的好處。對我而言，最不為人知的是，那些早期歲月塑造了我的企業家直覺，以及我一生中關於變革的思考。

These early economic struggles made the need for personal change rather obvious. It was not hard to convince myself that with a new instant family of four, I was going to have to make some critical changes quickly. I knew I could find lots of ways to survive and make a living. I picked up odd jobs (thank you Mrs. Kalmbach and Mrs. Crane) and my wife worked equally hard to survive some tough, early, lean years. Through those struggles, we both developed stronger mindsets that showed us that we could accomplish things. Those circumstances required personal change. Change was hard but had to be done. Having a growth mindset allowed us to embrace the discomfort of change because we could see the benefits of the change on the horizon. Unbeknownst to me, those early years were shaping my entrepreneurial instincts and how I thought about change for the rest of my life.

短短幾週之後，我被餐館解雇，這促使我申請了教師的工作（這是我最初在大學學習的內容）。意識到改變的必要性後，我更加努力地做出改變，以創造更光明的未來。幸運的是，我找到一所小型私立學校，非常適合我當老師。我很快就發現自己跟隨父親的步伐，走上了穩定舒適的道路。

After just a few short weeks, I was fired from my restaurant job, which pushed me into applying for teaching jobs (which is what I had been trained for in college in the first place). Realizing the need for change, I pushed harder to make the change necessary for a brighter future. Fortunately, I found a small private school that was a great fit for me as a teacher. I soon found myself following my father's footsteps into the comfort of consistency.

我的教學生涯雖然算不上特別掙錢，卻為我提供了財務的穩定性，並且非常充實，使我處於一個可以永遠塑造我的企業家精神的環境中。我開始從事不同的業務時，我發現自己遵循著與以往一樣的職業道德。這些追求可能是出於養育全家五個孩子的需要，但更深層的動機並非財務方面的，而是追求成就。

My teaching career, though not particularly lucrative, provided me with financial consistency and proved very fulfilling, placing me into an environment that would forever shape my entrepreneurial spirit. I found myself applying the same work ethic that I had noticed previously, as I began to start different business pursuits. These pursuits may have arisen out of the need to provide for my family of five children, but the deeper motivation was not as much about finances, as is was about finding fulfillment.

在二十年的全職教學生涯中，我也發展了其他業務。我接受了成長型思維模式——這是機遇使然，並從全職教學中走了出來，將更多的精力投入到發展我的商業興趣上。具有諷刺意味的是，父親此時將我的許多選擇視為「風險」，但在我看來，這些改變是有必要的。這就是我證明德懷克所描述的**思維差異**的證據。我擁有一種成長型思維模式，而我父親是典型的固化思維模式。（**我得說，我並不認為一種思維模式一定是正確的，而另一種思維模式是錯誤的。我父親是一個非常忠實自律的人。我的紀律性可能遠不如他，但是在某些領域缺乏紀律使我在其他領域蓬勃發展。我因為他的穩定性帶給我的一切而深愛著他。**）

During my 20 years of full-time teaching, I simultaneously developed other business pursuits. I embraced the growth mindset that opportunity presented and stepped away from full-time teaching to pour more efforts into developing my business interests. Ironically, my father saw many of my choices at this time as "risky", yet in my mind, I saw them as necessary change. This was my proof of what Dweck would describe as *the mindset difference*. Mine was a growth mindset, whereas my dad's was a classic fixed mindset. *(Let me say that I do not think one mindset is necessarily right and the other wrong. My dad was an incredibly faithful and disciplined man. I am probably far less disciplined than he, but that lack of discipline in some areas makes me thrive in other areas. I loved him for everything his consistency did for me.)*

我所必須經歷的改變對我而言至關重要。它完全喚醒了我的企業家精神，並開始了我作為商務人士的第二職業。對我來說，改變只是因為遵循了我的成長型思維模式。它並非沒有風險，但我的風險承受能力遠大於我父親。

The change I had to go through was essential for me. It fully awakened my full entrepreneurial spirit and started me on my second career as a businessman…of sorts. For me, change resulted from simply following my growth mindset. It was not void of risk, but my risk tolerance was far greater than my father's.

我講這個故事是因為這與個人改變有關。我當時必須進行一些艱難的個人改變。由於我的成長型思維模式和對風險的承受能力，這些變化得以發生。改變一個人（尤其是自己）並不總像改變多個人那樣具有挑戰性。如果教師將班級的性格視為有害或破壞性的，則他必須以成長型思維模式來努力實現群體的改變。需要改變公司文化的公司領導者或經理也需要一種成長型思維模式，以便為所需的文化變革設定清晰的願景和過程。我們可以發現變革是艱難的，有時甚至是讓人不適的。但是，如果可以訓練成長型思維模式，並將經歷的不適視為實現成長之必需，那麼自我或團隊的成功改變就有可能發生。

I tell this story because this is about personal change. I had to make some difficult personal changes. These changes were propagated because of my shaping growth mindset and emerging tolerance for risk. Changing one person (especially oneself) is not always as challenging as changing more than one person. A teacher who sees the personality of the class as one that is detrimental or destructive must embrace a growth mindset to work towards group change. A company leader or manager that needs to change a company culture will also need a growth mindset to set out a clear vision and process for the culture change desired. We can all recognize that change is hard and, at times, uncomfortable. But, if a growth mindset can be trained, and the discomfort experienced seen as necessary for fulfilling growth, then successful change in self or the group is possible.

帶領團隊走向變革
Leading a Group Toward Change

當團隊領導認為有必要進行變革時，還必須仔細考慮如何要求成員接受變革。具有成長型思維模式的領導者不能期望團隊中的每個人都具有相同的思想和接受度。許多人看不到變革帶來好處的可能性，而認為變革是對穩定性和舒適性的惡化或威脅。領導如果不能讓團隊成員在**情感上**為即將發生的變革做好準備，那他們會發現團隊成員在任何時候都可能對變革產生**智識上**的抵制。

The group leader who sees change as necessary must also give careful consideration to how to ask for members to embrace the change. A leader who has the growth mindset cannot expect everyone within the group to be of the same mind and acceptance. Many people see change not for the possibilities they may present, but rather as a deterioration or threat to stability and comfort of consistency. Leaders who fail to *emotionally* prepare the group for the impending change can expect *intellectual* resistance to the change at every turn.

認真樹立變革願景至關重要。對於團隊成員而言，重要的是能夠聽到並且盡可能要看到變更的過程和結果是怎麼樣的。在進行變革之前，他們必須清楚地表達願景，這一點很重要。最初，那些擁有固化思維模式（甚至可能是成長型思維模式）的人可能會對變革的想法產生負面反應。他們可能在變革的方式方法上存在分歧，或者一開始就抵制需要變革這個觀點。領導者不能無視這些反應，也不能簡單地要求做出改變，而不設身處地地理解團隊中的每個人對改變的想法。優秀的領導者會找到辦法來驗證和表達對變革可能有多困難的理解，並且這樣做有助於塑造或至少揭示思維模式在這個過程中所起的作用。

Carefully casting a vision for change is essential. It is important for members of the group to hear, and probably see, the vision of what the change process and results may look like. It is important that they know the articulated vision before thrusting into change. Initially, those with a fixed mindset (or maybe even a growth mindset) may react negatively to the idea of change. They may disagree on the means, method and mode of change, or resist the philosophical vision that change is needed in the first place. Leaders cannot ignore these reactions, nor can they simply mandate the change without showing empathy for how individuals in the group will deal with the idea of change. Good leaders find ways to validate and express understanding for how difficult change can be, and in doing so, they help shape, or at least reveal, how mindset plays a role in the process.

有時候，可以透過簡單地對成員表明改變的需求或讓其發聲來化解變革阻力。富有同情心地表達關切，這代表了領導層的關心和考慮，這種做法可能會使許多人感到安慰，同時也分散了其他人的擔憂。但是，如果希望獲得全面的理解和支持，可能仍需更多的保證和說服。

Sometimes resistance can be headed off at the pass by simply providing an acknowledgment or vocalization for the range of feelings members are likely to have. Empathetically stating this reflects care and consideration on behalf of the leadership and doing so may give comfort to many while also diffusing the concerns of others. But more reassurance may still be needed if you hope to get full buy-in and support.

我們可以考慮的一種有效的策略，就是和對團隊有明顯影響的主要領導人（團隊的推動者和參與者）私下會面。與主要領導人會面可能使得他們支持你的計劃。指導和管理他們的反應可能有助於團隊整體對變革的看法和接受度。希望他們能將它傳遞給他們所能影響的人。至少，這個舉措將幫助他們了解團隊的想法。

One effective strategy to consider would be to meet privately with key leaders (the group movers and shakers) who have a clear & obvious impact on the group. Meeting with key leaders may empower them to support your initiatives. Guiding and managing their reactions may help the overall tone and acceptance of the message, vis-à-vis the larger group. The hope is that they would pass it on to those they influence. At the very least, it will help them get a sense of the pulse of the group.

在教室中，這可能意味著與一些具社交影響力的學生坐在一起，他們可能會利用自己的身份來幫助傳播訊息。在工作場所中，這可能意味著需要找到一些能準確反映整個團隊想法的有影響力的人員。這也就是「分而治之」的策略。領導者必須給策略足夠的時間，以考慮如何提出所需進行的變革，並在被問起時能預知團隊成員的潛在反應。優秀的領導者能把準團隊的思想脈搏，很少會因團隊的反應而感到震驚，因為他們了解那些他們領導的人的個性。

In a classroom, this may involve sitting with a few socially influential students who might use their status to help spread the message. In the workplace, this might include finding a few influential workers who could accurately reflect the overall group pulse. This is the "divide and conquer" strategy. It is necessary for the leader(s) to give quality strategy time to considering how to ask for the change needed and anticipate the potential reaction of group members when asked. Good leaders have their finger on the group pulse and are rarely shocked or surprised by the range of responses because they know and understand the personalities of those they lead.

另一個需要考慮的關鍵因素是團隊成員有多少時間來消化變革的想法。在某些情況下，變革的發生必須比任何人所希望的快得多。按照先前提出的先發制人的方法，可以簡單地進行感同身受式的承認，即儘管大家都希望團隊成員有更多的時間來吸收和處理即將發生的變化，但時間緊迫，根本沒有辦法這樣做。因此，不得不立即發生改變，而這比任何人願意接受的速度都更快。傳達這一訊息仍然可以驗證你的感受，但幾乎沒有動搖和表示異議的空間。大多數團隊成員希望做的，就是知道領導者能夠驗證並認識到團隊對變化的感受。一個團隊中，不是所有人都是成長型思維模式或固定思維模式，兩者永遠是融合在一起的。請尊重所有感受，並就如何在整個過程中共享、實施和處理變化而提出周到的計劃。這將有助於團隊成員更好地消化和吸收變化。他們可能仍然不全都喜歡變化，但是相比於獨裁的方法，感同身受的方法可能更讓人樂意接受。

Another key consideration is how much processing time the group members are given to digest the idea of change. There are always situations that arise when change must happen more quickly than anyone may prefer. Following the same preemptive approach previously suggested could simply include an empathetic acknowledgement that although more time for members to absorb and process the impending change is the desire, the time constriction simply does not permit it. Therefore, immediate change must happen faster than anyone will necessarily be comfortable with. Giving this message still validates the feelings, but gives little room to wiggle and show dissent. A key thing that most group members want is to know that the leader validates and recognizes the group's range of feelings about change. No group has a membership of all growth mindset or fixed mindset members. There will always be a blend of both. Treat all feelings with respect and present a thoughtful plan as to how the news of change will be shared, implemented, and handled throughout the process. This will help the group members to digest and absorb change better. They still may not all like it, but it may be more palatable with an empathetic approach versus a dictatorial approach.

畢竟,團隊成員希望能信任領導他們的人。領導者不僅因摁擁有領導職位而贏得尊重。團隊成員希望因摁自己的感情以及他們的服務而受到讚賞和重視。甚至連那些成長型思維模式的成員也可能在一定程度上因為變革的想法而感到威脅。許多領導者認為變革的必要性一直是顯而易見,而被要求改變的人們卻認為變革是有害且令人恐懼的。當然,領導者並非總是能讓團隊中百分之百的人信服改變,這可能是一件好事。但是,領導者應努力確保在必須進行改變之前,團隊中百分之百的人感受到傾聽和重視。

Ultimately, group members want to trust those who are leading them. Leaders do not just earn that respect because of the leadership title they possess. Group members want to feel appreciated and valued for their feelings, as well as for their service. Even those growth mindset members may feel threatened by the idea of change, to a degree. Many leaders see the change needed as clear as day, while those being asked to change view it as detrimental and frightening. Granted, it is not always possible for a leader to convince 100% of the group that change may be a good thing but, the leader should work hard to ensure that 100% of the feelings of those represented are heard and valued before forcing change to occur.

認真考慮如何引入或實施變革是值得做的,並且需要花費時間。把準「團隊成員脈搏」的領導者可能知道大多數團隊成員將如何接受或拒絕這種變化，但是對於大型公司而言，獲得關鍵部門領導的傾聽可能對於獲得真實觀點至關重要。只有在將受影響的接收者至少能夠分享願景和改變背後的原因時，才是實施變革的最佳方式。了解團隊成員的成長型或固化思維模式將使變革的訊息能夠以更體貼的方式呈現。

Careful consideration as to how change is introduced or rolled out is worthwhile, and it requires an investment of time. Leaders who have the "pulse of the people" may know how it will be received or rejected by most of the group members, but for larger companies, hearing from key divisional leaders is probably crucial to have a true perspective. Change is best implemented when the recipients who will be impacted can at least share in the vision and in the reason behind the change. Knowing the growth and fixed mindset perspective of those in the group will allow the message of change to be presented in a more thoughtful and considerate way.

一些簡單的思路
Simple Thoughts of Consideration

1. **精益求變**——我曾經聽過「精益求變」一詞。我真的很喜歡聽到這個詞語時想到的畫面。傾向於變革的公司或領導者通常會組建一支充滿關鍵成長型思維的領導者團隊。不是因為改變而改變，而是為了相關性和創新而改變。顯而易見，蘋果、阿里巴巴、騰訊、微軟、亞馬遜都是變革的偉大範例。而西爾斯公司則是一個反面案例。曾經在某個時期裡，美國公司西爾斯憑藉其PRODIGY產品的創新合作而有望成為亞馬遜那樣的公司。但是，由於西爾斯並不傾向於變革，因此它對時代文化的演變沒有作出反應。如今，西爾斯僅剩不到五百家門店，並且由於相關性的缺乏和對創新的抵制而逐漸走向衰敗。

1. **Lean Into Change** - I once heard the term, "lean into change". I really like the image that comes to my mind when I hear that. Companies, or

leaders, who lean into change usually build teams full of key growth mindset leaders. It is not that they change for the sake of change but instead for the sake of relevancy and innovation. Apple, Alibaba, Tencent, Microsoft, Amazon are all clear mega-examples of leaning into change. Sears would be an example of the opposite. At one time, the American company – SEARS - was in the driver's seat to become Amazon with their innovative collaboration with their PRODIGY product. But, because Sears was not leaning into change, it did not react to the evolving culture of the times. Today, Sears has fewer than 500 stores remaining and is slowly being suffocated due to lack of relevancy and resistance to innovation.

2. 變革文化——上文說過，很多人像躲避瘟疫一樣避免改變本身。很多時候，改變被視為對一致性、舒適性和獨立性的的攻擊。文化變革的基礎源於領導者在聘用或引入團隊時所做出的選擇。文化往往是由人格塑造的，而不是程序。領導者應著重於讓合適的人「上車」，即使領導者不能完全確定「汽車的去向」。在旅途中尋找可以適應並做出改變的人員要比讓每個人都了解目的地但無法到達目的地要好得多。對於老師來說，應該意識到變革的文化是發生在每個班級成員的個性之內。

2. The Culture of Change - I already shared that many people avoid change like the plague. Very often, change is viewed as an assault on everything that stands for consistency, comfort and independence. The foundation of culture change emanates from the choices leaders make in whom they hire or add to the group. Culture is most often shaped by personalities, more than procedures. Leaders should focus on getting the right people on the bus, even if the leader is not totally sure where the bus is headed. Acquiring people who can adapt and make modifications during the trip is far better than having everyone understand the destination, but not be able to get there. For the teacher, realize the culture of change is within the personalities of who is in the class.

3. 心態很重要——除了把《心態》這本書作為所有員工的必讀書籍之外，那些招聘人員或直接負責團隊建設和培訓的領導者還應該精通了解誰在塑造文化的「車」上。固定思維模式的人可以改變，但他們可能會以不同的方法來看到這樣做的價值和需要。同樣，成長型思維模式的人可能更容易接受改變，但是當需要整合文化時，他們也可能更容易分心。最重要的是，業務的開展既需要成長型又需要固定思維的個體才能組成團隊。了解與你你一起工作的人的心態很重要。

3. Mindset Matters - Aside from making the book *Mindset* mandatory reading for all employees, those who do the hiring, or the leaders directly responsible for team building and training should be well versed in knowing who is on the culture-shaping bus. Fixed mindset individuals can change, but it may just take a different approach for them to see the value or need to do so. In the same way, growth mindset people may change more easily, but they can also become more easily distracted when culture consolidation is necessary. The bottom line is that business requires both growth and fixed mindset individuals to be a part of the team. Understanding the mindset of those you work with does matter.

總結
Summary

領導者對變革的看法可以透過口頭進行表達，但需要確定的是，那些接受領導的人需要在聽到變革之前先觀察到變革。除少數例外，領導者需要生動表達自己對改變的感受。領導者應始終為期望的行為樹立榜樣，因此，他們必須願意成為變革的第一部份。公司或團隊的文化始於高層，領導者為變革和進步奠定基調。如果領導者自己的成長型思維模式都不靈活、適應力不強也不流暢，那麼對於周圍的人來說，這是肉眼可觀察的。這些領導者時刻關注著團隊的動向，因此他們通常知道傳達變革有多麼困難或輕鬆。即使在溝通良好的願景中出色地提出變革，除非該團隊成員認為對變革的誠意和支持始於提出變革要求的人，否則他們將對變革進行抵制。如果你想領導團隊，請表現出同理心，但也要完全透明，並且自己也要願意接受改變。如果你要讓人們放棄穩定性、獨立性、自治性和舒適性，那麼請驗證他們的感受。讓他們知道變革是困難的，但是在過程和結果中他們會獲得成長。

A leader's own opinion about change can be verbally communicated, but, most assuredly, those they are leading need to observe it before they hear it. With few exceptions, leaders will vividly portray their own feelings about change in how they conduct themselves. A leader should always model desired behaviors and, therefore, must be willing to be the first part of change. The company or group culture starts at the top, and those who lead set the tone for change and progress. If leaders are not flexible, adaptable, and fluid in their own growth mindset, that will be obvious to those around them. These leaders have their finger on the pulse of the group so they often know how hard or easy communicating change will be. Even when change is brilliantly laid out in a well-communicated vision, it will be resisted unless the group feels that sincerity and support for change starts with those who are asking for it. If you want to lead, show empathy, but also be fully transparent and willing to embrace the change yourself. Validate the feelings of those you are asking to give up independence, autonomy, and comfort in consistency. Let them know you understand change is hard, but that there is growth waiting for them in the process and in the results.

教師需要注意課堂文化。這文化是集體中的每一個體的性格所塑造的。大多數情況下，班級氛圍是無法透過剔除一個或幾個成員而去除或改變的。與工作場所不同，你無法輕易開除學生。改變班級文化是具有挑戰性的。改變班級文化通常是全年進行的過程，具體而言，它是透過提出和執行明確的期望和後果而得到強化的。改變班級文化是最早教育孩子成長型和固定思維模式的機會之一。這是他們一生的寶貴教育。

      Teachers need to be mindful of the class culture. It is shaped by the individual personalities that make up the collective whole. Most times, removing or changing the dynamics by removing one or a few members is not possible. Unlike in the workplace, you can't easily just fire a student. Changing a class culture is challenging. The process of changing the class culture is often a yearlong process strengthened by presenting and enforcing clear expectations and consequences. Changing class culture is one of the earliest opportunities to educate children on the ideals of the growth and fixed mindset. This is valuable education for their life.

關於影響的名言
Impact Quotes

- 成長是痛苦的。變化是痛苦的。但是沒有什麼比停留在不屬於你的地方更痛苦的了。
  "Growth is painful. Change is painful. But nothing is as painful as staying stuck somewhere you don't belong."
- 那些不能改變主意的人，不能改變任何東西。
  "Those who cannot change their minds cannot change anything."
- 萬事唯有先難，方能後易。
  "All things are difficult before they are easy."
- 未來的事情比我們□在身後的要好得多□——孔子
  "There are far better things ahead than any we leave behind." -- Confucius
- 改變是不可避免的。成長是可選擇的。——約翰.C.麥克斯韋
  "Change is inevitable. Growth is optional" -- John C. Maxwell

It 要素
The "It" Factor

Image credit: The It Factor @ itfactorbiz

　　你是否想過，為什麼成年之後你能記得一部份老師，而其他老師則記得不清楚呢？我對許多老師有一些基本的記憶，但對少數老師有強烈的記憶。我三年級的時候有一個老師，這個老師一定是很出色的，因為作為一個「活躍的」男孩，我在她的課堂上感到自己是有能力的。我還可以輕鬆地想起我的打字老師（閱讀這篇文章的年輕人根本不知道打字機是什麼東西），因為她在嚴格、友好和愉快之間找到了很好的平衡。對於那些以前聽過我故事的人來說，我一直很在意一位老師——唐.馬丁代爾所扮演的角色，他在我的生活中扮演著具有影響力和改變一生的角色。儘管我在高中的學習成績不佳，但他還是設法提高了我的運動能力和領導能力，並給了我從事教育事業的希望。他的鼓勵，可以說，改變了我的人生道路。為什麼我還記得這些老師對我的影響，但卻無法記住所有的老師呢？我認為，有影響力的老師會因為具有「it」因素而與他們的學生建立連結。

　　Do you ever wonder why, as an adult, you can remember some of your teachers more than others? I have some basic recall memories of many of my teachers but intense memories of a select few. I had a 3rd grade teacher that must have been rather exceptional because, as an "active" boy, she made me feel capable in the classroom. I can also easily recall my typing teacher (young people reading this have no idea what a typewriter even is) because she managed a beautiful balance between being strict, yet friendly and pleasant. For those who have heard my story before, I have been very vocal about one teacher - Don Martindale - who played an influential and life-changing role in my life. Despite my less than stellar academic high school performance, he managed to encourage my athletic and leadership skills and gave me hope for a possible career in education. His encouragement literally altered the path of my life. Why do I remember the impact these teachers had on me, but I do not recall all my teachers the same way? I think impactful teachers make a connection with a student because of having the "it" factor.

在順利完成本科、研究生學習並走上我的第一份教學崗位後，我的生活飛速前進，在那裡我發現自己全神貫注於與學生的聯繫。像大多數老師一樣，儘管我嘗試對所有學生進行相同的教學，但我發現我與一些學生相處得比其他學生更好。我盡力以「影響」學生的方式教學生，就像我的老師影響我那樣，我知道自己作為老師的性格（常常以諷刺挖苦的方式來讓自己顯得有趣）對某些學生而言並不具有吸引力，但我敢肯定，這有助於建立一種舒適感和聯繫感，使我的角色超出教授學科知識的老師，讓他們知道有對他們有更大的幫助，能夠幫助他們成長並適應中學時代。當我考慮如何描述或定義「it」因素是什麼時，我認為「it」在於教師如何與學生建立有意義的聯繫並產生影響，超越其所教授的課堂內容。學生和老師之間的聯繫成功地達到更高的水平，這使老師能夠對學生進行有力的指導、建議、愛護，和時不時地幫助和管教他們，使學生能夠為人生做好準備。

Flash forward my life after having navigated successfully through college, grad school and into my first teaching job where I found myself focusing heavily on my connection to the students. Like most teachers, although trying to teach all students the same, I found that I got along with some students better than others. As hard as I tried to "impact" students the same way that my teachers had influenced me, I knew that my personality as a teacher (often using sarcasm to be funny) was not a personality style that some of my students probably found appealing. But I am sure for some, it helped to create a comfort and connection that allowed my role to be less about the subject taught and more about me helping them to grow up and navigate through their middle school years. When I think about how to describe or define what the "it" factor is, I think that "it" rests in how the teacher makes that meaningful connection with students and having that impact extend beyond the material that is being taught. The student and teacher connection that successfully hits a different level puts the teacher in a powerful position to guide, advise, love, and at times help discipline the student, enabling the student to be better prepared for life.

為什麼有些老師似乎有「it」因素而有些老師卻沒有呢？我認為，這個問題的答案更多與師生關係的「化學反應」有關。我肯定記得自己和有些學生的聯繫比其他學生更加牢固。由於這種聯繫，我認為我們之間建立了更深的信任和尊重，進而形成有意義的經歷和聯繫。對於其他人，如果我們的性格不合，則儘管他們可能已經學習了我在班上所教的學科內容，但他們可能沒有將我添加到具有「it」因素的老師名單中。與盡可能多的學生建立真誠的聯繫對我而言是即艱鉅又理想的目標。作為老師，除了和與我們相處融洽的學生建立聯繫之外，我們應盡量不只選擇和我們更為接近的人，而要竭盡全力確保與所有學生建立潛在的聯繫。我們的工作始終是教育每一名學生。為此，我們必須了解他們，並以他們作為一個人和學習者的身份對待他們。

Why do some teachers seem to have it and others don't? I think the answer to that question has more to do with the "chemistry" of the relationship between teacher and student. There were certainly students I can recall with whom I had stronger personality connections than with others. And because of that connection, I think a deeper trust and respect developed between us and, in turn, forged a meaningful memory and connection. For others, if our personalities did not mesh, then although they may have learned subject information taught in my class, they may not have added me to their list of teachers who had the "it" factor. Building authentic connections with as many students as possible was my difficult, yet desired, goal. We as teachers should try NOT to pick and choose who we want to be drawn closer too, but rather stretch ourselves to ensure we tap into potential connections with all students, not just those we seem to get along better with than others. Our job is always to teach each individual student. To do so, we must get to know them and meet them where they are as a person and as a learner.

　　我在一所學校工作了二十年。在那段時間裡，我可以誠實地說，我愛自己曾經教過的幾乎所有班級的學生。當然，有個別學生讓我的記憶尤其深刻，但是當我回顧我的整個職業生涯時，除了一個班級的學生之外，我幾乎對所有學生都有愉快的回憶。這個班級的特點被少數幾個男孩造成了負面的影響。那是一所小規模的學校，課堂比正常班級小（這可能表明這幾個男孩消極情緒，迫使其他學生選擇了轉校）。他們藐視權威，特別是對老師。他們彼此討厭，也討厭周圍的人，對試圖靠近他們的老師也心懷討厭。簡而言之，由於這幾個男孩的行為方式，沒有人喜歡他們。

　　　　I worked at one school for 20 years. During that time, I can honestly say I loved almost all the classes of students I ever taught. I remember specific students more than others, but when I survey my entire career, I have pleasant memories of all but one class of students. This class was negatively characterized and manipulated by a small handful of boys. Being a small school anyway, this class happened to be a smaller than normal class (probably indicative of the negativity within these few boys which may have forced other students to find another school). They carried a persona of contempt for authority and especially towards the teachers. They were nasty to each other, nasty to those around them, and nasty to the teachers who tried to draw close to them. In simple terms, because of how a few boys acted, they were unlikeable.

按照我們的一貫傳統，我們每個學年都從八年級的過夜露營之旅開始，以幫助學生們彼此建立聯繫。這次旅行是在戶外進行，學生們在帳篷裡睡覺，做飯，在大自然裡徒步旅行，參加高空繩索課程，當我們作為老師與學生互動時，這也是非常重要的「沉澱時間」。這麼多年來，在每次的露營旅行後，結果始終是相同的——這段美好的時光將學生們凝聚在一起，並為整個學年奠定積極的基調。但是，今年會有所不同。

As was our longstanding tradition, we began each school year with an 8th grade overnight camping trip to help bond students together. The trip was done outdoors, complete with students sleeping in tents, making our own food, hiking in nature, participating in a high ropes course, and it also had the very important "down time" when we, as teachers, could interact with the students. In all the previous and subsequent years of this trip, the result was always the same - a spectacular time that bonded students together and set a positive tone for the rest of the school year. However, this year would be different.

學生們總是享受這段休息時光，在此期間，老師與學生們一起踢足球或打籃球。這段時光總是充滿樂趣和歡笑，它使學生有機會在我們不那麼嚴肅的時候透過「娛樂與遊戲」的方式看待他們的老師。但是，在這個特殊的年份裡，有一群男孩不僅試圖贏得比賽，而且在此過程中羞辱了我們。我們甚至感到他們似乎試圖毆打我們！

Students always enjoyed this downtime during which we teachers would play football or basketball together with the students. It was always filled with fun and laughter, and it gave the students a chance to see us, as teachers, in a "fun & games" element when we were not so serious. But, in this particular year, there was a group of boys who were not just trying to win the game but to humiliate us in the process. We felt as if they were trying to beat us physically!

　　大約二十分鐘後，我們提前結束了橄欖球比賽，因此沒有人受傷。我們認為籃球可能不如橄欖球那麼具有戰鬥性，所以嘗試了這項運動，但結果是，我們很快就意識到他們把籃球打得更像橄欖球！那場比賽也很快結束了，以避免我們受到傷害。在兩場比賽中，這群男孩都在嘲笑我們。本來初衷是與我們建立聯繫，但卻迫使我們之間陷入了令人討厭的困境。在之前和之後的所有年月裡，我們從來沒有一群學生有他們那樣的表現。因此，像以前的所有野營旅行一樣，這一年也為一整年奠定了基調。但是，與前幾年不同，這種基調給人以非常消極和令人討厭的感覺，並且從未消失。

　　We ended the football game after only about 20 minutes, so we did not get hurt. Feeling that basketball might be less combative than the football was proving to be, we tried that sport only to quickly realize they were making basketball look more like football! That game also ended rather quickly, to avoid us getting hurt. During both games, this group of boys was snickering and mocking us. What was meant to bond us, drove a nasty wedge between us, instead. In all the years before, and after, we never had a group of students behave the way that they did. Consequently, like all the prior camping trips, this one also set the tone firmly for the entire year. However, unlike all the previous years, this tone had a very negative and nasty feel to it that never went away.

　　即使在撰寫本文時，我仍可以輕易回憶起班上少數可恥又討厭的學生的名字和面孔！我也可以回想起同一個班級裡的一些快樂、積極而又可愛的學生，但不幸的是，由於種種錯誤的原因，這些男孩的面孔更加令人難忘。

Even now as I write, I can easily recall the names and faces of the few members of that class who were mean and nasty! I can recall a few of the happy, positive, and sweet students within that same class, but unfortunately, the faces of those boys are far too memorable, for all the wrong reasons.

我非常努力地與他們建立聯繫。與八年級學生有很多聯繫，這讓我感到很榮幸：我教了他們美國歷史、衛生、體育以及足球和籃球。我也擔任班主任和輔導員，因此與其中一些學生度過了寶貴的時光。我以為他們可能只是不喜歡學術課程，如果是這樣，那麼我當然可以與他們建立聯繫，成為他們的籃球或足球教練。不，他們還是相同的反應！這也是我二十七年的教練生涯中唯一的一次在比賽結束時不得不將一支球隊從地板上拉下來並且不與對手握手的原因，因為我的一些球員已經準備好與另一支球隊的成員打架了。（請記住，他們是來自郊區一所富人中學的八年級學生。）作為教練和老師，我很尷尬，因為這些男孩子的表現與以往毫無二致。那支球隊在兩項運動中只贏了區區幾場比賽，這一點也不奇怪。

I had tried very hard to bond with them. I had the luxury of having many points of contact with 8th grade students: I taught many of them US History, Health, PE, and coached soccer and basketball. I was also homeroom teacher and an advisor, so the time spent with some of these students was significant. I thought maybe they just didn't like academic classes and, if that was the case, then surely I could bond with them as their basketball or soccer coach. Nope! Same response. This would also be the only time in my 27-year coaching career that I had to pull a team off the floor at the end of the game and not shake the opponent's hands because some of my players were ready to fight members of the other team. (Remember, these were 8th graders from a wealthy, well-to-do middle school in suburbia.) I was very embarrassed, as a coach and as teacher, that these boys acted the way they did. Not surprisingly, that team only won a few games…in both sports.

在這種情況下，一個班級的特徵遭到少數可悲的人的統治，他們以消極的態度對待他人，這破壞了許多老師及其同學的整個學年。我肯定看不到「it」因素。我可以肯定地說，這些難忘的男孩中沒有一個把我列入對他們有影響的老師。要具有「it」因素，必須存在對等聯繫，而不是單向聯繫。就像老師可以嘗試差異化的教學方式一樣，我們也必須嘗試差異化的聯繫方式。如果不能建立聯繫，那麼整體而言，影響力就微乎其微。

In this case, the class was powerfully characterized and dominated by a few miserable individuals who treated others with negativity and, in doing so, ruined a school year for a lot of teachers and their classmates. The "it" factor was not visible in me for sure. I feel safe to say that none of these memorable boys would have me on their list of impactful teachers. To have the "it" factor, there must be a reciprocal connection, not a one-way connection. Just like the teacher may try differentiated teaching styles, so too must we try differentiated connection styles. If the connection is not made, the overall impact is minimalized.

培養關係
Cultivating Relationships

我喜歡教中學生的原因之一，是他們希望與老師建立積極的聯繫。我認為許多學生，甚至工作場所的許多員工都是如此。人們被人際關係所吸引，因此，大多數人在感受到連結時就會喜歡上它。我們都有一種與生俱來的強烈願望，希望能感受到特別的事物。這就是為什麼家庭感覺在人生中有如此強大的影響力。人類都想屬於某一個群體。如果老師可以與學生建立聯繫並幫助其建立健康而有影響力的關係，那麼老師便能夠改變學生的人生。

One reason I loved teaching middle school students was that they wanted to have positive connections with their teachers. I think that is true of many students and even many employees in the workplace. Humans are drawn to personal connections and, therefore, most love it when they feel connected. We all have an innate and powerful desire to feel a part of something special. It is why the feeling of family is such a powerful influencer in life. Humans want to belong to a group. If a teacher can connect with a student and help forge a healthy and impactful relationship, that teacher can literally change the life of a student.

這發生在我身上！它不是一夜之間發生的，而是老師堅定不移地以極大的愛心、耐心和努力來指導我的信念。值得慶幸的是，老師認為值得在我身上花時間，與我建立聯繫，幫助我的發展。作為一名成功的教練，他了解連結的影響力。對他而言，重要的是，我感受到某種東西，這反過來又使我對自己的信仰比以往任何時候都更強。他促進了這種聯繫，反過來又促進了我的個人成長和自信。

This was done for me! It didn't happen overnight, but it was cultivated by one teacher's steady commitment to mentoring me with much love, patience, and effort. Thankfully he believed that I was worth the time spent investing in a relationship that would help me to develop. As a successful coach, he understood the impact that connection can have. It was important to him that I felt a part of something and, in turn, it helped me believe in myself more than I had before. He cultivated that connection and in turn, cultivated my personal growth and self-confidence.

建立聯繫需要時間，而老師需要與他們面對面的學生進行真實而體貼的努力。我發現我與中學生相處融洽，因為，老實說，我只比他們成熟一點點！我喜歡開玩笑、玩遊戲，並且和我的學生玩得開心。當然，我也嘗試在課堂上教他們重要的東西，但是我一直覺得，我更重要的角色是與他們建立聯繫。對我而言，滿足感的提高並不是因為我教授的內容，而是因為建立了良好的關係。這些關係使我能夠為這些學生的初中學習提供幫助，並希望他們未來能過上幸福的生活。這對他們和我而言都是無比珍貴的。**（這是附帶的故事，顯示了一位老師可以對學生產生的影響。我開始像我的老師曾為我所做的那樣去影響我自己的學生。）**

Connection takes time and it takes an authentic and sensitive effort on the part of a teacher to meet the students where they are. I found that I got along well with middle school because, truthfully, I was only slightly more mature than they were! I loved to joke, play games and have fun with my students. Certainly, I tried to teach them important things in the classroom too, but I always felt my more important role was finding ways to connect with them. I felt my fulfillment came less because of the content I taught, and more because of the relationships that were forged. Those relationships allowed me to help these middle school students navigate through middle school and hopefully, toward a happy future life. That was invaluable, both to them and to me. *(The side story to this is it shows the impact one teacher can have on a student. I set out to influence students exactly as my teacher had done for me.)*

一些老師／領導者擔心與他們領導的人「走得太近」，擔心這會削弱他們的權威或影響力。他們認為，如果與自己領導的人過於親密、友善或自在，那麼他們將無法有效地領導這些人。是的，總是存在走得太近的危險，這可能導致雙方都無法遵守界線。其他人則避免了與教師和學生之間某一方處於弱勢地位的關係。在有些故事中，一些惡言相向的老師利用了這種師生關係，使其他人處於高度戒備的狀態。為了達到平衡，一些老師避免任何建立聯繫的嘗試，而只作為書本內容的傳授者。這樣可以避免學生與老師之間出現任何混亂，甚至也可能避免錯誤的指控，因為這可能會破壞專業人士的聲譽和職業生涯。

Some teacher/leaders are apprehensive about getting "too close" to those they lead for fear it diminishes their authority or influence. They think if they are too close, friendly or comfortable with those they lead, then they won't be able to lead them effectively. Yes, there is always a danger of someone getting too close, possibly resulting in either party not being able to respect the boundary line. Others avoid a relationship for the vulnerable position in which it puts the teacher and the student. There are stories where some abusive teachers have taken advantage of such student-teacher relationships, which put others on high alert. To counterbalance, some teachers avoid any attempt at connection, and simply remain as the giver of content. This avoids any possibility of confusion between the student and the teacher, as well as even the false accusation, which can ruin the reputation and career of a dedicated professional.

在確定「聯繫」對你意味著什麼時，務必仔細評估你的領導風格。我認為我的領導風格就是基於聯繫的。我想與自己的學生和員工保持聯繫，因為我希望他們知道我在乎他們，因為他們以及他們熱愛從事的事情對我而言很有價值，所以我認為對這種關係的投入至關重要，因為這表明人們珍惜他們作為一個人的價值。我認為這種聯繫不會削弱我的教學或領導能力。實際上，我想說它的效果正好相反。我相信，因為我了解他們，所以我可以利用這種深厚的關係並提高他們對工作績效的期望值。我認為，與接受領導的人建立健康關係的領導者不會因此失去影響力或尊重。

When deciding about what "connection" means to you, be sure to carefully evaluate your leadership style. I identify my leadership style as relationship-based. I want to have a relationship with my students and employees because I want them to know I care about them. Because who they are, and what they like to do is valuable to me, I see the investment in the relationship to be of the utmost importance because it shows them that I value who they are as a person. I do not feel this connection weakens my ability to teach or lead. In fact, I would say it has the opposite effect. I believe that because I know them personally, I can leverage that cultivated relationship and raise their own level of expectation about their job performance. I do not think a leader who builds healthy relationships with those they lead loses leverage or respect by doing so.

總結
Summary

當老師（領導者）願意為培養人際關係而投入時，對於學生或他們領導的人來說，結果可能是強有力的。由於建立起來的關係，老師／領導者可以用更有意義的方式進行教導、帶領、建議、指示和管教。成為老師的意義不僅僅在於教授學科內容，就像領導不只是發號施令一樣。努力建立健康和真實的關係需要老師／領導者付出努力。成功取決於你的個性和領導風格。如果做得好，它可以改善所有參與者的人生，使老師更有效，領導者更有力，也能使接受者的感受得到重視和聯繫。

When teachers (who are leaders) are willing to invest in cultivating a connection relationship, the results can be powerful for students or those they lead. The teacher/leader can mentor, guide, advise, instruct, and discipline in a much more meaningful way because of the relationship established. The significance of being a teacher is not just about delivering the information in the subject they teach, just like leading is not just about giving orders or commands. Working to build healthy and authentic relationships requires effort on the part of the teacher/leader. Success depends on your personality and leadership style. When done correctly, it enhances the life of all involved, making the teacher more effective, the leader stronger and the recipient feeling valued and connected.

因為一位老師與我建立了聯繫，所以我的人生方向發生了變化。他使我感到與人聯繫並受到重視，從而永遠改變了我的人生。反過來，我也希望延續這種東西，並且對至少一名學生——當然我希望不只是一名學生——做到同樣的事。

Because one teacher cultivated a connecting relationship with me, the direction of my life was changed. He made me feel connected and valued, thereby altering my life forever. In turn, I hope I paid it forward and did the same for at least one, but hopefully more than just one, student.

領導他人就是影響他人。我的老師是領導者，因為他對我產生了深遠的影響。他不僅將自己的角色看作是教授歷史、健康和體育知識的知識提供者，而且還擔任人生導師。他擔任我的籃球和足球教練，不僅傳授了我每天使用的運動技能，而且還幫助我培養了領導才能。因此，我最終走上了歷史，健康和體育教學的道路也就不足為奇了。另外，我也執教足球和籃球，和他完全一樣。因為他在我身上進行了投入，所以我致力於對其他人進行投入。建立聯繫對於我現在所做的一切至關重要，因此，我既謙虛又心懷感激。

To lead is to influence. My teacher was a leader because he influenced me in a profound way. He saw his role as not only the knowledge-giver hired to teach History, Health, and PE, but also as a life mentor. He served as my basketball and soccer coach, which helped instill not only sports skills, but also leadership skills, that I use every day of my life. It should be no surprise that I also ended up teaching History, Health and PE. In addition, I coached soccer and basketball exactly as he did. Because he invested in me, I sought to invest in others. Cultivating a connecting relationship is essential to everything I now do and, as a result, I am both humbled and grateful.

我的課堂很無聊嗎?
Is My Classroom boring?

Image credit: So Bored Smiley

　　我不記得任何老師說過他們的課堂很無聊。但是,在我與無數的學生交談中,他們告訴我他們的許多課程都無聊透頂。怎麼會這樣呢?學生只是不切實際或脫離現實嗎?還是說,真正不切實際或脫離現實的是老師們自己?

　　I cannot recall a time when I spoke with a teacher who professed that his/her classroom was a boring place for students. Yet, I talk to countless students who tell me many of their classes are boring. How could this be? Are students simply unrealistic or disengaged? Or, could the teachers themselves be unrealistic or disengaged?

　　現實是,作為老師,我們每個人都或多或少有無聊的時候。甚至可以肯定的是,當我們很無聊、我們的課程或者我們設計的學生活動很無聊的時候,我們是能認識到的。作為教師,我們可以認識到我們無法使每個課程計劃都讓人充滿興奮和精力,以此保持所有學生的充份參與。我們並沒有將「無聊」作為任何課程計劃的目標,但是我們有時難免都會這樣。儘管我們應該讓無聊的時刻限制在最低水平,但對許多人而言,無聊已成為習慣，而對學生來說，無聊**確實**已經是習以為常了。

The reality is, as teachers, we all have times when we are, or have been, boring. It may even be true that we recognize when we are boring, our lesson is boring, or our designed student activity is boring. As teachers, we recognize it is impossible to make every single lesson plan filled with excitement and energy to keep all students fully engaged. We do not set "boring" as the target objective of any lesson plan, but we all have those moments. Whereas we should seek to limit the boring moments to a "rare occasion" basis, for many, being boring becomes a routine, and for students, boring *is* the routine.

面對現實吧，對於生活中的大多數事情，簡單地在工作中開啟「自動駕駛」模式要容易得多。在這些時刻，例行公事的感覺舒適而輕鬆，而我們通常可以毫不費力地如此前行。無論我們從事什麼職業，陷入常規都會輕易導致慣例的形成。停留在慣例中成為了一種生活方式。我們需要問自己的問題是：「我是願意停留在目前的慣例中，還是願意付出努力擺脫慣例呢？」要走出慣例需要大量的努力，但是對於你和你的學生而言，結果將是值得的。停留在某種領導慣例中會降低我們的效率，並降低我們對所領導的人的影響。我們將變得懶惰，因為停留在慣例中是無比輕鬆的事情。

Let's face it, for most things in life, it is so much easier to simply put our work efforts on autopilot. In these moments, routine feels comfortable and easy, and we can often move along with little to no effort. Regardless of our occupation, falling into the routine can easily lead to a rut. Remaining in that rut then becomes a lifestyle. The question we need to ask ourselves is, "Is the rut we are currently in where we plan to remain, or are we willing to put in the effort needed to steer out of it?" To steer out is going to involve a lot of hard work and effort, but the results will be well worth it for you and your students. Remaining in a leadership rut reduces our effectiveness, and it reduces the influence we have on those we lead. We become lazy because the routine rut is an easy place to remain.

作為一名教師，設計獨特而有創意的教學計劃是一項艱鉅的工作，需要犧牲時間、精力和資源。在中國，許多老師每天的工作時間很長，幾乎沒有時間花在家庭或備課上。此外，一天中老師需要準備的課程往往不只一堂。我還記得以前教書的日子裡，我不得不在同一天備五堂不同的課。當然，不能期望我在同一天把五堂課都上得很棒！確保學生在課堂上的每一次經歷都令人興奮、引人入勝且令人難忘的工作和奉獻精神基本上是無法維持的。即使老師們有這樣做的動力，執行所需的時間管理和計劃也需要付出巨大的努力。

As a teacher, designing unique and creative lesson plans is extremely hard work and requires a sacrifice of time, energy, and resources. Many teachers in China work very long hours in a day, leaving little time for family or lesson preparation. In addition, teachers have more than just one lesson to prepare for in a day. I remember days of teaching when I had to deliver five unique lesson preps in the same day. Surely it could not be expected of me to deliver five great lessons on the same day! The amount of work and dedication it takes to ensure that every classroom experience for the students is exciting, engaging, and memorable is almost impossible to sustain. Even if the motivation to do so were present, the time management and planning needed to execute it would take a heroic effort.

當我反思教學生涯的頭兩年時，我清晰地記得我只是想比學生領先兩到三個課時。在最初的幾年裡，我基本上只是在學生學習之前進行學習而已！老實說，有時候我發現自己在用「輔導」活動來拖延或佔用教學時間，因為我不確定接下來該教什麼內容。這是好的教學嗎？當然不是！我不過是在盡力而為罷了。我是第一個承認有時候我的課對我的學生而言很無聊的老師。從那以後，我就寬恕了那些曾在早年讓我覺得無聊的老師。我缺乏的是經驗。

　　When I reflect on my first two years of teaching, I remember vividly that I was just trying to stay two or three class periods ahead of the students. In those early years, I was basically learning the material just a little before they were! Honestly, there were times when I found myself making up some "filler" activities to stall or take up instructional time because I was unsure of what content I had to teach next. Was this good teaching? Of course not! I was managing the best that I could. I am the first to admit that sometimes my class was a boring place for my students. I have since forgiven myself for being a boring teacher in those early years. What I lacked was experience.

　　如果你是一位年輕的老師，那麼我希望你做的第一件事，就是原諒自己課堂無聊的時候。當然，你可以記住這種情況，我不怪你。現在，你需要原諒自己。像我當初一樣，你可能也是一名剛走上教學崗位的老師，只比你的學生領先幾節課而已。這是可以理解的，並且與提高所需的經驗直接相關。如果你的課堂是由於這種情況而無聊，那麼要寬恕就並非難事了。但是，如果你認為自己是一位經驗豐富的老師，但你的教室仍然很無聊，那麼，要寬恕就可能額外困難了。

　　If you are reading this as a young teacher, the first thing I want you to do is forgive yourself for the times you, too, are boring in the classroom. Surely, you can remember a time when this has happened to you. I forgive you. Now you need to forgive yourself. Like me, you may be a new teacher prepping and staying just a few lessons ahead of your students. This is understandable and directly related to experience needed in order to improve. If your classroom is boring due to this type of scenario, then forgiveness should not be difficult. However, if you consider yourself an experienced teacher and your classroom is still boring, then forgiveness might take additional effort.

班傑明.富蘭克林曾說過：「教育的成本很高，但是與無知的成本相比，卻顯得微不足道。」我認為無知的一種表現就是忽略你本已知道的事實，而不是對無知的更傳統的定義——不做或不知道你尚未學到的東西。根據這一定義，如果你沒有學到某些東西，可以說是無知。但是，當你明明知道某些東西但卻不採取任何措施時，就可以說是**冷漠**了。只有掌握了知識，你才能選擇冷漠。隨著我們獲得寶貴的經驗，我們有責任對它做點什麼。隨著經驗的積累，我變得更加善於利用課堂時間，同時我在課程設計方面也變得更好了，以便適應學生的需求和我的目標。

"The cost of an education is high, but that pales in comparison to the cost of ignorance." (Ben Franklin) I think one perception of ignorance involves ignoring what you know to be true, as opposed to the more classic definition of ignorance - not doing or knowing what you have not yet learned. By definition, you can be considered ignorant if you have not yet learned something. But you can be considered *indifferent* when you know something, but do nothing about it. Only after you have knowledge can you be indifferent. As we gain valuable experience, we are then responsible to do something with it. As I gained experience, I became much better at making the most out of the classroom time, but I also became better at designing lessons to fit my students' needs and my objectives.

在老師／領導者培訓課程上，我經常談到對教學或領導很重要的兩個關鍵詞：**目的地和方向**（請參閱「目的地和方向」一章）。簡言之，目的地描述的是學習目標。這可以是需要學習的技能或內容，也可以是團隊的領導目標。不管怎麼說，目的地是我希望我的學生完成的「十字準心」的中心。就方向而言，我指的是到達目的地的指導策略。光指明道路還不夠。老師和領導者在學習過程中需要進行仔細而周到的指導。這就是為什麼引導技巧對於任何老師或領導者都是必不可少的。

In my teacher/leader training workshops, I often talk about two key words that are important to teaching or leading : **destination and direction**.

(Refer to "Destination and Direction" chapter.) Simply stated, destination describes the targeted learning objectives. These objectives could be the skills or content needed to be learned, or they could be the leadership objectives for the group. Nonetheless, destination is at the center, in the "crosshairs", of where I wanted my students to end up. By direction, I am referring to the guided strategies used to reach the destination. Pointing the way is not enough. Teachers and leaders need to be a careful and calculated guide in the process of learning. This is why facilitation skills are essential to any teacher or leader.

為了指引方向，人們利用並設計活動來引導自己到達目的地。對於老師而言，應始終設計和選擇定向活動，以保持學生的參與度並強化預期的學習效果。有效地開展這些活動需要出色的引導技巧。成為一名優秀的引導者是無法替代的。擁有引導者經驗，意味著你可以更好地指導你所領導的人，因為你具備信心、技能和專業知識來預測可能的發展趨勢。作為老師，獲得的經驗越多，我的目標和方向就變得越清晰、越有效，因為我可以預測它可能會如何發展。我知道如何提出更好的問題，並透過問答來提高學生的參與度，甚至在短時間內設計一些學生活動，這些活動對我來說可能仍然是出於填充時間的目的，但對於學生來說卻仍然是健康的學習經歷。當「目的地」明確時，我的指導「方向」會更好。老師可以設計創造性的活動來增加學生的參與度時，便減少了學生感到無聊的機會。

To guide the direction, activities are utilized and designed to help lead toward the destination. For a teacher, directional activities should always be designed and chosen that keep the students engaged and reinforce the intended learning. Carrying out these activities effectively requires excellent facilitation skills. There is no replacement for experience in being a good facilitator. Having experience as a facilitator means you can better direct those you lead because you have the confidence, skill, and expertise to anticipate how it is likely to go. The more experience I got as a teacher, the sharper and more effective my destination and direction became, because I could predict how it was likely to go. I knew how to ask better questions, get more student engagement through responses, or, even on short notice, design some student activities that may have been filling time for me, but still healthy learning experiences for the students. When my destination was clear, my direction was better. When a teacher can design creative directional activities that increase student engagement, the result is reduced opportunities for student boredom.

有時，由於對「方向」的渴求，學生的參與度會達到難忘的程度。有時被認為佔用課堂時間的活動，反而催生出最好的學生活動。我記得上一堂課時，「方向」錯誤反而變成了令人難忘的方向性時刻，學生們在期間展現了極高的參與度。

Sometimes, memorable moments of student engagement came as a result of directional desperation. There were times when the need to fill class time spawned some of my best student engagements. I remember one class when directional disaster was turned into a memorable directional moment of high student engagement.

在一個漫長假期來臨之前的兩天，我們完成了一個大單元的學習，我也知道自己最好不要在假期前夕嘗試引入新的學習材料。很明顯，學生們心裡已經開始放假了。我迅速而心焦地想用創意活動消磨時間，在找構想的過程中，發現了簽署《美國獨立宣言》的歷史人物傳記的整套資源。我知道我們最終要學習有關這傳奇文檔的歷史，腦海中便突然出現一個場景。我想像我的學生坐在星巴克那樣的氛圍中，喝熱可可，吃零食，隨意討論這份文檔的價值。我知道學生會喜歡星巴克這個主意，但是他們會喜歡這個討論歷史的想法嗎？

Having finished a large unit of study two days prior to a lengthy holiday break, I knew better than to try to introduce new material on the eve of a vacation. It was clear the students were already on a mental holiday. In a fast

& frantic search to creatively fill time, I stumbled across a resource packet of biographies of historical figures who signed the American Declaration of Independence. Knowing we were going to eventually learn about the history surrounding this legendary document, an image of a scene popped into my mind. I imagined my students sitting in a Starbucks-like atmosphere, drinking hot cocoa, eating snacks and casually discussing the value of the document. I knew the students would like the Starbucks idea, but would they embrace the discussion of history idea?

趁著把水燒熱的時間,我找到了一個燒水的壺,一些在野營時留下的熱巧克力小包,並準備足量的簽署者傳記的複印講義。上課的時候,我熱情地向學生們宣佈我們要舉辦一個**歷史咖啡廳**!僅憑我的語氣,就聽起來神奇而有趣,幾乎使我相信這是經過仔細考慮和計劃的「方向」活動。令我驚訝的是,每個學生都急著開始閱讀自己手上的傳記。他們甚至還主動提出為明天的「課堂咖啡廳」活動帶零食!

With barely enough time to get the water hot, I located a hot water urn, some hot chocolate packets that were left from a class camping trip and made enough copies of the signer's biographies. As I entered class, I enthusiastically announced to students we were having a HISTORY CAFÉ! The tone of my voice alone made it sound magical and fun, almost convincing myself that it was a carefully thought out and planned directional activity. To my surprise, each student anxiously started reading their given biographies. They also started offering to bring in snacks for tomorrow's café!

第二天(學校放假前的最後一天),學生們迅速湧入教室。每個人都做了一個名字標籤,有些甚至帶來了一些簡單的道具來宣傳他們的簽署人物。我讓他們閱讀並充份了解他們的人物性格,以便用第一人稱視角來講述他們各自的歷史角色,以及他們當初簽署此一歷史性文件時所冒的風險。等水燒開的同時,我看到了學生明顯高漲的參與度。

The next day (the final day of school before holiday break), the students flooded quickly into the room. Each had made a nametag, some even brought in some simple props to promote their signer. I had tasked them to read and understand enough about their character to speak in the first person about their historical role and about the risk they took to sign this historic document. While the water was heating up, I couldn't help but see the obvious level of student engagement.

水燒開時，學生們開始享受熱可可的溫暖，並假裝文件的原始簽署者已經透過他們的聲音復活了。正如我之前在忙亂時的靈光乍現中所想像的那樣，大家分享小吃，進行歷史對話。完美嗎？算不上！難忘嗎？當然！無聊嗎？沒那回事！你不知道嗎，當我在學年結束對學生進行調查時，大多數學生都將歷史咖啡廳視為那學期最喜歡的課程之一！

By the time the water was hot, students began to enjoy the warmth of the hot cocoa as they pretended as if the original signers of the document had come back to life through their voices. Snacks were shared and historical conversation took place, just as I imagined in my moment of desperation. Was it perfect? Not at all! Was it memorable? For sure! Was it boring? Not even close! Wouldn't you know it, when I surveyed students at the end of the year, most students commented on the history café as being one of their favorite classes of the term!

並非每個計劃外的方向性時刻都會產生一個難忘的時刻，但在當時那個情況下，我受到了上天的眷顧，因此我將歷史咖啡廳延續了多年。在每個咖啡廳的場合，我都想辦法來對它進行改進。我想讓你學習的課程不是關於「即興表演」並把某些東西堆在一起，而是要冒險嘗試一些可能與常規不同的東西。例行程序很無聊。要確保始終挑戰自己，以擺脫常規。

Not every unplanned directional moment spawns a memorable one, but in this case, the universe came together in my favor, and I continued the History Café for many years. With each café occasion, I tried to find ways to improve it from the time before. The lesson I want you to learn is not so much about "winging it" and throw something together, as it is about being willing to take the risk to try something that might be different and well outside the routine. The routine is boring. Push yourself to steer out of the routine by making sure you always challenge yourself.

在中國的培訓中，我結識了許多才華橫溢且經驗豐富的老師。當我發現學生們苦於「**無聊之常規**」時，我可以看到他們有多麼不自在。我問他們：「你的學生入學時是否能保證，他們每天都會坐在同一個座位上？你構建的課堂流程是否很容易預測？你是否總是按設計規律來授課和安排課程？用來衡量他們學習水平的問題是否也遵循類似的模式或風格？你的測評僅僅是以前測評的複製嗎？」當我的問題完成解答時，我可以看到許多老師認罪似的蔫在座位上。同時，年輕的老師們開始坐得更高，好像鬆了一口氣似的，因為他們意識到經驗豐富的老師們也像他們一樣在無聊的課堂裡苦苦掙扎。兩者之間的區別在於，年輕的老師渴望適應和修改他們的教學方法，而經驗豐富的老師則意識到，擺脫常規的束縛需要進行大量的工作。我發現新老師比有經驗的老師更渴望擺脫常規。

I have met many talented and experienced teachers in my trainings throughout China. I can see their level of discomfort when I reveal that students find "**the routine to be boring.**" I ask them, "Do your students enter your class with reasonable assurance that they will sit in the same seats each day? Do you structure your class procedures with great predictability? Are your lessons delivered and framed with regularity of design? Do the questions asked to gauge their learning follow a similar pattern or style? Are your assessments mere clones of the previous?" As I finish the line of questions, I can see many teachers sheepishly slouch in their seats in an admission of guilt.

At the same time, young teachers begin to sit up taller in their seats, seemingly relieved because they realize experienced teachers struggle with a boring classroom just like they do. The difference between the two is that the younger teachers are anxious to adapt and modify their teaching methodology, whereas the experienced teachers realize the amount of work needed to steer out of the routine rut is significant. I find new teachers more eager to steer out of the rut routine than experienced teachers.

我真誠地分享了自己在常規教學中的掙扎。我也承認，自己曾經用「自動駕駛模式」慣性滑行／上課。在有些時候，這是由於我的懶惰，而其他情況則是由於缺乏經驗。青年教師只需要經驗，而經驗豐富的教師則需要找到動力來誠心地尋求變革。對他們來說，慣例似乎已經成為一種生活方式，擺脫慣例所需的努力比留在慣例中要困難得多。人們正是由於這兩個非常不同的原因而留在了相同的常規慣例中。

I share, honestly, about my struggle teaching in the rut routine. I freely admit that I had times of coasting on autopilot. In some of those times, it was because I was lazy, while other instances were from lack of experience. Young teachers simply need experience, whereas experienced teachers need to find the motivation to launch a sincere effort to change. For them, the rut routine seems to have become a lifestyle, because the effort required to get out of the rut is harder than staying in it. These are two very different reasons for being in the same routine rut.

努力創造富有參與性的課堂體驗
Strive to Create an Engaged Classroom Experience

「參與」這個詞一直吸引著我。在美國文化中，當一對戀愛中的年輕夫婦決定準備好結婚時，他們就會「訂婚」（譯者註：英文中的「參與」與「訂婚」是同一個詞）。從文化上講，這時男子要給未婚妻戴上戒指，表示她已經有主了。戒指是一種視覺標誌，顯示出他們之間的關係與尋常人相比已處於不同的水平。我想表明兩者的相似之處是，真正的學生參與意味著老師和學生之間的教學處於與別人不同的水平。參與意味著老師不僅負責傳授考試所需的知識，更意味著就相關材料進行更高程度的互動。

The word ENGAGEMENT is something that has always appealed to me. In the United States culture, when a young couple in love decides they are ready to commit to marriage, they "get engaged." The culturally common practice is for the man to present his fiancé with a ring, signifying that she is now taken. The ring is a visual display that the relationship they have is at a different level as compared to anyone else with whom they may be seen. The parallel I want to establish is that authentic student engagement signifies a different level of learning between teacher and student. Instead of the teacher being solely and simply responsible for communicating knowledge needed for test results, engagement implies a higher level of interaction with the material.

現代教學法鼓勵老師謹慎地結合針對學習而進行的測評和為了學習而進行的測評。有些測評關注於**知識的習得**，而其他測評則著眼於**學習過程本身**。參與式課堂是教師設計方向（活動）的方式之一，可以達到廣泛的學習風格，並同時訓練硬性和軟性（影響）技能。參與式學習是指，學生對學習負有主動權甚至承擔相應責任。當學生參與課堂時，他們不僅非常活躍、高度參與，而且彼此之間也在互相學習。

Modern pedagogy practice encourages teachers to use a careful blend of assessment OF learning and assessment FOR learning. Some assessments assess knowledge gained where other assessments are given to increase the knowledge. An engaged classroom is one where the teacher is designing the direction (activities) that reach a broad spectrum of learning styles, as well as training both hard and soft (impact) skills. Engaged learning is when the student has some ownership and even responsibility for learning. When students are engaged, they are not only highly active and involved, but they are also teaching each other.

我希望避免讓教室陷入無聊，這也讓我有能力找到其他方法來吸引或重新吸引我的學生。為此，我使用簡單的遊戲來打破常規，並保持課堂環境的活躍和新鮮。我注意到，即使只這樣做三到四分鐘，也足以加快學生大腦血液流動並重新吸引他們的注意力和腦力。對於那些觸覺學習者來說，就算要坐八分鐘也是太久了（我當學生的時候也是一樣），我發現他們透過活動，重新投入了學習狀態，並激發了他們的興趣和好奇心。當然，這對於教學而言算是暫時離題，但我認為這是寶貴的過渡時間，從長遠來看，這為我提供了更富有成效的教學時間。我相信這項的投資是值得的。

My personal desire to avoid having a boring classroom also empowered me to find other ways to engage or re-engage my students. To do so, I used simple games to break up the routine and to keep the environment active and fresh. I noticed that even doing this for 3-4 minutes was enough to get the blood flowing and re-engage both their focus and their brains. For those tactile learners for whom sitting more than 8 minutes was too long (like I was as a student), I found they re-engaged and reinvigorated their interest and curiosity. Sure, it took a little bit of time away from instruction, but I looked at it as valuable transitional time, which provided me with more productive instructional time in the long run. I believe it was an investment well spent.

老師如何擺脫常規？
How Can a Teacher Get Out of the Routine Rut?

變革需要建立新的健康模式。你不能繼續做導致你陷入習慣性的例行教學中的事情。你是否曾經看過講述某人戲劇化的減肥歷程的電視節目呢？減去四百磅用不著的脂肪並不是短期內就能輕鬆完成的任務。其間的轉變是精神和身體兩方面的，需要耗費時間和精力。實際上，如果沒有正確的精神狀態，想要的身體轉變將不會如願發生。減重的工作實際上比增重還要多。如果一個人不對自己進行重大改變，那麼他想要的改變就不會發生。

Change requires the establishment of new healthy patterns. You cannot continue to do the things that led you to teach in a rut routine. Did you ever watch television shows highlighting an individual's dramatic weight loss journey? Losing 400 pounds of unneeded body fat is no quick fix or easy task. The transformation is mental and physical, and it takes time and commitment. In fact, if the mental attitude is not properly fixed, the physical transformation desired will not follow. The work to lose the weight is substantially more effort than it was to add it on. A change cannot occur if the person does not make drastic changes.

改變生活方式。一個人為了實現向所需結果的完全轉變（你的目的地），必須破壞既定的模式。要改變既定模式，只能透過引入能養成良好習慣的新習慣（方向）來實現。如果你在常規的模式中開展教學，請了解當前狀況以及把你引入該狀況的模式。這誰都怨不了，只能怨你自己。要認識到，是你任由不健康的模式發展，才最終導致當前的結果。產生新結果的承諾將要求進行轉型變革，包括建立全新的、僅由你的行動支持的健康模式。改變需要由你自身做起。要下定決心，以便在思維上創建新模式。

Changing lifestyle patterns. For a person to achieve a total transformation for the desired results (your destination), established patterns must be disrupted. Patterns can only be changed by the introduction of new habits (direction) that lead to healthy routines. If you are teaching in a rut routine, take ownership of the current condition and the patterns that got you there. It is nobody's fault but your own. Recognize that you allowed unhealthy patterns to develop that produced the current results. The commitment to producing new results is going to require a transformational change involving establishing new, healthy patterns supported only by your actions. You need to be the change. Get your mind set so that you mentally create new patterns.

原諒你自己。我發現，原諒他人比原諒自己要容易得多。承認是你放任自己的模式導致了當前的結果。不要再責怪「體制」、學生、行政部門、教育局、個人情況等等。眼前的結果源自你自己所做的選擇。承認這一點，然後找到一種原諒自己的方法吧。經過這個過程，你可以獲得解放並大聲說：「我原諒自己的懶惰模式。」

Forgive yourself. I personally find it easier to forgive others faster than I can forgive myself. Recognize that the patterns you have allowed have produced the current results. Stop blaming the "system," the students, the administration, the education bureau, personal circumstances, etc. The results are based on choices you made. Own up to it and find a way to forgive yourself. The process can be liberating and empowering to say out loud, "I forgive myself for my lazy patterns."

制定一個計劃。有句話說得好：「人們並不計劃失敗。他們失敗源於沒有計劃！」有一點很容易理解，那就是你所追尋的目的地需要明確的方向指引。如果要到達任何地方，你不僅必須將終點位置可視化，而且還必須識別出沿途需要轉彎的地方。在制定完善的教學計劃之前，要先制定一個自我改進的計劃。找出不良習慣（寫下來），然後列出能使你擺脫不良習慣的新習慣（也寫下來）。執行此過程中，你將擁有一份書面記錄，以幫助你衡量自己的成長並提升你的責任感。你的教學改進應遵循相同的計劃。寫下使你陷入困境的不良習慣，並寫下新的方向，以引導你到達新的理想目的地。

Make a Plan. There is a great saying, "People don't plan to fail. They fail to plan!" It is simple enough to understand that the destination you seek requires clear direction. If you want to get anywhere, you must not only visualize where you want to end up, but also be able to identify the necessary turns to make along the way. Make a self-improvement plan before making an improved teaching plan. Identify the bad habits (write them down) and then list the new habits that will get you out of it (write them down as well). When you do this, you will have a written record to help you measure your growth and provide you with some accountability. Your teaching improvement plan should follow the same plan. Write down the poor habits that got you in the rut, and write down the new directions that will lead you to reach your new and desired destination.

責任。美國著名棒球員和教練約翰.伍登說過：「一個人力量太小，不足以實現卓越。」沒有人可以獨自改變世界。進行持久改變需要一些幫助和責任感。有效的問責可以用願意成為問責伙伴的導師形式出現。導師可以在需要時提供指導、肯定和建設性的批評。你務必仔細選擇自己的問責伙伴。通常，朋友或配偶不是最好的選擇，因為他們離你太親近了，並且只會給你鼓勁，而不是向你提出挑戰。你的導師不能是只微笑並同意你所說或所做的一切的橡皮圖章。只有選擇了合適的導師，你才會有機會。選擇錯誤的導師將保證你的失敗。

Accountability. "One is too small a number to achieve greatness." (John Wooden) No one person changed the world on his/her own. Making lasting changes requires some assistance and accountability. Effective accountability can come in the form of a mentor who is willing to be an accountability partner. Mentors can provide guidance, affirmation, and constructive criticism when needed. Your accountability partner needs to be carefully chosen. Usually a friend or spouse is not the best choice because they are too close to you and will simply enable you, as opposed to challenge you. Your mentor cannot be a rubber stamper who only smiles and agrees with everything you say or do. Pick the right mentor and you have a chance. Pick the wrong mentor and you guarantee your failure.

可衡量的目標。 如果人們認為一項任務太艱鉅，許多人會選擇迴避而不是冒險失敗。如果你設定了不切實際且無法衡量的目標，那麼你每次都會失敗。把你想要達到的目標寫下來。合適的導師可以幫你開始挑戰和修正目標，但前期工作必須你自己來做。有些人認為養成新習慣需要二十一天。我不相信這個說法，但我確實認為練習和制定按時間衡量的目標時，三週是合理的時間。將它們分成這樣的時間長度可以讓人有足夠的時間來關注結果，同時又沒有太多的時間可以忽略目標。此外，限定時間範圍可以使你的思考和評估保持清醒狀態。

Measurable Targets. If humans think a task is too hard, many will opt for avoidance rather than risk the possibility of failure. If you set unrealistic and immeasurable targets, you will succeed in failing every time. Write down goals and targets you want to reach. The right mentor can help challenge and revise your goals, but you must do the initial work. Some believe it takes 21 days to establish a new habit. I am not convinced that is true, but I do think 3 weeks is a reasonable length of time to practice and develop time-measured goals. Breaking them into this length of time allows for enough time to pass to notice results, but not so much time to lose sight of your goals. Plus, limiting your time frame allows you to keep your reflections and assessments fresh.

面對風險。 不採取行動不是風險。它是另一個壞習慣。有些人因為害怕失敗而不採取行動。你必須認識到，不作為的風險比失敗的風險要大得多，並且會打敗自我。最初，一個新的課堂活動可能會失敗，但是你至少要承擔這個風險。不要因為擔心失敗而害怕風險。相反，你要怕的應該是連失敗的機會都沒有抓住過。透過失敗，我們在分析結果時，將學到寶貴的經驗和知識。將你的計劃付諸實踐是有風險的，但保持例行程序也是有風險的。透過練習，對風險的適應將變得越來越容易。

Face the Risk. Inaction is not a risk. It's another bad habit. Some people do not act because they fear failure. You must feel that the risk of inaction is far greater and self-defeating than the risk of falling short. A new classroom activity may fail, initially, but at least you took the risk. Do not fear the risk because you fear failure. Rather, fear never having taken the opportunity to fail. Through failure, we learn valuable lessons and knowledge when we analyze the results. Putting your plan into action is risky, but so too is continuing in the rut routine. Adjusting to the feeling of risk becomes easier with practice.

在設計方面進行協作。 如果你想成為最好的房地產開發商，那就不要試圖向其他行業的人學習房地產知識。相反，要做到最好，找到在自己領域內被公認為最好的人，並請求與他們會面，以便請他們給你提些建議。同樣，如果想要成為最好的老師，你可以去找最偉大、最受尊敬的老師，並邀請他們共進午餐。告訴他們你正在制定一個改變自己教學習慣的新計劃，並且希望他們幫助你弄懂使他們成為偉大老師的原因。（如果你這樣說，他們甚至可能會自願幫你買午餐！）你和什麼樣的人來往，就會成為什麼樣的人。想致富嗎？那就與有錢人來往。想破產，那就和破產的人來往。想成為一名出色的老師？那就與出色的老師來往吧，這樣你就可以目睹他們的工作。請求他們讓你看足以提高學生參與度的課程計劃。問他們哪些活動在學生中很受歡迎？詢問他們的學業測評，**針對學習的測評**和**為了學習而進行的測評**都要。詢問他們是否願意在項目上與你合作，以便你可以向他們學習。直擊他們的自我是獲得他們知識的一種好方法。關鍵是與你尊敬的人合作，以幫助你改進教學模式。

Collaborate on the design. If you want to be the best real-estate developer, you do not try to learn about real estate from someone in a different industry. Instead, to be the best, find people who are considered to be the best in their field and ask them to meet with you so you can ask their advice. Likewise, to become the best teacher, find the best and most respected GREAT teacher you can and offer to take them to lunch. Tell them you are making a new plan for changing your teaching habits, and you want their help in discovering what has made them a great teacher. (If you say it that way, they will probably even pick up the lunch tab!) You become like those you hang around. Want to be rich? Hang out with the rich. Want to be broke, hang out with those who are broke. Want to be a great teacher? Hang out with the great teachers so you can see what they do. Ask to see lesson plans that produce high student engagement. Ask them what activities they find popular among the students? Ask about their assessments, both FOR and OF learning. Ask them if they would be willing to collaborate with you on a project so that you can learn from them. A stroke of the ego is a great way to gain access to their knowledge. The key here is to collaborate with someone you respect in order to help produce improved patterns in your teaching.

繪製結果圖表。在教學（或生活）中嘗試新的且具有挑戰性的方向後，請繪製結果圖表。你可以將其作為日記來完成，也可以僅作為私人成長圖來完成，但是稍後進行反思是頗有價值的。拿出你幾個月或幾年前寫的東西，就可以對成長有健康的看法。無論你是回顧新課程還是方向性活動，該過程都極具價值。無論是每週一次或每兩週一次都可以，最重要的是確保持續書面成長記錄。快速回顧可以揭示新的模式，或者讓你發現舊習慣的死灰復燃。繪製結果圖表可以加倍提高你的成功率。

Chart Your Results. After you try new and challenging directions in your teaching (or life), chart your results. You may accomplish this as a diary or simply as a private growth chart, but it is valuable to reflect on it later. Pulling out something you have written months or years earlier provides healthy perspective on growth. Whether you review each new lesson or directional activity you try, the process is valuable. Whether you do it on a weekly or bi-weekly basis isn't as important as making sure you keep a written record of your growth. A quick look back can reveal the new patterns or allow you to spot old habits resurfacing. Charting the results increases your success rate exponentially.

總結
Summary

當你思考「我的課堂很無聊嗎?」這個問題時,請對自己誠實,如實回答。我不認為有誰一開始就想讓自己的課程無聊。沒有歌手／作曲家一開始就打算寫一首糟糕的歌。沒有任何領導者希望自己效率低下。沒有任何運動員把最後一名作為目標。我們可能不會以無聊為出發點,但是,很可能我們所有人都有無聊的時候,雖然自己不願承認,在很大程度上,那是已經存在的不良習慣導致的。

When you contemplate the original question, "Is my classroom boring?", be honest with yourself and answer the question truthfully. I really do not think anyone sets out to be boring. No singer/songwriter sets out to write a bad song. No leader wants to be ineffective. No athlete sets a goal to come in last. We may not set out with the intention of being boring but, it is possible that we all move in and out of being boring more than we care to admit, largely because of pre-existing bad habits.

你可能已經知道問題的答案。你可以根據學生的反應來衡量自己的課程是否無聊。如果他們看起來並沒有融入課堂或者看起來很無聊,那麼答案已經顯而易見。如果你不確定自己的課堂是否無聊,那麼請對學生進行調查,無須為此感到羞恥。誠實和反思的自我檢查是一項寶貴而有價值的任務。

There is a chance you already know the answer to the question. You can gauge whether you are boring by the reaction of your students. If they appear disengaged or look like they are bored, then the answer is obvious. There is no shame in taking a survey of students if you seem to be unsure whether or not your classroom is a boring place to be. Honest and reflective self-examination is a valuable and worthwhile task.

如果你在教學中陷入了「例行公事」的模式，那就必須決定是保持現狀還是勇敢前進。與養成「慣例」比起來，掙脫「慣例」需要付出更多的工作。要下決心認識到，要對既定的習慣和模式進行徹底的改變，因為它們完全不利於打造一個令人興奮的課堂。你需要制定改善計劃。可以從原諒自己開始。然後，列出不健康的習慣，並願意冒險嘗試新事物。尋求導師與你合作並幫助你設定可衡量的目標。繪製結果和進度圖表，讓你可以看到自己在該過程中的成長和奮鬥。這都需要付出努力。如果你付出了必要的努力和奉獻，結果自然會到來。當你掙脫常規時，你終將能夠用一個明確的「不是！」來回答最初的問題「我的課堂很無聊嗎？」。

If you have slipped into the rut routine in your teaching, you must decide whether you want to remain in the rut or steer out of it. Getting out is going to be more work than it took to get into the rut. Set your mind to the realization that steering out will require a drastic change in the established habits and patterns that were not conducive to the creation of a stimulating classroom. You will need to make a plan to change. Begin by forgiving yourself. Then, list the unhealthy habits and be willing to take more risks to try new things. Seek out a mentor to collaborate with and to help you set measurable goals. Chart your results and progress so you can see the growth and struggle of the process. It will require hard work. But if you put in the necessary hard work and dedication, the results will emerge. When you steer out of the rut routine, you will emphatically be able to answer the initial question, "Is my classroom boring?", with an emphatic "NO!"

動機的魔力
The Magic of Motivation

Image credit: Forbes

　　我發現,人們對年底的反應是對人類行為的非常有趣的心理學研究課題。在美國,我們在十一月的最後一個星期四慶祝感恩節。假期的傳統包括一頓豐盛的家庭聚餐(「宴席」這個詞要準確得多),這含有大量的卡路里。實際上,僅此一餐,美國成年人平均就攝入了超過三千卡路里的熱量!加上幾片山核桃派或南瓜派,一頓飯可以將其增加到四千卡路里。如果還不夠的話,感恩節就預示著「節假日美食季」的開始,該季節將持續四週,直到新年前夕。

　　I find people's reactions to the end of the calendar year to be a very interesting psychological field study of human behavior. In the United States, we celebrate Thanksgiving on the last Thursday in November. The holiday tradition includes a large family meal (the term feast is far more accurate) that has a ridiculous number of calories attached to it. In fact, the average American adult consumes in excess of 3,000 calories on that one meal alone! Add a few slices of pecan or pumpkin pie and one can push that to 4,000 calories in one single meal. If that weren't bad enough, Thanksgiving signals the start of the "holiday eating season" that will last for the next 4 weeks leading up to New

Year's Eve.

　在這個假期裡，將有無數的家庭和工作派對，人們會吃得更多，以至於到最後，你覺得自己別說吃，就是看食物都不想看了！然後，新年來臨，就像宿醉一樣，美國人開始清醒地思考個人的健康習慣。他們突然試圖恢復鎮定，並不可避免地宣稱自己想要恢復健康！對新目標的大膽宣言就是所謂的「新年新希望」。由於之前四週大吃特吃，在身體上留下了多餘的脂肪，因此大多數人的新年新希望都是將身體重新塑造成原來的樣子，甚至想比以前的身材更好。這些決心會導致健身房會員人數激增，因為節假日後減肥已成為大家痴迷的新潮流。這些希望大多數都不能實現，到了二月底就更不用說了，因為人內心的動機消失的速度比假日大餐所吃的最後一塊甜派要快。

　　During this holiday season, there will be countless family and work parties that involve more eating, to the point you almost never want to see or eat food again! Then, as soon as the New Year kicks in, like a bad hangover, Americans start to sober up regarding personal health habits. They suddenly try to regain composure and inevitably proclaim they want to get back into shape! This bold proclamation of a new goal is what we call a New Year's Resolution. Because the previous 4-week feeding frenzy has left unwanted fat all over the body, most of these resolutions are about sculpting the body back into what it once was, or even making it better than ever before. These resolutions cause a significant spike in gym memberships, as losing the holiday weight becomes the new personal obsession. Most of these resolutions fail to make it to fruition, let alone the end of February, as the internal motivation needed soon vanishes faster than the last piece of pie eaten at the holiday meal.

　許多人起初是有動力的，但很少有人能夠有自律的精神去堅持實現真實而持久的改變。為什麼有些人可以下定一個新年決心並最終實現，而另一些下了相同決心的人卻慘敗收場？一些人的動力比其他人強嗎？

導致變化的動機是對人類行為的有趣研究。有些人可以設定目標，然後透過必要的步驟來採取行動，而其他人則做不到。理解這背後的原因可能有助於我們更好地了解學生的課堂表現。

Many people start out motivated, but few sustain the discipline needed to effectuate true and lasting change. Why is it that some people can make a New Year's resolution and follow it through to fulfillment, but others, who may start out with the same objective, fail miserably? Do some people have better motivation than others? Motivation that results in change is an interesting study in human behavior. Some individuals can set a goal and then take the necessary steps to follow it through with action, but others cannot. Understanding why this is true may help us understand our students' classroom performance better.

我不認為動機中有什麼「魔法」。動機不是要喝下的魔力藥水，也不是發生在某些人身上卻不發生在其他人身上的奇蹟。請任何人解釋他們的自我動機，我保證你聽到的回答不會包含「魔法」或「奇蹟」這樣的字眼。典型的答案可能包括自律、問責、決心、毅力、專注之類的詞語。這些詞語被視為確保維持動力所需採取的絕佳指標。是什麼使某些人能夠維持動力而其他人卻慘敗收場？回答這個問題需要更多的自省。

I do not believe there is "magic" in motivation. Motivation is not a magical potion to be consumed or a miraculous occurrence that happens to some, but not to others. Ask anyone to explain their self-motivation and I guarantee responses will not include the word "magic" or "miracle". Typical answers are likely to include words such as: self-discipline, accountability, determination, perseverance, focus, or others. All these words would be considered excellent indicators of what it takes to ensure that motivation is maintained. What makes some able to sustain motivation while others fail miserably? Answering that question requires a bit more philosophical self-examination.

像許多人一樣，我發現動機的起源有內在的和外在的。確定成功是內在力量還是外在力量導致的結果並非易事。實際上，起初似乎是清晰的，內在的動機可能是由不那麼明顯的外部因素所推動的。作為老師和父母，我們將外在動機應用於學生和孩子，並認為我們正在幫助他們將其轉化為內在動機。在某些情況下可能會發生這種情況，但我們自認為激發內在動機的努力可能只是在灌輸對失敗的恐懼而已。

Like many, I see the origins of motivation coming from intrinsic and extrinsic sources. Determining if success is the result of intrinsic or extrinsic forces is not a simple task. What may have started out as clear, intrinsic motivation may have, in fact, been fueled more by less obvious external factors. As teachers and parents, we apply extrinsic motivation on our students and children, thinking we are helping them channel that into intrinsic motivation. That may happen in some cases, but it is likely that our effort to inspire intrinsic motivation simply instills fear of failure.

我最近問了一位年輕的中國大學生，是什麼促使她保持自己忙碌的日程。除了成為全日制醫學生之外，她還想辦法打工。她說：「我做服務生賺錢，以便繼續接受大學教育，成為兒科醫生。」透過詢問，我發現她至少還要學習六年，並且還需要花很多錢才能實現自己的目標。我問她，當目的地距離遙遠時，她如何讓自己聚焦於最終的目標。她回答說：「因為這就是我選擇的人生。」

I recently asked a young Chinese university student what motivates her to keep the very hectic schedule she endures. In addition to her being a full-time medical student, she is also managing to work a job. She said, "I work as a waitress to earn money, so I can continue my university education to become a pediatric doctor." Through questioning, I found out she has at least 6 more years of study and a lot of money yet to spend in order to reach her goal. I asked her how she keeps the end-goal in focus, when the destination is so far off in the distance. She replied, "Because it is what I have chosen to do with my life."

　　我想知道她是否能夠維持必要的動力，以支撐這漫長而艱難的求索之路，最終實現目標。她的動機中有多少是內在的，外在的又有多少？我知道她為了實現這個夢想而肩負著家庭的重擔。她還有兩對祖父母和一對辛勞的父母，他們付出大量財力以確保實現自己的人生目標。我想知道這種外在動機是否比她想要做兒科醫生的個人目標更能激發她的奮鬥。她害怕失敗嗎？如果她不能讓家人感到自豪又怎麼辦？如果她失敗了，那麼他們投入在她身上的所有時間和金錢都會付諸東流！我遇過很多像她一樣的學生。可悲的是，我遇到的許多人都還在上初中和高中，所以他們還要承受很多年的壓力。外部動機並不總是能激發內部動機。

　　I left wondering if she can sustain the required motivation to stay the long and difficult course towards achieving her goal. How much of her motivation was internal, and how much was external? I know she was bearing the heavy weight of family expectations to fulfill this dream. She also had 2 sets of grandparents and 1 set of hard-working parents directing lots of financial resources to ensure she accomplishes her goal. I wondered if this external motivation fueled her more than her personal goal of wanting to do the work of a pediatric doctor. Did she fear failure? What if she cannot make her family proud? If she fails, then all the time and money they poured into her would be lost! I have met many students just like her. Sadly, many I meet are in middle school and high school, so they still have many more years of this pressure yet to endure. External motivation does not always inspire internal motivation.

　　在最近的一些閱讀中，我看到了這樣的說法：「思想產生感覺，感覺導致行動，而行為帶來結果。」我認為，這是維持個人動機、實現既定目標的秘訣。在採取行動並取得成果之前，我們需要深刻地感受。感覺—行動—結果。那些認為自己選擇的飲食習慣和生活方式導致不必要增重的人，在採取行動之前，要先有需要改變的感覺。當然，人們只有在努力工作和改變生活方式後才能獲得結果。首先必須深刻地意識到需要改變。內部和外部動機會影響這些感覺，但是如果人們沒有需要改變的感覺，這種動機就註定不會持久。

In some recent reading, I came across the statement that "thoughts lead to feelings, feelings lead to action, and actions lead to results." I think, herein lies the recipe for being able to sustain the personal motivation to accomplish set goals. We need to have deep feelings impacted before action can be taken and results can be achieved. Feelings-Actions-Results. The individual who feels their eating habits and lifestyle choices are leading to unwanted weight gain would need to FEEL that change is needed before ACTION can be taken. Certainly, RESULTS can only be obtained after the hard work and lifestyle changes are implemented. One must first FEEL deeply that change is needed. Internal and external motivation can impact those feelings, but without the individual feeling that change is needed, the motivation will not be sustained.

我在教育中注意到的一個巨大危險是，學生對學習的熱愛被成功的「動力」壓得喘不過氣。當我採訪學生為什麼喜歡或不喜歡學校時，他們的不喜歡很少與「工作」相關，而通常與成功之類的「壓力」有關。這種動機不是來自內心（內部），而是來自外部。許多學生感到學習不愉快，因為他們試圖滿足他人對其學業表現的期望。獲得某些結果的壓力成為了焦點，而不是真實、好奇或參與性學習。在最近的一項研究中，百分之七十四的五年級學生感到他們參與了自己的學習過程。但可悲的是，只有百分之三十二的十一年級學生回答說他們參與了自己的學習過程。學校（和父母）是否應該激發孩子們的好奇心和對學習的熱愛，使他們感到對學習的參與呢？初中和高中學生參與度的下降應該是令人震驚的，並且應該警示人們注意到整個教育體系的變化，而不僅僅是低質量的教學或表現欠佳的學生。我認為問題出在學生為了的高分而感到壓力，這個動機是不對的。

One great danger I see in education is when the love of learning in the student is suffocated by the imposed "motivation" to succeed. When I interview students about why they like or dislike school, their dislike is rarely related to "the work" and more often linked to the "pressure" felt to succeed. This motivation is NOT coming from within (internal), but rather from external sources. Many students do not FEEL learning is enjoyable because they are trying to meet someone else's expectations for their educational performance. The pressure to achieve certain results becomes the focus, not authentic, curious, or engaged learning. In a recent study, 74% of 5th graders felt engaged in their learning. Sadly, only 32% of 11th graders responded that they are engaged in the learning process. Shouldn't schools (and parents) be inspiring children's curiosity and love of learning so that they feel engaged in learning? The decline in student engagement in middle and high schools should be alarming and indicative of something systemic to the overall educational process, not just poor-quality teaching or poorly performing students. I think the problem lies within the misaligned motivation of pressure students feel to score high marks.

錯位的動機起初可能是無辜的，但由於成績表現驅動的期望可能會使學生產生冷漠，因此它可能會適得其反。結果是緩慢而痛苦地撲滅了學生們的好奇心，讓他們無法為了熱愛學習而學習。在一個好心的老師都說他們想激勵學生成就卓越的時代，許多人無意間參與了對夢想有條不紊的粉碎。我們突然之間發現，學生學習不再因為熱愛，而是為了結果而學習。成績成為學生的個人標識，而競爭成為激發學生努力的最有力的動力。加上父母對學生在高中「努力學習」的壓力，以便將來上一所偉大的大學、獲得一份高薪的工作、享受幸福的生活等。這樣，曾經在早期學習過程中享受到的純粹就被破壞性的外部壓力所取代，這些壓力消滅了真正的內在動力。

  The misaligned motivation may start out innocent enough, but it can quickly backfire, as performance-driven expectations potentially create apathy in the student. The result is a slow and painful extinguishing of personal curiosity, making it impossible for the student to learn for the love of learning. In a time when well-meaning teachers all say they want to inspire their students to become something great, many inadvertently participate in the methodical crushing of dreams. Suddenly, learning is not for the love of it, but for the results of it. Grades become the personal student identifier, and competition emerges as the most powerful motivator to inspire student effort. That can be coupled with the parental pressure for students to "work hard" in high school, so they may attend a great university, get a good-paying job, enjoy a happy life, etc. With this, the pureness once enjoyed in the early learning process is replaced by damaging external pressures that kill true internal motivation.

  我忘記了在高中時學到的很多東西，但是由於某種原因，我還記得幾個比較奇怪的話題，它們在當時激發了我的好奇心。我記得十年級時的公民項目課程，我們在那個課程裡學習了德皇威廉一世。我似乎記得我們做過一些獨立研究，關於威廉一世的歷史或故事引起了我的興趣。最終，我抱著極大的興趣學習了這個課題，但對我的學習成績卻絲毫沒有考慮。

  I do not remember many things I learned in high school, but for some reason, I remember a couple of rather odd topics, which even back then, sparked my curiosity. I remember a 10th grade civics project where we studied Wilhelm I. I seem to recall that we did some independent study, and something about the history or story of Wilhelm piqued my interest. It ended up being a topic that I studied with great interest, but with little consideration about the grade I might receive for my learning.

在研究生院時，我參加了全班研究美國內戰的項目，但是老師並未要求我們進行傳統的（無聊的）研究，而是要求我們設計一個以內戰為主題的虛擬樂園。不論出於何種原因，這都讓我感到非常震驚，我深入研究了分配給我的兩個主題：地下鐵路和安德森維爾監獄。（譯註：前者為十九世紀幫助非裔奴隸逃亡的秘密路線網路，後者為美國內戰期間南方邦聯軍隊的戰俘營。）我對這些主題進行了深入研究，以至於項目完成近十年後，我從教學工作中休假時，選擇了駕車前往美國南部。你最好相信這次自由行的一個主要目的地便是在安德森維爾監獄。

In graduate school, I was part of a class-wide project to study the American Civil War, but instead of the traditional (boring) research, we were asked to design a fictitious Civil War-themed fun park. For whatever reason, that struck a chord with me, causing me to dive deeply into my 2 assigned topics: The Underground Railroad and Andersonville Prison. I dug so deeply into those topics that, nearly 10 years post project completion, I took a sabbatical from my teaching job and opted for a driving tour into the American south. You better believe one major destination on this self-directed tour was a stop at the site of Andersonville Prison.

老師是如何向我介紹這兩個主題，並激發我的內在動力，對它們進行了比其他課題更深入的探究呢？我沒有只是為了獲得好成績而進行深入研究。我發現了一些有趣的東西，所以我學它完全就是因為這對我來說很有趣。這便是內在的動力。

What was it about the way the teacher presented these 2 topics to me that inspired my intrinsic motivation to explore deeper than other topics? I did not dig deeply because I wanted a good grade. I found something so interesting that I learned it because it was interesting to me. That is intrinsic motivation.

我並不認為老師在項目介紹中做了任何獨特或有創意的事情，但確實有些「魔法配料」使我對學習產生了好奇。它始於一種興趣。這種感覺驅使我好奇地學習更多，並做出有效的行動。我的行動導致了結果。動機來自於我學習的欲望，而不是成績這一外在動力。這種感覺來自我內心，而不是來自成績差的威脅。我最終學習並培養了一種興趣，這種興趣因我的感受而激起並得到了增強。這就是我動力的源泉。教育者具有影響學生好奇心的巨大能量。如果成功，好奇心可以激發被稱作動機的內部行動。

I do not think the teachers did anything unique or creative in their project presentation, but there was some "magic sauce" that spiked my curiosity to learn. It started with a feeling of interest. That feeling drove my curiosity to learn more and produced effective action on my part. My actions led to results. The motivation came from my desire to learn, not the external force of grades. The feeling came from within me, not from the threat of a bad grade. I ended up learning and nurturing an interest that was piqued and enhanced through my feelings. This was the source of my motivation. Educators have tremendous power to influence student curiosity. If successful, that curiosity can provide the internal action called motivation.

有一天，愛因斯坦四歲或五歲的時候，他不得不因病缺課。為了不被生病的愛因斯坦所困擾，他的父親給他帶來了一個指南針以分散他的注意力，後來回憶起此事時，他說這令他興奮不已。愛因斯坦產生了濃厚的興趣，想知道是什麼魔力讓指南針工作的。這魔力是指南針的顯示嗎？恐怕不是。真正的魔力是他的好奇心，只是這個物件揭開了他的好奇心而已。愛因斯坦對驅使這個物體工作的奧秘感到無比好奇。他後來寫道，他內心深處隱藏著某種東西，迫使他去發現它起作用的原因。產生這種感覺的原因並不像引起和喚醒他的好奇心的感覺那麼重要。一旦覺醒，這種感覺就會導致行動，從而帶來結果。在這種情況下，愛因斯坦的真正內在動機已經被激發出來，並沒有被任何學習測評壓到窒息。

One day, when Albert Einstein was 4 or 5 years old, he had to stay home sick from school. So as not to be bothered by the sick child, his father brought Albert a compass to distract him, which he later recalled made him tremble with excitement. Einstein was magically taken into an overwhelming feeling of interest and connection with the hidden force that made the compass work. Was it the presentation of the compass? Probably not. The magic was his curiosity that was uncovered by the object itself. Einstein was curious as to the mystery behind what made that object work. He later wrote that there was something deeply hidden in him that compelled him to discover the reason why it worked. What created that feeling was not as important as the feeling that stirred and awakened his curiosity. Once awakened, the feeling led to action, which led to results. In this case, Einstein's true intrinsic motivation had been elicited, and not suffocated by any assessment of learning.

處理感覺絕非易事，它需要強大的情商來維持。識別、管理和控制我們的情緒並非心志不堅的人所能做到。我們都經歷過情緒的「低谷」和絕望的時刻。這些時刻使我們重新剝開自己情緒的洋蔥皮，以找出我們所相信的，我們所感受到的和我們想要的事物的核心到底是什麼。有時候你會想放棄，但是如果你深知並理解自己的感受，那麼與低谷的情緒進行談判也是可以忍受的。

Managing feelings is not at all easy or simplistic, and it requires strong emotional intelligence to sustain. To recognize, manage and control our emotions is not for the faint of heart. We all experience emotional "valleys" and times of despair. These times are trying, and they make us peal back the onion layers of our emotions to find out what is at the core of what we believe, how we feel, and what we want. There are going to be times you want to give up, but if you intimately know and understand your feelings, then negotiating the valley is bearable.

一個人註冊成為健身房會員之後，並不願意因為不想改變自己的身體而放棄鍛煉。他們之所以放棄，是因為「失望低谷」和真正的身體轉變所需的努力很難。他們不能讓自己的感覺支配他們的行動。為了保持敏銳的情商，必須不斷地監控和管理自己的情感。恢復體形所需的艱苦工作只是努力的一部份。這些最初會使我們感動的深刻感受，只是朝著目標邁出的一步而已，而非事情的全部。即使你遇到諸如艱苦掙扎、自我懷疑或恐懼之類的障礙，你也有能力戰勝這些情緒並保持執著，這將決定你成功的廣度。當你面對這些時刻的挑戰時，管理你的情商至關重要，因為你的成功和整體效率就在於這一點。

A person does not sign up for a gym membership and then give up working out because they don't want to change their bodies. They give up because the "valley of disappointment" and effort needed for true body transformation is difficult. They fail to let their feeling dictate their actions. Feelings must be constantly monitored and managed in order to keep a sharp EQ (emotional quotient). The hard work necessary to get back into shape is only part of the endeavor. Those deep feelings, which may initially get us moving, are just one step toward the goal, not the whole journey. Your ability to channel those emotions and remain committed, even when you come up against obstacles like hard work, self-doubt or fear, will determine the breadth of your success. When you are challenged by these moments, managing your EQ is crucial because your success and overall effectiveness lie within.

2012年一月，彼得.伯格曼在《哈佛評論》的一篇文章中指出：「思想對於動機而言至關重要。」儘管頭腦會激發動機，但頭腦在後續過程中什麼也做不了。後續行動結合的是毅力和決心。創造參與變革欲望的情感首先來自我們的思想。「度過低谷」的決心來自我們的頭腦，它表達著我們成功或失敗的意願。我們的學生正在設法弄清並管理他們對不符合外部期望產生的恐懼情緒。許多學生無法對自己的成功或失敗產生連結。他們的情商很低，因為沒有人教過他們如何識別或管理自己的情商。他們只是被告知要「努力學習並做到最好，這樣你才能擁有良好的工作和幸福的生活」。同時，那個學生看著這一訊息的傳達者（老師或父母），可能會問，為什麼這會使他/她感到高興？他們內部沒有主動權或動機。只有好意而已，但外部壓力可能會也可能不會產生結果，它們往往無法提升學生充份參與學習的好奇心。

In a Harvard Review article, Peter Bergman (January 2012) points out that "The mind is essential to motivation." Though the mind initiates motivation, the mind does nothing on the follow-through. The follow-through is an action that combines grit and determination. The feelings that create the desire to engage in change come first from our mind. The determination to "weather the valley" comes from our mind telling our will to succeed or fail. Our students are trying to figure out and manage their fear of not meeting external expectations. Many students have no connection to the feelings of their own success or failure. They have very low emotional intelligence because no one is teaching them how to recognize or manage their EQ. They are simply being told to "work hard, study hard, and be the best so you can have a good job and good life." Meanwhile, that student looks around at the message giver (teacher or parent) and may question why that would make him/her happy?" There is no ownership or motivation from within. There is just well meaning, but external, pressure that may or may not produce results, but often fails to increase a student's curiosity to engage fully in their learning.

教師必須盡可能地呼籲學習者並幫助他們管理和駕馭他們對成功和失敗的情緒洪流，但他們也必須透過激發學生的好奇心來幫助他們充份參與學習。如果他們能夠激發好奇心，那麼學習的動機就會從學習者的內心生長。這將產生高度投入的學習者，因為他們會對學習的前景感到興奮。這種興奮將產生行動進而帶來結果。因此，教師不是以學業等級或成績為動機，而是以學習者的好奇心為動機。隨著好奇心的增長，老師需要謹慎地幫助學生識別和處理情緒，毫無疑問，學生之間的打分和比較將是不可避免的事情。這也就是為什麼從教師到學生的情商開發和管理是教師/導師角色中至關重要的部份的原因。

Teachers must appeal to the learner where they can to help them manage and navigate the flood of emotions they have about success and failure, but they must also help them engage fully in the learning by spiking their curiosity. If they can ignite the curiosity, the motivation to learn will grow from within the learner. This will produce a highly engaged learner because they will feel excited about the prospect of learning. This excitement will produce actions that lead to results. The teacher, therefore, is not using academic grades or results as the motivator, but rather the learner's curiosity. As the curiosity grows, the teacher needs to be mindful of helping the student identify and manage the emotions along the way because, undoubtedly, grading and student-to-student comparison are going to be inevitable. This is why the EQ development and management from the teacher to the student is such an important and critical part of the teacher/mentor role.

對於教師來說，一個好的起點是自己首先成為高情商的好榜樣。認識、理解和管理自己的情緒，這樣你才可以幫助他人認識、理解和管理他們的情緒。這就是影響力！情商低的老師不會影響學生的好奇心，他們也不知如何影響學習者的人生。這些老師只是簡單地翻閱書本材料，讓學生們下次考試的時候用得上這些東西。這就延續了不明智「學習」的惡性循環。學習者沒有參與度，也沒有好奇心。這恰好迎合了記憶型的學習者。學生認為他在「學習」，但他卻錯過了教育的真正本質，教育的本質始於好奇心和內在動機，並以擁有完整的教育經歷為滿足的。

A good starting point for teachers is to first be a shining example of high EQ. Recognize, understand and manage your own emotions so that you can help others recognize, understand and manage their own emotions. That is influence! Teachers with low EQ do not impact student curiosity and have no idea how to influence the life of a learner. Those teachers simply plow through the material so the student can regurgitate information on another exam. This continues the vicious cycle of disingenuous "learning". There is no learner engagement and no curiosity spike. This just caters to the learner who happens to be a good memorizer. The student thinks he is "learning", but he is missing out on the true essence of education, which involves the pathway beginning with curiosity and intrinsic motivation, and ending with the fulfillment of having a complete educational experience.

總結
Summary

　　為什麼有些人擁有堅持追求目標的動力，而有些人卻沒能實現相同的目標？真正的內在動力源於感覺。感覺會導致行動，進而帶來結果。內在動機是最好的動機類型，因為有內在動機的人會感受到渴望，付出努力並創造結果。外部動機可以產生結果，但也附帶損害，例如讓人害怕失敗和承受巨大壓力。在理想的情況下，為了獲得最佳的學習效果，應激發學生的好奇心，然後讓他們挑戰自己，以便出於內在興趣而不是為了成績而學習。教師需要有多種測評方法，以確保他們能教育並且全面影響學習者的風格，而不僅僅是讓他們死記硬背。這是艱苦的工作，但學生的幸福和成功都取決於它。

　　Why do some people sustain their motivation towards a goal while others with the same goal fail to achieve? True internal motivation is born out of feelings. Feelings will lead to actions that produce results. Intrinsic motivation is the best type of motivation because the individual feels the desire, puts forth the effort and accepts the results. External motivation can produce results, but has collateral damage as well, such as fear of failure and intense pressure. Ideally, for optimal learning, a student's curiosity is piqued, and they then challenge themselves so learning is achieved from intrinsic interest and not grades earned. Teachers need to have multiple methods of assessment to ensure they are teaching and reaching all styles of learner, not just the memorizer. It is hard work, but the happiness and success of your students depend on it.

那麼，我們如何激勵學生呢？首先要認識到他們的感覺會導致行動並帶來結果。這些感覺的來源必須來自每個學生內心。太多的人沒有個人動機，只不過是善意的父母和老師給他們施加了義務和壓力的動機。老師需要熟練地關心和教導學生如何管理他們自己的情商。幫助他們認識並表達自己的感受，以便他們可以更好地表達和管理它們。老師和校長必須幫助父母了解如何教育子女，以免給他們造成不必要的壓力，這些壓力會令學生的參與逐漸降低。如果我們想讓學生參與學習並且感到快樂，就必須幫助他們擁抱並認識他們自己的感受。這將導致行動並帶來結果。

So how can we motivate our students? Recognize that their feelings will lead to actions that produce results. The source of those feelings must come from within each student. Too many have no personal motivations, only the motivations of obligation and pressure put on them from well-meaning parents and teachers. Teachers need to be proficient at caring for and teaching students how to manage their EQ. Help them recognize and verbalize their feelings, so they can be better versed at expressing and managing them. Teachers and Headmasters must help parents understand how to support their children, so that unwanted pressures, which contribute to stress and suffocate true student engagement, are not placed upon them. If we want students to be engaged and happy learners, we must help them embrace and recognize their feelings. This will lead to actions and results.

- 彼得.伯格曼，「你的問題不是動機」，《哈佛評論》，2012年一月四日。

  Peter Bregman, "Your Problem Isn't Motivation", *Harvard Review*, January 4, 2012. (https://hbr.org/search?term=peter bregman)

勇氣、膽量還是運氣？
Grit, Guts or Luck?

> "It takes grit & guts to be and do the abnormal and extraordinary!"

Image credit: Tirzah Libert

勇氣＝勇敢和決心；性格的力量
Grit = Courage and resolve; strength of character
膽量＝不屈不撓
Guts = Fortitude
運氣＝幸運事件的發生機率
Luck = The chance happenings of fortunate events

　　我經常反思自己的人生，思考其間的一些重要事件，情況、選擇和發生過的事情，這些都有助於構成我的人生故事。我們每個人都有一個「故事」，請了解並欣賞它與你的身份的獨特聯繫，這一點非常重要。你的人生故事是由塑造你生活的重要事件組成的。我意識到我的人生故事並不引人注目，但它是「我的」故事，並且由於它對我來說是獨一無二的，所以我常常想知道我是如何走到這一步的？我絕不是在暗示我已經成功了，或者說我有什麼特別之處，但是我的確有一些很棒的人生經歷，它們幫助我成為了如今的我。實際上，它們是定義和促使我成為我的一些事件。由於我將要討論「成功」的概念，因此，我首先將其定義

為：最大限度地發揮才能、技能、努力、奮鬥和環境，以取得令個人滿意、愉悅和滿足的結果。

I often reflect on my life and consider significant events, circumstances, choices, and happenings that help make up my story. Each of us has a "story" and it is important to know and appreciate it for being uniquely connected to who you are. Your story is composed of the contributing events that shape your life. I realize my story is not spectacular, but it is "my" story and since it is unique to me, I often wonder how it is that I got here? I am in no way suggesting that I have "made it", or that I am anything special, but I have had some great life experiences that have all helped shape me into the person I have become. These are, in fact, defining and contributing events that made me who I am. Since I am going to be discussing the concept of "success", let me first lay out my definition as: *maximizing one's talents, skills, hard work, efforts, and circumstances to achieve results that, in combination, bring personal satisfaction, pleasure and contentment.*

在去旅行或開始新的工作項目之前，我曾多次聽到朋友或祝願者的「祝你好運」一詞。在這種情況下，「祝你好運」一詞既常見又適當。我知道他們是一番好意，但我也會喜歡聽到這樣的話：「願你的辛勤工作帶給你想要的結果。」或「繼續完全按照自己的意願做，你會做得很棒。」但是，當人們說「祝你好運」時，幾乎就好像在暗示成功或失敗是取決於隨機機率的，並且成功和失敗對技能的依賴程度還不如對偶然性的依賴程度。運氣對個人取得成功能起到多大的作用呢？

Many times, I have heard the words, "good luck" from friends, or well-wishers, before I leave for a trip or start a new work project. The words "good luck" are both common and appropriate in situations like these. I know they mean well, but I would also enjoy hearing phrases such as: "May your hard work produce the results you want." or, "Continue to do exactly what you have been doing and you will be great." But, when people say, "good luck", it is almost as if they are implying that the only chance of success or failure rests on a random set of circumstances and, that success and failure are less dependent upon skill than upon happenstance. How much of a role does luck play on an individual achieving success?

作為一個喜歡看體育比賽的人，我在體育運動中見過很多好運的例子。例如，我們可以想像一位籃球運動員，他在八十四英尺外絕望地投籃，只有籃球完美入網，他們才能贏得比賽。那個球員可能練了八十四次，一次都沒成功。在這種情況下，完美的軌跡和距離產生了幸運的結果。我曾在一個足球場上見識過運氣，一個球員失了球（所謂的笨手笨腳），而那個長橢圓球（所謂的橄欖球）由於其幾何形狀而開始隨機彈跳。一番彈跳之後球恰好完美地飛入了一名防守球員的懷抱，後者將其接達得分。運氣體現在哪裡？ 那個球員以正確的角度和速度靠近球，乾淨俐落地接住球，然後帶球奔跑，這當然離不開技巧，但是「反彈的運氣」與人的努力、技巧或計劃都沒有關係。當你玩的彩票遊戲從一百個乒乓球中吸出六個，上面印有隨機數字時，也會發生同樣的運氣。幸運的是，你恰好就選了那六個獲獎的數字。隨機抽取數字球的過程沒有任何技巧可言。有人可能會爭辯說，選出獲獎數字也沒有什麼技巧可言。如果體育賽事和彩票中有運氣，那是否意味著人生中也有運氣呢？

  As one who enjoys watching sports, I have seen many examples of luck in athletics. For example, consider the basketball player who heaves a desperation shot from 84 feet away, only to have it swish in the net perfectly to win the game. That player can practice that shot 84 times and never make it once. On this occasion, the perfect trajectory and distance produced lucky results. I have seen luck on a football field when one player drops the ball (called a fumble) and the *prolate spheroid* (a.k.a football) begins to bounce randomly because of its geometrical shape. One of these bounces happens to elevate perfectly into the arms of a pursuing defensive player who runs it in for a touchdown (score). Where is the luck here? Having that player take the correct angle and speed towards the ball, grasping it cleanly and then running with it certainly has skill involved, but the "luck of the bounce" had nothing to do with human effort, skill, or planning. The same sample of luck occurs when the lottery game you are playing sucks up 6 out of 100 ping pong balls with random numbers printed on them. As luck would have it, these are the same exact 6 numbers you chose for the win. There was no skill in the random draft of the balls. Some may argue there wasn't any human skill in even picking the winning numbers. If there is luck in sports and in the lottery, does that mean there is also luck in life?

作為一個有信仰的人，我不確定我是否相信運氣。但我覺得，許多並非我應得的事情，也不在我計劃之內的事情，可能發生在我身上。作為這些事件的接受者，我感到非常幸運並且心存感激。但是事實上，很多時候我們都將運氣歸因於一種情況，那就是我們已經付出了真誠的努力和練習，減輕了失敗的可能性。實際上，我們所投入的練習和計劃讓我們值得好的結果。成功或失敗取決於心態。

As a person of faith, I am not sure I believe in luck. But I feel that many undeserved things may happen to me that I did not earn or otherwise plan. As the recipient in these times, I feel quite lucky and grateful. However, there are many times we attribute luck to a situation when, in fact, we have put sincere effort and rehearsal into mitigating the possibilities of failure. The practice and planning invested has in fact earned a result. Success or failure depends on a mindset perspective.

我到中國旅行已經十多年了。我的第一次中國之行僅僅是為了拜訪幾個把孩子送到我夏令營的家庭。從那時開始，人們把我介紹了出去。我繼續回到中國，結識更多的人，擴大人脈，這些年來，我很幸運地造訪了十個不同省份的一百多個城市。我不再為自己的夏令營做宣傳，但是我的業務已經擴展到了教育諮詢、演講嘉賓和教師培訓。我是否要將這種業務增長和機遇僅僅歸因於運氣呢？不！我更願意認為這是毅力和勇氣的結果，是它們幫助我建立了這些聯繫。

I have been traveling to China for more than 10 years now. My first trip to China was simply to visit a few families who had sent their children to my summer camp. From there, introductions were made. I continued to return to meet more people, expand connections and, all these years later, I have been fortunate enough to visit over 100 cities in 10 different provinces. I no longer find myself promoting my summer camp, but I have expanded into education consulting, guest speaking, and teacher training. Do I attribute this business growth and opportunity simply to luck? No! I would give more authority to the notion that it was a result of grit and guts that helped me to forge and build these connections.

我深夜在路上開車，輪胎扁了，這是運氣嗎？如果 我碰巧在行李箱裡放了我的備胎、手電筒和安全照明彈，這是運氣嗎？我正好扎到那顆釘子，它的位置很合適，恰好可以刺破輪胎，這是「運氣」使然，但是可以說，我預先做好了一些計劃，以確保無論何時發生這種情況，即使我感到不便，我都已經做好了準備，這裡面就包含著技巧和勇氣。

Is it luck that I am driving down the road late at night and I get a flat tire? I happen to have my spare in the trunk along with a flashlight and a safety flare. Is it luck? It may be luck that the nail I ran over was perfectly positioned to puncture the tire, but, arguably, there was some element of skill and grit that I invested in pre-planning to make sure when that scenario occurred, even though I was inconvenienced, I was still prepared.

運氣裡面確實沒有任何人為的計劃或技能。這是隨機發生的事情，例如足球、籃球或彩票數字球都與技能無關。當我獲得「好運」時（無論好運到何種程度），我當然會感到高興，但我寧願不依靠運氣過自己的生活。相反，我寧願希望自己的勇氣和膽量能產生我想要的結果，而不是指望它偶然發生。

　　Luck is really the absence of any human planning or skill. It is a random happening, like the bounce of a football, basketball or lottery ball that skill had nothing to do with. I am certainly happy when I am the recipient of "good luck" (to whatever extend it may be luck) but I would prefer not to live my life relying on luck. Instead, I prefer to live a life where my grit and guts produce the results I desire, and not leave it to happenstance.

　　有時，當與一位朋友聊天，發現他們剛從溫暖的熱帶地區度假歸來時，我聽到自己說：「哇，你真幸運！」我試圖警醒自己，並意識到運氣可能與此無關。要省下所需的錢需要勇氣和技巧，需要制定必要的計劃，也需要假期以便他們可以去他們選擇的目的地。仔細的預先計劃與運氣無關。一個好運的例子是，如果在假期結束時，當他們去支付酒店賬單時，他們被告知他們「碰巧」（運氣）是第兩萬個入住該酒店的客人，而酒店為此選擇的慶祝方式是給他們免去全部住宿費，這次住宿將是完全免費的！沒有計劃，技巧或毅力可以幫助他們獲得這種獎勵。這就純粹是運氣！

　　Sometimes, when speaking to a friend who reveals they recently returned from a vacation in a warm, tropical place, I have heard myself say, "Wow, you're so lucky!" I try to catch myself and realize that luck probably had nothing to do with it. It required grit and skill to save the necessary money, make the necessary plans, and take the desired vacation to the destination of their choice. Careful pre-planning had nothing to do with luck. An example of luck would be if, at the end of the vacation, when they went to pay the hotel bill, they were told they "happen to be" (luck) the 20,000th guest to ever visit that hotel. To celebrate, the hotel is awarding them by covering the entire cost of the stay. The stay would be completely free! No planning, skill, or grit would have been used to receive this reward. This would be pure luck!

我們使用「運氣」這個詞，便忽略了我們所投入的勇氣和膽量。這兩個詞我都喜歡。勇氣的定義之一是「勇氣和決心，性格堅強」。勇氣即是韌性。它需要決心、毅力，有時還需要克服不利條件。我希望人們認為我是一個有勇氣和膽量的人，而不是一個幸運的人。我希望成為一個願意付出必要的努力的人，當遇到不利條件時，我希望自己表現出毅力和決心。這樣，我就可以接受可能出現的結果。也許我還是需要一些運氣，但因為我有勇氣和膽量，我可以更容易地對任何運氣心存感激，同時也對自己的決心和努力感到滿意。我願意相信自己的努力，而不是運氣。

When we use the word luck, we overlook the grit and guts that were invested. I love both of these words. One of the definitions for grit is "courage and resolve; strength of character". Grit is toughness. It requires determination, perseverance and, at times, going up against unfavorable odds. I want people to think of me as a person who possesses grit and guts, rather than luck. I want to be one who is willing to put in the necessary hard work and effort, and when up against unfavorable odds, shows perseverance and determination. In doing so, I can then accept the results that may come along. Maybe there is still some luck involved, but because I have grit and guts, I can more easily be grateful for any luck involved, but also satisfied with the determination and effort I put forth. I want to trust my effort, not my luck.

如果體育界存在運氣，那麼教育界也存在運氣嗎？作為一名教育工作者，當我試圖教導我的學生在準備個人的學習和生活時，要依靠自己的勇氣和膽量。我不希望他們抱著考好成績的幻想而鬆懈下來。我敦促他們採取必要的準備措施，以獲得更多的成功機會。有了勇氣和膽量，學生可以從任何運氣中受益，也不會在遭遇「壞運氣」時崩潰。老師應該鼓勵學生盡可能地學習和準備（也就是教給學生毅力），這樣當學生被問到一個意料之外的考試問題（運氣不好）時，他們不會崩潰。

If there is luck in the world of sports, can there also be luck in the world of education? As an educator, I tried to teach students to rely on developed grit and guts in their personal preparation for studies and for life. I did not want them to sit back and hope for a good grade. I urged them to take the necessary preparatory steps to keep the odds of success favorable to them. With grit and guts, the student can be the beneficiary of any luck involved, and also not be devastated when "bad luck" occurs. Teachers should encourage students to study and prepare as best they can (that is teaching grit), so that when an unexpected exam question (bad luck) is asked, students are not devastated.

有了堅定的決心，就有了毅力。有了膽量，處理意外情況就成為了可能。當勇氣和膽量都很明顯的時候（不管遇到好運氣還是壞運氣），結果都可以被更好的接受。培養勇氣和膽量是人生中的偉大計劃。依賴運氣只能帶來徒勞的挫敗感，最終無法讓人滿意或得到信任。等待運氣不能成為計劃。

With well-established grit, perseverance is present. With the demonstration of guts, dealing with the unexpected is possible. When both grit and guts are evident (even if good or bad luck is involved) the results can be better accepted. Developing grit and guts is a great game plan for life. Relying on luck is a futile frustration that ultimately cannot satisfy or be trusted. Waiting for luck is not a plan.

向學生傳授勇氣和膽量並不容易，因為要同時學習兩者，就必須經歷挫敗帶來的失望。太多的家長不希望他們的孩子經歷挫折、失敗或坎坷，所以他們會立即介入，責怪老師或學校。父母擔心孩子的不適感會給他們的一生留下創傷。傳遞給家長的適當訊息應該是，支持老師將更好地幫助孩子理解他們可能需要在哪些方面做得更好，以減輕厄運發生時的情況，或在好運發生時心存感激。克服失望需要勇氣和膽量。太多的學生在這兩方面都缺乏。

Teaching grit and guts to students is not easy because, to learn both, one must experience the disappointment of failure. Too many parents do not want their child to experience frustration, failure, or a set back, so they immediately step in to blame the teacher or the school. Parents fear the discomfort in their child will scar them for life. The appropriate message to parents should be that supporting the teacher will better help the child understand where they may need to do a better job to mitigate instances when bad luck happens or appreciate it when good luck occurs. Overcoming the disappointment requires grit and guts. Too many students lack evidence of either.

結果導向的教育與勇氣和膽量的教育背道而馳。學生成績越來越重要，並最終決定學生、教師和學校的成敗。由於教育的重點在於結果，我們並不能正確地教授勇氣和膽量。家長和學生都不願承受掙扎帶來的不適，而這對於勇氣和膽量的教育是必不可少的。即使是那些非常努力的學生，他們花了大量時間準備，他們可能顯示出了膽量，但依然缺乏勇氣。任何輕微的成績下滑（或出現壞運氣）都會使學生和家長崩潰。

Results-driven education is heading in the opposite direction from teaching grit and guts. Student grade results are taking on a greater importance and ultimately are used to determine the success of the student, teacher, and school. With the focal point of education being on the results, we fail to properly teach grit and guts. Parents and students do not want to endure the discomfort of the struggle, which is needed to teach grit and guts. Even for those very hardworking students who spend tremendous time preparing, they may show guts but lack grit. Any slight deterioration in results (or the presence of bad luck) renders the student and parents devastated.

總結
Summary

我很幸運地教導了一些非常堅毅而勤奮的學生，然而他們的成績從來沒有高過「B」。雖然他們的一些同學可能獲得了更高的分數，但他們並沒有發展或學習到與我的這些B級學生一樣的勇氣和膽量。結果，B級的學生學到了勇氣和膽量，而高分學生則只是得到了更高的分數。如今，那些B級學生（以及其他像他們一樣的學生）經營著成功的企業，這些企業之所以變得強大，是因為他們的勇氣和膽量，而非他們的成績。

I was fortunate to teach some very gritty, hardworking students who never earned higher than a "B" for a grade. Although some of their classmates may have earned higher grades, they did not develop or learn the same level of grit and guts as some of my "B" students. As a result, the B students learned grit & guts, whereas the higher scoring students simply got higher grades. Today, those B students (and others like them) are now running successful businesses that have grown strong because of their grit and guts, not because of the grades they received.

儘管我自己的高中成績很差，但我確實學到了勇氣和膽量。這種教育是透過體育運動和比賽而得來的，這些都為未來的商業投資和計劃打下了基礎。當然，好運和厄運都時有發生，但我的勇氣和膽量幫助我忍受、堅持，讓我對好運和厄運都心存感激，並讓我因為自己的努力工作而獲得滿足感和成就感。我學到的勇氣也來自於無數次的失敗。業務失敗和糟糕的決策則導致了業務計劃和新想法的改進。失敗並沒有把我毀掉。它激勵我做得更好或改變我現有的方法。是勇氣和膽量讓我做到了這一點，而不是運氣。

In spite of my own poor high school academic record, I did learn grit & guts. This education came through athletics and competition, which then parlayed into future business investments and initiatives. Sure, there are times that both good and bad luck events occur, but my grit and guts help me endure, persevere and appreciate the good and the bad, as well as give me satisfaction and fulfillment because of my hard work. My learned grit also grew out of a lot of failure. Business failures and poor decisions led to improved business plans and new ideas. Failure did not ruin me. It inspired me to do it better or shift my approach. Grit and guts did this, not luck.

教學生如何培養勇氣和膽量，同時對好運氣和壞運氣都心存感激。它們一個涉及到可行的計劃，另一個只是依賴於偶發事件。二者之一可以打磨或摧毀你的勇氣，並影響你的膽量。培養勇氣需要膽量，但付出的努力都是值得的。這樣一來，當幸運降臨時，你就可以簡單地心存感激。如果你有勇氣，那麼任何壞運氣都只會讓你變得更有膽量。如果你有勇氣，又趕上了好運氣，那麼你會更加心懷感激地迎接它。

Teach students how to develop grit and guts while also appreciating both good and bad luck. One involves a workable plan and the other simply relies on happenstance. One can sharpen or destroy your grit and impact your guts. Developing grit takes guts, but it is worth the effort. Then you can simply appreciate luck when it happens. If you have grit, then any bad luck simply teaches you to have even more guts. If you have grit, and good luck happens, then you appreciate and welcome that even more.

每個人都需要一個行動計劃來培養個人的勇氣和膽量。學生和老師都同樣需要它。強大的領導型教師需要在學生身上進行投入，引導和指導他們，這樣他們才能在兩個方面同時獲得發展。相信自己的勇氣和膽量可以帶你到達個人發展的新高度。依賴運氣會讓你變得脆弱、軟弱，最終壯志難酬。

Each person needs a game plan to develop personal grit and guts. Students and teachers need it equally as much. Strong lead teachers need to make the investment in their students to guide and mentor them so they can develop both. Trusting in grit and guts can take you to new heights of personal development. Relying on luck leaves you vulnerable, weak, and ultimately unfulfilled.

目的地 vs. 方向
Destination vs. Direction

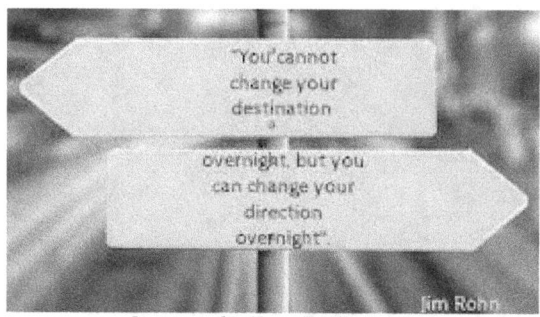

Image credit: Home Professionals

　　我可以輕鬆地回憶起我第一份教學工作早期的情形。我從大學畢業並獲得了學位和證書,表明我已有資質走上教學崗位,我認為我已經準備好在經驗豐富的資深老師的信任下開展我的第一份課堂教學工作!好吧,並不是這麼回事!我所擁有的只是一些教學的理論知識罷了,我的實踐教學(大學期間完成了兩次實習)讓我獲得了一點課堂經驗,獲得了大學學位、教師資格證以及過度的自信。現在回想起來,我顯然缺乏了最重要的東西——經驗。我可能已經合格並很興奮,但是我顯然是缺乏經驗!我像大多數其他一年級老師一樣,發現那年的教學工作非常困難,有很多過渡學習內容。就像我父親說的,那是「艱苦的磨練」,天哪,我被磨練得七葷八素的!

　　I can easily recall the initial days of my first teaching job. Having graduated from the university with a degree and certificate indicating I was authorized to teach, I assumed I had been prepared to enter my first classroom job with the confidence of an experienced veteran teacher! Well, I was NOT! What I had was some teaching theory knowledge, a little bit of classroom experience because of my practice teaching (having completed two placements in schools), a degree from a university, a teaching certificate, and a heavy dose of overconfidence. As I look back now, I clearly lacked the most important thing of all - experience. I may have been qualified and excited, but I was certainly not experienced! Like most other first year teachers, I found that year of teaching quite difficult, with a lot of transitional learning. As my father said, it was the "school of hard knocks" and boy did I get knocked around!

如果我能向你形象地描述我當時感受的話，請想像一個人在海洋中顫抖，陷入水流的漩渦，同時拼命地抓著一個物體，卻還是幾乎嗆水。每次我都以為自己能摒住呼吸，但當我更加努力地保持漂浮時，另一輪波浪拍過來，將我吞沒。那真是令人筋疲力盡的事情，我的教學生涯就這麼開始了！

If I could give you an image illustration of how I felt, it would be a person bobbing in the ocean while desperately clinging to an object barely able to keep my head above the swirling waves. Each time I thought I would catch my breath, another wave would wash over me as I tried even harder to stay afloat. That would be exhausting and terrifying, and thus my teaching career was launched!

那一年的大部份時間裡，我發現自己和學生相比，就只提前學了一到兩個課時的內容。基於我的經驗，我瘋狂地計劃著最好的課程。我進行了勇敢的嘗試，以增加創造力，我認為它們可能會激起學生對學習體育和美國歷史的好奇心和必要的參與度。那時，我認為我的目標是上完每一章和每個單元的內容，最終完成期末考試。我把考試作為目標。我並沒有看到我的課程將如何作為預備課程，幫他們適應高中時期更為廣泛的學習，更不用說是如何幫助他們為人生做好準備。最終，我心裡並沒有一個正確的目的地。

Most of that year, I found myself staying 1-2 book lessons ahead of my students. Based on my inexperience, I was frantically planning the best lessons I could. I was making a valiant attempt to add the creativity that I thought might inspire the engagement necessary to make middle school students curious about learning PE and U.S. History. At that time, I thought my destination was to complete each chapter and each unit that would culminate with a final exam. The exam was my destination. I did not see the bigger picture of how my course would fit into their bigger picture of high school preparation, let alone how I could better help them prepare for life. Ultimately, I did not have the correct destination in mind.

回想起來，我當時心裡很難有正確的**目的地**，因為我並不知道如何開發教學的這一個方面。我希望我的學生了解歷史事件與相關人員的行為之間的因果關係。但是，由於沒有必要的經驗來提供構思周到的課程和測評，我發現自己的教學效率很低。那時，我不得不把自己評為一名典型的新手老師。用口頭語來說，我當時只是「跟著感覺走」！幸運的是，經過短短幾年的經驗積累，我開始理解**目的地和方向**的真正含義，以及這些詞語在塑造我的教學風格和方法方面的重要性。

In retrospect, it was hard for me to have the correct **destination** in mind because I had no idea how to develop that aspect of my teaching. I wanted my students to understand the cause/effect relationship between events in History and the actions of people involved. However, without the necessary experience to deliver well-conceived lessons and assessments, I believe I was ineffective. I would have to rate myself, back then, as a typical rookie teacher. In colloquial terms, I was "flying by the seat of my pants"! Fortunately, after a few short years of experience, I began to understand the true meaning of **destination and direction** and how important those terms are in shaping my teaching style and methods.

請允許我用兩個詞深入探討我想表達的意思：目的地和方向。**目的地**是老師教授任何學科內容的最終結果或宏觀目標。（目的地**不是**測試或評估。) 例如，也許當我講授有關美國內戰的內容時，我真正打算讓學生們了解的是戰爭的社會、政治和經濟原因，以及戰爭的結果如何塑造了美國這個現代化國家。目的地歸根到底是我們希望在我們所教的課程中得到的結果。如果比作一張地圖，那它就是你旅程的最終目的地。

Let me dive deeper into what I mean using the two words: destination and direction. **Destination** is the end-result, or macro objective, a teacher has for teaching any subject content. (The destination is NOT a test or assessment.) For example, perhaps when I taught the content about the American Civil War, my intended destination for my students was to understand the social, political, and economic reasons for the war and how the results shaped the United States as a modern nation. Destination is ultimately the WHERE we hope to end up in WHAT we are teaching. If it were a map, it would be the final destination of your trip.

要到達目的地需要很多轉彎。這就是對「**方向**」這個詞的理解。如果將其與教學聯繫起來，方向指的是教育者用來實現其宏觀目標的日常技巧。如果目的地是**哪裡**和**什麼**的話，那麼方向便是**這個**和**那個**。它們共同作用，相互依存。方向性項目可以是任何設計的團隊活動，方向性問題、工作表、項目、辯論，甚至是將知識推向目的地的視頻片段。

Getting to the destination requires many turns along the way. This is how to understand **direction**. To relate it to teaching, direction is the day-to-day techniques educators will use to reach their macro objective. If destination is the WHERE and WHAT, then direction is the THIS and THAT. They go together and are dysfunctional without each other. Directional items could be any designed small group activities, guiding questions, worksheets, projects, debates or even video segments that move the knowledge toward the destination.

參加我的工作坊的老師總是能得到「職位晉升」！在培訓的開始，

我總會很高興地告訴他們，他們都已經得到了晉升。他們不再僅僅被稱為老師，而已經被提拔為課堂裡的CEO。在這個領導職位上，老師將承擔教室之內所有活動的「建築師」和「設計師」的職責。建築師設計一棟建築物時，他們知道項目最終完成後的樣子。為此，他們還要決定使用的材料以及構建過程的步驟順序，以便按正確的工序完成工作。在課堂裡，CEO（老師）選擇開展哪些方向性活動以及何時開展這些活動，因為他們心裡清楚最終產品是什麼樣的。和任何優秀的建築師一樣，他們借助包含所有建築物詳細訊息和所含系統的藍圖開展工作。以此類推，藍圖便是課程和目的地。方向則是完成建築所需的材料和步驟。而CEO顯然是老師。

Teachers who attend my workshops are always promoted! Early in my training session, I happily inform them that they have all been promoted. No longer are they just known as a teacher, but rather they are promoted to the position of CEO of their classroom. In this leadership position, the teacher assumes the responsibility as the architect and designer of all that gets built inside those classroom walls. The architect designs a building knowing what the final project will look like when completed. To accomplish that, they also decide the materials used as well as the sequential steps in the building process so that things are completed in the proper order. In the classroom, the CEO (teacher) chooses which directional activities to use and when they should happen, because they know what the finished product should look like. Like any good architect, they work from a blueprint that contains all the building details and systems to be included. In this analogy, the blueprint is the curriculum and destination. The materials and steps taken to complete the building are the direction. The CEO is obviously the teacher.

當我從經驗不足的新人轉變為經驗豐富的CEO時，我注意到我為學生學習而設定的「目的地」已經有所改善。當我對他們有所了解並明白了如何利用自己的領導力時，我對如何閱讀自己試圖建立的藍圖有了更好的理解。隨著對最終產品理解的提升，我得以改進自己的建築設計，以便用正確的材料和體系促進成長和學習。有了更清晰的視野，我對方向有了更好的了解，於是得以改善學生的學習體驗。我開始明白，教學不僅僅是為學生提供考試要記住的內容和訊息而已。我需要他們了解和理解這些訊息，但更重要的是，要讓他們知道如何應用自己學到的訊息，以便他們不會在學了三天之後就把它們忘記。目的地和方向對於每位老師來說都至關重要。請始終把它們置於日常計劃的最前端，以便在你作為「首席建築師」，打造課堂傑作時，它們始終處於學生學習經驗的最前端。

As I transformed from an inexperienced rookie to a more experienced CEO, I noticed that my "destination" for student learning improved. As I got to know them and how to utilize my leadership, I had a better understanding of how to read the blueprint for what I was trying to build. With my finished product better understood, I could improve my architectural design so that I had the correct materials and systems that would enhance growth and learning. With a sharper vision of where I was going, I had a better sense of direction so I could improve the student learning experience. I began to understand that teaching was far more than just giving students content and data to remember for the exam. I needed them to know and understand data, but more importantly, how to apply the data learned so it was not just forgotten 3 days later. Destination and direction are essential for each teacher to grasp. Keep them at the forefront of daily planning so they are at the forefront of the student learning experience while you build your masterpiece as the CEO architect.

每個CEO都需要知道目的地和方向，但他們還必須具備有效完成旅程所需的領導技能。簡而言之，一個好的CEO要學會如何與學生建立聯繫和溝通。這有助於增強方向性的曲折迂回。我作為老師的最佳技能不是我對書本內容的熟練掌握，而是我理解中學生思想和個性的能力。因為我可以在他們的社交和情感層面上與他們建立聯繫，所以我也能夠透過創造性和引人入勝的方向性活動成功地將他們送達目的地。成功的老師與學生保持聯繫；正如成功的CEO與他們所領導的人建立聯繫那樣。

Every CEO needs to know the destination and direction, but they must also have the leadership skills necessary to effectively complete the journey. Simply stated, a good CEO learns how to connect and communicate with students. This serves to enhance the directional twists and turns. My best skill as a teacher was not my masterful command over the content, but rather my ability to understand the minds and personalities of middle school students. Because I could connect and relate to them at their social and emotional level, I was also able to be successful in delivering them to the destination through creative and engaging directional activities. Successful teachers connect with their students; just like successful CEOs connect with those they lead.

這時，你可能懷疑自己是不是領導者，因為你感覺自己並不像什麼CEO。我講領導者僅僅定義為能影響他人的人。領導者不一定非得擁有多麼高的頭銜。領導者不一定是指職務。它只是指能夠影響他人的人。有效的領導者不僅要樹立清晰的願景，而且要讓他們帶領的人「認可」。當他們認可時，他們將跟隨你到達願景中所述的目的地。在領導的帶領下，你一路歷經所有的方向性曲折將他們最終引向願景。

At this point, you may doubt that you are a leader because you do not feel like a CEO. My definition of a leader is simply one who influences others. A leader does not necessarily have to have the supreme title. Leadership is not necessarily a job title. It just refers to anyone who influences others. Effective leaders not only cast a clear vision, but also get those they lead to "buy in". When they buy in, they will follow you to the destination set out in the vision. You lead them toward the vision through all the directional twists and turns taken under your guidance as a leader.

我的大部份「CEO」教育來自我當教練的時候。我在教學生涯中，我花了很多年的時間教授籃球、足球和網球。在體育運動中，任何一支球隊的目標都是獲得最高程度的認可。然而，隨著賽季的開始，每次練習和比賽都成了朝著目的地邁進的方向性步驟。知道如何使團隊到達目的地包括許多因素，這些因素可能會導致整體的成功或失敗。偉大的教練也是偉大的建築師。他們看到了願景，但也知道如何領導團隊一步一步積累，逐步實現團隊的目標。

Much of my "CEO" education came when I was a coach. I spent many years of my teaching career coaching basketball, soccer, and tennis. In sports, the destination of any team is to earn the highest level of recognition attainable. However, as the season begins, each practice and game played becomes a single directional step towards the destination. Knowing how to get a team to the destination includes many factors that can contribute to overall success or failure. Great coaches are great architects. They see the vision, but also know how to lead the team with the incremental steps needed to move the team towards reaching its goal.

帶領團隊獲勝的教練會告訴你，成功不僅僅在於教練的計劃，甚至也不在於球員的執行力。還必須對參與者進行強有力的管理（即領導指引）。獲勝的球隊經常會說，球隊就是一個家庭或者是緊密聯繫的一群人，他們能夠專注於球隊的利益而不顧自我。像老師一樣，教練也需要了解團隊中球員的個性、技能和情感。教練必須獲得球員的認可，這樣一來，他們在朝著建築師的願景前進時才會建立牢固的紐帶。優秀的教練和優秀的老師透過了解他們所領導的每個人，對他們的球員／學生進行投入。優秀的教練和老師了解讓一群人朝著集體和個人目標努力的心理。

Winning coaches will tell you that success is not just about the coach's plan or even the player's execution. There also must be a strong management (leadership guidance) of the players. Winning teams will often comment that the team is a family or deeply connected group of individuals who were able to put personal ego aside for the good of the team. Like a teacher, a coach also needs to understand the personalities, skills, and emotions of the players on their team. The coach must get player buy in, so they create a strong bond together as they move towards the vision cast by the architect. Great coaches and great teachers invest in their players/student by knowing everyone they lead. Great coaches and teachers understand the psychology of getting a group of individuals to strive towards a collective and personal goal.

經常有人問我:「我怎樣才能成為一名出色的老師?」其實並沒有一種模板可以讓教師、領導者或引導者輕易應對任何情況並突然成為一名出色的領導者。讓我驚訝的是,儘管我在中國進行了大量的領導力培訓,從沒有兩個人走的是相同的道路。儘管他們存在相似之處,但是每個團隊和情況都是獨一無二而且截然不同。團隊會發展出相似的「團隊規範」和行為,但是由於每個團隊的動態始終是獨一無二,因此每次培訓都給人不同的感覺。不變的要素只是我培訓內容中安排的那些核心活動。我的目的地永遠是固定的,儘管我的方向可能會根據情況而略有變化。但是,令每次培訓課程獨一無二的最大原因是每個參加者的個性。

I am often asked, "How can I be a great teacher?" There is no template for a teacher, leader, or facilitator to simply apply to any situation and suddenly become a great leader. I am still amazed that, given the large number of leadership trainings I have done in China, no two have gone the same way. Even though there are similarities, each group and situation are uniquely different and distinct. Groups develop similar "group norms" and behaviors, but because the group dynamic is always unique, each training feels distinct. The elements that remain fixed would be activities that are at the core of my training content. My destination is always fixed, though my direction may change slightly based on circumstances. But the biggest reason that each training session is unique comes in the individuality of each person that attends.

我的最終目標是讓老師們**看到**並**感受到**他們如何共同朝著我想要的目的地前進。儘管每次培訓都只有短短的兩天時間，作為「建築師」，我設計了方向性活動，但在這樣做的過程中，我了解了團隊成員的獨特個性。我必須根據這些個性進行領導。我必須處理它們帶來的優勢和劣勢。有些人參與願意強，並經常參與到培訓中來，而另一些人則對我的領導能力提出了更大的挑戰。請記住，正如出色的教練所做的那樣，你必須管理團隊中的每個人，以便他們可以共同取得成就。

　　My end goal is to have teachers SEE and FEEL how the group moves together towards my desired destination. Although each session is only two short days together, as the architect, I design the directional activities, but in doing so, I get to know the unique personalities of those in the group. It is these personalities that I must lead. I must manage the strengths and weaknesses that they bring to the process. Some participate willingly and frequently, while others present a bigger challenge to my leadership skills in getting them to buy in. Remember, like a great coach, you must manage the individuals on the team so that they can achieve something together as a group.

　　每個個體以及團隊的集體成長過程被稱為團隊成長過程。當一個團隊聚在一起時，變化就會發生。作為這一過程中有意識的建築師，我設計了以人為本的活動，以此向目的地前進。我不能簡單地背誦固定的腳本，因為它不能幫我建立起我想要實現的個人聯繫。我很高興看到培訓會的開展並接受在團隊成長過程中引導方向性過程的挑戰。有些參與者能比其他人更先看到團隊成長的發生，我可以從這些參與者的表情中看出這一點。他們的眼睛閃爍出光芒，笑容變得更燦爛，並且他們在此過程中的參與度已提升到了更高的水平。他們現在進入了認可階段，並親眼目睹了團隊成長過程。

　　The process of growth in everyone, as well as in the collective group, is called the Group Growth Process. Anytime a group comes together, change is going to occur. As the intentional architect of this process, I design people-centered activities to achieve movement towards my destination. I cannot simply recite a fixed script because it does not make for the personal connection that I am trying to achieve. It is so much fun for me to see the workshop unfold and to accept the challenge of facilitating the directional process through this Group Growth Process. I can literally see the expression on the faces of participants who begin to see it ahead of the others. Their eyes light up, a bigger smile takes over and their level of engagement in the process moves to a more heightened place. They now are at the point of buy-in and have seen and felt the Group Growth Process for themselves.

要明白，無論你是否採取任何措施，團隊成長過程都會發生。成長是不可避免的。但是，為了確保團隊的成長是積極的並朝著你預期的方向發展，你必須對流程進行管理。這就是引導的藝術。你知道目的地在哪裡。你可以設計方向性活動，並透過影響力來管理參與者的個性。這就是領導。

Understand that the Group Growth Process is going to happen whether you do something about it or not. Growth is inevitable. However, to ensure that the growth is positive and moving towards the direction you intend, you must manage the process. This is the art of facilitation. You know the destination. You design the directional activities, and you manage the personalities through your influence. This is leadership.

在西方教育中，「教育『全人』」（情感、身體、精神、智力）是掛在嘴邊的口頭禪。對老師的期望除了教育整個班級（指班上所有的孩子）之外，他們也必須教育每個孩子。教育每個孩子需要不同的學習技巧，以適應每個學習者的學習風格和挑戰。這真是個挑戰啊！試圖使所有團隊成員向目的地邁進的領導者需要一定的一致性和統一性。但是，當我們在指導過程中開展富有創造力和吸引力的活動時，學習的個性和體驗對於每個學習者而言都是獨一無二的。教師需要了解他們的班級，以及班級中每個人各不相同的學習風格。

"Teaching the 'whole' child" (emotional, physical, spiritual, intellectual) is a strong mantra in western education. In addition to a teacher being expected to teach the whole class (referring to all the children in the class), it is also essential that they teach each individual child, as well. Teaching each child requires differentiated learning techniques to meet the learning styles and challenges within each learner. What a challenge! A leader attempting to get all the group members headed towards their destination requires some conformity and uniformity. But, when we enact creative and engaging activities in the direction process, individuality in learning and experience is unique to each learner. The teacher needs to know the class, as well as the different learning style in each personality within the class.

例如，行動型學習者和聽覺型學習者在理論上都朝著老師確定的方向前進。儘管屬於同一班級的成員（即屬於相同的團隊成長過程），但每個人對每個方向性活動的參與和反應都將是獨一無二的。這就是使教學和領導如此令人驚嘆同時又充滿挑戰的原因！老師可以謹慎地指導班級朝著一個明確的方向發展，但也必須精心管理所有學生的個性（學習風格）。優秀的老師會不斷反思和評估學生的學習過程，就像我不斷評估培訓參與者的參與程度一樣。它成為老師和學生之間未經事先編排的舞蹈，並與更大的團隊融為一體，當它起作用時，便是一種純粹的美。

For example, the kinesthetic learner and the auditory processing learner are theoretically heading in the same direction established by the teacher. Although members of the same class (ie. the same Group Growth Process), each individual's engagement and response to each directional activity will be uniquely different. That is what makes teaching and leading so amazing and so challenging at the same time! Teachers can carefully steer the class in a clear direction but must also delicately manage all the individual personalities (learning styles). Great teachers constantly reflect on, and assess, the learning processes of their students, just like I constantly assess the level of engagement with my training participants. It becomes an un-choreographed dance between teacher and student, mixed in with the larger group, and when it works, it is a thing of sheer beauty.

我的每個培訓研討會都是相似的，但又各有獨特之處。同樣，每個班級的學生都是相似的，但同時又是獨特的。一位出色的領導者，就像一位出色的教練，必須進行管理和投入，認識每個人，以便最大程度地發揮團隊的潛力。就像偉大的體育運動員有成為優秀得分選手或打進明星聯盟的目標一樣，學生也有個人要實現的目標。一位了解學生的老師會了解並重視學生的個人目標，並努力幫助他們實現目標。但是老師也要管理那些個人的追求，並設法使他們理解，他們是更大的團隊的一部份，而團隊也必須努力發揮其潛力。偉大的領導者也是偉大的引導者。他們管理和培育每個人與眾不同的特徵：我們所有人都具有的情感、身體、精神和智力需求。這樣一來，每個人都會感到自己得到了重視和滿足，能夠實現自己的個人目標，但是他們也將感受到與更大的團隊的集體目標的聯繫和責任。這也滿足了人類成為家庭 / 團隊成員的願望。發生這種情況時，團隊成長過程會不斷發展，並揭示出幫助他們引領成功的引導者的才能和技能。

Each of my training seminars is similar, but they are also uniquely different. So, too, is each class of students similar, but uniquely different. A great leader, like a great coach, must manage and invest in getting to know each individual so he/she can maximize the potential of the group. Just like great sports players have goals to be great scorers or All-Stars, so too, students have individual goals to achieve. A teacher who knows the students, understands and values those personal goals and will work hard to help them be achieved. But the teacher also manages those individual pursuits and tries to get them to also understand that they are part of a larger group that also must strive to reach its potential. Great leaders are great facilitators. They manage and nurture the characteristics that make people distinctly human: the emotional, physical, spiritual, and intellectual needs that we all have. In doing so, everyone will feel valued and fulfilled, and able to achieve their personal goals, but they will also feel connected and responsible for the collective goals of the larger group. This also feeds the human desire to be part of a family/team. When this occurs, the Group Growth Process evolves and reveals the talent and skill of the facilitator who helped lead them towards success.

如果你正在閱讀本書但不是老師，那也沒關係。目的地和方向也適用於企業領導或人生的諸多不同領域。也許你是大型或小型公司的CEO，或者小型員工團隊的經理。無論如何，若缺乏明確的目標（有時在業務中被稱為「願景」），領導者很少會成功。如果你不知道要讓你的公司或你管理的公司走向何方，你又怎麼把他們送到目的地呢？在業務過程中，目的地描繪的是CEO想把公司帶向何方的遠景，方向則是在考慮願景的情況下做出的日常運營決策。好的領導者清楚目的地，然後與他們領導的人一起工作，以幫助大家實現這些目標。商業和教育在領導能力上頗有相似之處。

If you are reading this but are not a teacher, it's ok. Destination and direction are also applicable to business leadership or many different areas of life. Maybe you are the CEO of a big or small company, or the manager of a small team of workers. Regardless, without a clear destination (sometimes termed in business as "vision") those who lead can rarely be successful. If you do not know where you want your company, or those you manage, to go, how can you possibly get them there? In business, destination is the vision that delineates where the CEO wants to take the company, and direction is the day-to-day operational decisions made with the vision in mind. Good leaders know the destination, and then work with those they lead to help them achieve those goals or objectives. Both business and education have parallels in leadership.

你也可以從育兒的角度研究這個問題。結婚後，兩個具有獨特個性特徵以及個人目標的人合併成為一個組合。這也是團隊成長過程的一個例子。這兩人將根據他們的溝通和協作方式而成長和變化。不久之後，他們可能會在團隊中添一個孩子。在這一點上，具有獨特需求和需求的另一個獨特個體進入了這個團隊。管理所有這些需求和個性肯定需要統一的領導！這種情況下，目的地是幸福而充實的家庭生活。方向則是父母為達到目的地而設計和進行的所有事情。在家庭中，要使團隊成長過程變得快樂和成功，領導者必須管理好個人的個性和夢想。平衡個人目標和實現團體整體利益的野心是父母領導力中的挑戰之一。

You may also examine this from the perspective of parenting. Once married, two individuals with unique personality characteristics, as well as individual goals, merge to form a unit. This, too, is a sample of the Group Growth Process. These two individuals will grow and change based on how they communicate and collaborate. A short time later, they may add a child to their group. At this point, another unique personality, with unique demands and needs, enters the mix. Managing all these needs and personalities requires unified leadership for sure! The destination is a happy and fulfilled family life. The direction is all the things that parents design and do to move towards that destination. In the family, for the Group Growth Process to be happy and successful, the leader(s) must manage the individual personalities and dreams. Balancing personal goals and ambition for the overall good of the group is one of the challenges in parental leadership.

總結
Summary

引導學生探索和理解是教育的本質。正是在指導的過程中，教師的創造力可以（並且應該）使學習環境充滿樂趣。正是在獨特的方向性曲折中,學習者被導向目的地。領導者是團隊成長過程中有意識的「建築師」,他們影響並管理著獨特的個體,但這樣做的重點是團隊的團結。儘管目的地和方向受領導者的影響,但參與者的個體獨特性對參與者的成敗起著至關重要的作用。這也是引導藝術所面臨的挑戰。

Leading students on a path of discovery and understanding is the essence of teaching. It is in the process of direction that teacher creativity can (and should) make the learning environment engaging and fun. It is in the unique directional twists and turns that the learner is guided towards the destination. The leader, the intentional architect of the Group Growth Process, influences and manages the unique individuals, but does so with a focus on the unity of the group. Whereas the destination and direction are under the leaders' control of influence, it is the participants who play a crucial role in the success or failure of the group because of their uniqueness as individuals. This is where the art of facilitation is challenged.

打磨引導技能,提高目的地和方向的清晰度,這需要大量的嘗試、錯誤和實驗。認識到團隊成長過程勢必會發生,你最好成為這一過程中有意識的建築師,以嘗試為個人和整個團隊達成所需的目標。

Sharpening both destination and direction requires lots of trial, error and experimentation as facilitation skills are built. Recognizing that the Group Growth Process will happen, it is better to be the intentional architect of the process to try to obtain your desired destination goal for the individuals and the group as a whole.

教學遠遠不只是傳達考試中應用的事實性內容而已。教師也是領導者,他們不僅要分享知識內容,而且可以以有意義和令人難忘的方式影響他們所領導的那些人。

Teaching is far more than just communicating factual content to be given back on an examination. Teachers are leaders who can not only share content knowledge, but also influence those they lead in a meaningful and memorable way.

教學生面對失敗——建立情商
Teaching Students to Fail – Building EQ

Image credit: Wanderlust Worker

　　九歲的時候，我勇敢地走上棒球場，為自己的家鄉而戰。我很驕傲地穿著我的金鶯隊隊服。我深感自豪，因為那是我最喜歡的美國職棒大聯盟球隊，而且碰巧我的球隊被選為金鶯隊。對我來說，我覺得這套制服使我成為了像李.梅或馬克.貝蘭格這樣的球員（該隊著名的職業球員）。當我走進擊球位進行揮棒練習時，我比任何九歲的球員都充滿了大聯盟般的信心。我看著對方的投手，心中對他不得不向我投球而感到抱歉，因為我打算將球擊得很遠。我覺得在我打出全壘打之後，他會讓他的球隊失望，這可能會讓他感到難過。我信心十足，幾乎沒有考慮到失敗即將降臨。當投手向我發起挑戰時，關鍵時刻到了。他在三次投球中發揮了最佳水平。經過三次揮棒落空，我果然就這樣迅速出局了。

　　I stepped up to bat as a brave 9-year old playing baseball for my hometown team. I was proudly wearing my Orioles team uniform. Proud because that was my favorite Major League Baseball team, and it just so happened that my team was chosen to be the Orioles. For me, I felt as if this uniform transformed me into a player like Lee May or Mark Belanger (famous professional players for that team). As I stepped into the batter's box to take my practice swings, I was full of all the major league confidence any 9-year old could have. I looked out at the opposing pitcher and felt sorry he had to pitch to me because I planned to hit the ball very far. I thought he might feel bad that he let his team down after I hit a homerun. With confidence sky high, I approached this at bat with little consideration of possible failure. The moment of truth approached as the pitcher challenged me. For three pitches he threw his best stuff. With 3 swings I proved to be one very quick out.

發生了什麼事？我心裡這樣想。我幾乎連眨眼的功夫都沒有，我揮了三次球棒，每次都沒打中。這可不是我心裡想的那種擊球方式啊。但是，它轉瞬之間便成為現實。我失敗了，而不是他！我走回休息區，因為讓我的團隊失望而垂頭喪氣。當我進行賽後思考時，我覺得當時那幾棒沒打好，但從那以後，肯定會有所改善。

What just happened? I thought. I barely had time to blink and I swung the bat 3 times, missing each pitch. That wasn't the way this at bat had played out in my mind. However, it quickly became the reality. I failed, not him! I walked back to the dugout hanging my head wondering, knowing I let my team down. As my postgame thoughts took over, I figured it was just a bad at bat and surely things would improve from that point forward.

一局接一局，一場又一場比賽，同樣的結局像惡夢般反復出現。然後有一天，奇蹟發生了！我走進擊球位（基於我以前的擊球失敗率，我當時的絕對自信值為零）。我盯著道奇隊的投手，他是聯盟中最好的9歲投手之一，顯得勢不可擋。他看起來更像一個半大的男人，甚至在當天是開車去參加比賽的！他發揮了強大的發球能力，投出了自己最好的快球。在球飛到本壘板的那一瞬間，我幾乎看不到以音速朝我飛來的那一團模糊的白色。我閉上眼睛，準備好迎接最猛烈的衝擊。幸運的是，以他的投球速度，我甚至沒有時間把球棒從我的肩膀上移開。那一球投得又高又偏內。太高了，擊中了我的擊球頭盔。令我驚訝的是，我還活著，並聽到裁判授予我進入一壘的機會！我接受了邀請，並且在那一年的四個賽季中第一次為球隊跑了壘。

Inning after inning, game after game, the same result played out like a recurring nightmare. Then one day, a miracle happened! I stepped into the batter's box (this time with absolutely zero confidence based on my previous proven failure at hitting). I stared at the imposing and mighty Dodger's pitcher. He was one of the best 9-year old pitchers in the league. He was more like a man-child and probably even drove himself to the game that day! He took his powerful windup and unleashed his best fast ball. In the mere split-second that the ball took to reach me at the plate, I could barely get a glimpse of the white blur coming towards me at the speed of sound. I closed my eyes and was prepared to take the biggest swing I could muster up. Fortunately for me, with the speed at which he threw, I did not have time to even move the bat off my shoulder. The pitch was high and inside. So high that it hit off my batting helmet. To my stunning surprise, I was still alive to hear the umpire award me a free pass to first base! I took the invitation and for the first time all year, I became a base runner for my team.

你讀的時候可能一直在期待奇蹟，期待這是我第一次打出全壘打，雙打，三打或至少單打的球。我也可以肯定的是，你可能會認為這個故事的寓意是關於透過失敗的毅力，有一天，如果堅持下去，成功就會到來。這是一個很好的建議，對於許多人來說，這是一個英勇的動力，可以防止他們放棄夢想。但是，在我的情況下，我在小聯盟社區棒球運動中的失敗的結果是我父親給了我很有益的忠告，「兒子，也許你應該換一項運動？」

You may have been expecting the miracle that, for the first time, I had hit the ball for a homerun, double, triple or at least a single. I am also certain you might think the moral of this story is about perseverance through failure, and that, one day, if you stick with it, success will arrive. That is good advice, and it is a valiant motivator for many, preventing them from giving up on their dream. However, in my scenario, my failure in little league community baseball led to my dad giving me some great words of advice, "Son, maybe you should pick another sport?"

父母總是說:「你下決心做的任何事都可以做到!」或者,「如果你足夠努力,也許有一天你將成為美國總統。」或者,「不要因失敗而失望。只要繼續努力,好事就會發生。」這些話語都意味著鼓勵,但其中根本沒有蘊含太多現實或真理。

How many times does a parent say, "You can be anything you set your mind to!" Or, "If you work hard enough, maybe one day you will be President of the United States." Or, "Don't let failure slow you down. Just keep working hard and good things will happen." Those words and phrases are all meant to be encouraging but are not filled with much reality or truth at all.

我最近看到了一則有趣的新聞報導,該則新聞記錄了五年前五名九歲學生的視頻。在最初的採訪中,每一個孩子都對他們的美好未來表現出很高的信心。每個人都對自己在高中及以後所能取得的成就滿懷「自信」。一個說要成為職業舞蹈家,另一個說要從事執法工作,還有一個說要成為職業運動員。他們的笑容和他們自己預言的未來一樣燦爛。然後,在他們高中那年,這五個學生又被採訪了。採訪時向他們展示了五年前的視頻,視頻中他們臉上的表情十分清晰。當被問及五年後這個孩子現在在哪裡時,每個人似乎都說著那個曾經高度自信的孩子,現在卻不知道在承受著什麼壓力。他們說,他們在高年級時感受到的壓力使他們對未來的計劃沒有了把握。

I recently saw an interesting news report that video-recorded five 9-year old students 5 years ago. In that initial interview, each of the five children demonstrated high levels of confidence in their bright future. Each spoke with "major league" confidence about the great things they would accomplish in high school and beyond. One was going to be a professional dancer, the other would work in law enforcement and still another would be a professional athlete. Their smiles were as big and bright as the future they predicted for themselves. Then, in their senior year of high school those same five students were interviewed again. They were shown their video from five years earlier and the look on their faces was revealing. When asked where is that child now five years later? Each spoke as if elements of that once over-confident child now had no idea what pressures they were to encounter. They revealed that the pressures they feel now in their senior year have left them insecure about their future plans.

壓力不只是學業挑戰，而是更大的人生挑戰。社會壓力是巨大的，自第一次面試以來，這種壓力使他們最初的信心出現下滑。隨著想成為舞者的學生意識到別人比她更有才華，她的職業目標發生了變化。前途無量的職業運動員被從他的高中隊中除名，這似乎立即扼殺了他成為最佳運動員的夢想。在過去的五年中，他們經歷了失敗，而應對失敗成為改變人生的力量，而這種力量曾經是充滿信心的希望和夢想。

The pressure was less about the academic challenge but more about the challenge of dealing with life. Social pressure was significant, and it chipped away at their initial confidence since the first interview. Career goals had shifted as the dancer realized others were far more talented than she was. The hopeful professional athlete was cut from his high school team, which seemed to instantly kill his dream of being an athlete at the highest level. Over the past 5 years of life, failure was introduced and dealing with that failure became a life-changing force that altered once confident hopes and dreams.

我是五個孩子的父親，我知道，當我自己的孩子失敗時，我總是滿懷善意給出建議，讓孩子們堅持下去或者繼續努力。我不希望他們因失敗而放棄。我想成為一個不斷的鼓勵者，以便他們理解毅力可以帶來良好的結果。但也許這完全就是一條錯誤的訊息。只要人們下決心去做某件事，他們就能完成任何事情或實現任何夢想，真是這樣嗎？我們如何教導孩子們有關失敗的知識，將影響他們未來的希望和夢想。教育就包括著很多失敗，老師和家長需要注意失敗發生時我們所傳達給孩子們的訊息。

I am a father of five, and I know when my own children have failed, I have given each the well-meaning advice to stick with it or to keep working hard. I did not want failure to cause them to give up. I wanted to be a constant encourager, so that they would understand that perseverance could bring about good results. But maybe that message is the wrong message altogether. Is it true that if someone just puts their mind to do it, they can accomplish anything or be anything they dream to be? How we teach children about failure will impact their future hopes and dreams. Education includes a lot of failure, and teachers and parents need to be mindful of the message we give when failure happens.

回顧一下我那失敗的棒球試驗，父親給我的訊息是：「兒子，也許你應該換一項運動。」這就是很好的建議。他本可以告訴我再堅持一兩年，在某些情況下，成熟和更多的經驗可能確實會有所回報。但是，在這種情況下，對我來說，他的話給了我自由！我並沒有因為父親知道我明顯缺乏能力而喪失信心。相反，父親提出的換一項運動的建議使我開始學習足球和籃球，這最終成為我生命中兩項重要的運動。我將自己在球場上與隊友和教練共度的時光視為我夢寐以求的最佳人生經歷和職業培訓。透過運動，我學會了如何應對失敗。

Looking back at my failed baseball experiment, the message my dad gave me, "Son, maybe you should try another sport" was excellent advice. He could have told me to stick with it another year or two, and in some cases, maturity and additional experience could possibly pay off. But, in this case, his words were freedom to me! I wasn't crushed that my father did not have confidence in my obvious lack of ability. On the contrary, the suggestion from my dad to seek another sport led me to pick up soccer and basketball, which ended up being two significant sports in my life. I credit my time on the court and the field with teammates and coaches as the best life experience and professional job training I could have asked for. Through sports, I learned how to handle failure.

籃球運動員麥可.喬丹是有史以來最著名的職業運動員之一。我曾讀到他的一句名言，讓我印象深刻，他在其中透露了他對失敗的反應。他提到一個事實，在他傑出的職業生涯中，他有九千多次投球沒進。有二十三次，他的教練和團隊指望他再次投籃，從而有機會打成平局或贏得比賽。在他所經歷的每一次信任中，麥可.喬丹都失敗了。在超過三百場比賽中，他和隊友都沒能打敗對手。這是三百個麥可.喬丹的失敗。（公平地說，我相信他的隊友也發揮了作用。）然而，透過所有這些失敗，他認為失敗的機會是他最終成功的關鍵！我們可以從失敗中學到很多東西，特別是如果我們知道如何正確處理它，就更是如此。

One of the most famous professional athletes of all time was Michael Jordan, a basketball player. I was impressed when I came across a quote attributed to him where he revealed his reaction to failure. He relates the fact that in his illustrious career, he missed over 9,000 shots. Twenty-three times his coach and team looked to him to make a last second shot with a chance to tie or win the game. In each of those times of trust placed in him, Michael Jordan failed. More than 300 times, he and his teammates failed to defeat the opponent. These were also 300 Michael Jordan failures. (To be fair, I'm sure his teammates played a role as well.) Yet, through all these failures, he attributes the opportunity to fail as the key to why he succeeded! There are many lessons we can learn through failure, especially if we know how to deal with it properly.

當我們害怕失敗時，我們就從自己、孩子和學生那裡偷走了機會。它阻止我們獲得有價值的觀點和人生經驗。大多數學生不知道如何處理失敗。與此同時，大多數父母都不希望自己的孩子在失敗發生時感到不適。他們經常訴諸於指控，試圖把責任推卸到別人身上。我們不知道如何應對失敗，因此，我們不知道如何教育我們的孩子應對失敗。

When we fear failure, we are stealing opportunity from ourselves, from our children and from our students. It prevents us from gaining valuable perspective and life lessons. Most students do not know how to deal with failure. Compound that with the fact that most parents who do not want their child to experience discomfort when failure does happen. They often point fingers and look to deflect the cause to make it someone else's fault. We do not know how to deal with failure and, consequently, we do not know how to teach our children about failure.

當我反思自己人生中學到的最有價值的教訓時，我發現許多教訓之前都有過重大的失敗。積極的人生教訓可能不會在失敗後馬上出現，但它們似乎都以奇特的方式存在於那些失敗的時刻。我不會單純為了學會如何堅持而去經歷失敗。但我明白失敗乃成長的機會。我仍然可能不喜歡或無法享受自己的失敗，但如果我的成長心態是強大的，我可以更容易地堅持下去，並嘗試從中找尋我可以學到的課程。

As I reflect on the most valuable lessons in my life, I find many are preceded by rather impactful failures. The positive lessons may not come immediately after, but they seem to come strangely close to a time of failure. I do not set out to fail simply so I can learn how to persevere. But I have learned that failure is an opportunity for growth. I still may not like or enjoy my failure, but if my growth mindset is strong, I can more easily persevere and try to look for the lessons I can learn.

教育中有很多失敗。全球教育面臨的一個最艱難的困境是，很大一部份往往是結果導向。分數往往被用來衡量學習。分數和平均績點成為了判斷一個學習者成功或失敗的標誌。糟糕的成績不僅反映了學生的表現，也令人擔憂地暗示了老師的失敗。在大多數國家，老師要為學生取得的成績承擔巨大的壓力和責任。如果學生成績不夠好，許多老師都要承擔責任。學生、老師和學校都害怕失敗。

There is a lot of failure in education. One of the hardest dilemmas of global education is that so much of it tends to be results-driven. Grades tend to be used to measure whether learning is taking place. Grades and G.P.A. (Grade Point Average) become the identifier of an individual learner's success or failure. Poor grades do not just reflect the learner's accomplishments, or lack thereof, but alarmingly, they may suggest the teacher failed, too. In most countries, there is tremendous pressure and responsibility placed on teachers for the grades earned by the students. Many teachers are held accountable if students do not score well enough. Students, teachers, and schools are afraid of failure.

為什麼我們如此害怕失敗？失敗可不可以是一件好事？我們能從失敗中吸取有價值的教訓嗎？當然能！我不是說我們都能成為麥可.喬丹，但我確實認為我們都能從我們的失誤中吸取教訓，就像偉大的麥可.喬丹做到的那樣。喬丹學會了如何處理失敗，他做得比大多數人都好，把失敗變成了動力。

Why are we so afraid of failure? Can failure be a good thing? Can we learn valuable lessons through failure? YES! I am not suggesting we can all be Michael Jordan, but I do think we can all learn lessons from our missteps, as did the great Michael Jordan. MJ learned how to handle failure, better than most, by turning his failures into his motivation.

我們能改善自己對失敗的看法嗎？當然能。我相信，情感的成熟和高情商能讓我們重新審視失敗。因為我們可以清楚地識別我們的感覺，管理我們的情緒，保持心理和情感上的完整，這樣一來，我們便給自己更大的機會從挫折中受益。

Can we improve our personal perspective on failure? Yes. I believe that emotional maturity and a high EQ allow us to rewire our perspective on failure. Because we can clearly identify our feelings, manage our emotions, and remain mentally and emotionally intact, we give ourselves a greater opportunity to benefit from our setbacks.

讓學生為失敗做好準備
Equipping Students to Fail

請記住，我們恐懼的不應該是失敗本身，我們應該恐懼的是永遠不經歷失敗，因為我們可以在失敗中學習。我們應該讓學生做好失敗的準備。失敗的機會中蘊含著成長和學習，而不僅僅是失敗的結果本身。

Remember, our fear should not be of failure itself, but rather never having to experience failure, because in failure can be learning. We should be equipping our students to fail. There is growth and learning in the opportunity, not just in the outcome.

教育文化淹沒在競爭和成功之中。各地的教育部門總是想要宣傳他們有最好的地方學校，這對廣大家庭和學生極富吸引力。學校想成為最好的學校，希望自己被公認為本市最好的學校。校長們希望和學校一起被認為是最好的，這給他們帶來名聲和發展。老師希望被認為是最優秀的老師，這樣他們可以提高他們的地位和工資。父母希望他們的孩子成為最好的學生，將來能進入最好的大學，過上最好的生活。學生們瘋狂地努力成為班上的第一名，以使周遭的每個人都開心。這種循環或追求讓我想到了一句諺語「狗在追自己的尾巴」。須知狗轉得再快，也追不上自己的尾巴。

The education culture is drenched in competition and success. The local education bureaus want to promote that they have the best regional schools, and this attracts families and students. Schools want to be the best schools, so they can be recognized as the best in the city. Principals want to be recognized as best along with the school, which brings them notoriety and advancement. Teachers want to be considered the best teachers, so they can elevate their status and salaries. Parents want their students to be the best students, so they can get into the best universities and have the best life. Students frantically work to be number one in their class to make everyone else happy. This cycle or pursuit makes me think of the proverbial saying, "The dog is chasing its own tail". As fast as the dog may spin, it can never catch up to its own tail.

學校、家長和學生的部份追求是令人敬畏的。當然，我們都應該盡我們最大的努力去實現目標和夢想。但我擔心的是，當前人們的關注點沒有給失敗留出空間。在這種模式下，成功是唯一的選擇。一個六十人的班裡能有幾個第一名？一個城市能有多少所頂尖的學校？所有的焦點都集中在第一名的成功上，那麼剩下的競爭者的失敗呢？他們對失敗做好準備了嗎？他們知道如何管理自己的失敗嗎？這種失敗是有幫助的、有成效的，還是只是破壞性的、令人灰心喪氣的？

Part of the pursuit by schools, parents and students is awesome. Sure, we should all work to our fullest potential to achieve goals and reach dreams. But my fear is that the current focus has no room for failure. In this model, success is the only option. How many number ones can there be in a class of 60 students? How many top schools can there be in any one city? With all the focus on the success of the top one, what about the failure of the remaining competitors? Are they prepared for failure? Do they know how to manage their failure? Can this failure be helpful and productive or simply devastating and disheartening?

我記得有人告訴我,「如果你沒能取得成功,至少你成功地盡了最大的努力。」透過失敗可以實現個人成長,甚至學到有價值的東西。失敗的結果不一定是唯一的標識符或學到的教訓。用成長的心態來吸收失敗是有可能的,這樣才能吸取教訓,繼續實現轉變。了解失敗的一個好方法就是研究那些經歷了失敗的人。

I remember someone telling me, "If you fail to succeed, at least you didn't fail to give it your best effort." There can be personal growth, and even valuable learning, through failure. The results of failure do not have to be the only identifier or lesson to be learned. It is possible to absorb the failure with an attitude of growth mindset so that lessons can be learned, and transformation continued. One great way to learn about failure is to study those who have failed.

美國最偉大的發明家之一是湯瑪斯.愛迪生。愛迪生被認為是美國最偉大的發明家和商人之一,他在發電、大眾通訊、錄音和電影等領域發明了許多裝置。在所有這些裝置中,也許白熾燈泡是最有意義的。發明家當然了解失敗。他的一些著名的關於失敗的名言闡明了成長心態如何幫助我們在失敗發生時管理自己的人生。「生活中的許多失敗體現在人們放棄的時候並沒有意識到他們離成功其實有多近。」「我沒有失敗,我只是找到了一萬種行不通的方法。」

One of America's great inventors was Thomas Alva Edison. Considered one of the greatest American inventors and businessman, Edison developed many devices in fields such as electric power generation, mass communication, sound recording, and motion pictures. Of all these devices, maybe his work on the incandescent light bulb was most significant. An inventor certainly knows failure. Some of his notable quotes about failure shed light on how a growth mindset can help us manage life when failure happens. "Many of life's failures are people who did not realize how close they were to success when they gave up." "I haven't failed. I just found 10,000 ways that won't work."

這是多麼美好的失敗視角啊。我們中有多少人在嘗試了九千次、五百次甚至僅僅三次之後就放棄了？學生的課堂生活幾乎連一次失敗都容不下，更不用說多次失敗了！我們需要借助失敗來學習。當我把試卷發回去的時候，大多數學生只是看看自己的成績，抱怨或歡呼，然後把它收起來。最好的學生則會檢查他們的試卷，看看哪裡出了錯，甚至糾正這些錯誤來鞏固他們的學習。失敗的機會可以是值得學習的寶貴經驗，也可以是毀滅性的，有時甚至是驚天動地的事件。

What a beautiful perspective on failure. How many of us would have given up after 9,000, 500, or even 3 attempts? So much about a student's life in the classroom barely gives room for 1 failure, let alone multiple failures! We need failure to help us learn. When I used to hand test papers back, most students simply looked at their grade, moaned or cheered, and then put it away. The best students looked through their test papers to see where the mistakes were made and even corrected those mistakes to solidify their learning. The opportunity to fail can be a valuable experience from which to learn or, it can be a devastating, and at times earth-shattering, eventuality.

運動員了解如何失敗，因為他們失敗的機會太多了。在任何體育比賽中，都有輸贏之分。最好的教練和球員會從失敗中回顧比賽錄像，並試圖分析他們可以做得更好的地方。然後他們將這些改變納入他們未來的比賽計劃中。傳奇的大學籃球教練約翰.伍登曾告訴他的球隊：「失敗是成功的後門。」他明白，當你贏了的時候，你很少會想辦法去提高自己。獲勝的前提是你每件事都做對了，結果你贏了，而另一個隊輸了。然而，勝利可能導致自滿，並導致一種扭曲的觀點，即勝利等於完美。

Athletes know how to fail because they have so many opportunities to fail. In any athletic contest, there is a winner and a loser. The best coaches and players review the game film from a loss and try to dissect where they could have done better. They then build those changes into their future game plans. The legendary college basketball coach John Wooden would tell his team, "Failure is the backdoor to success." He knew that when you win, you rarely look for ways to improve. Winning assumes you did everything correctly and, as a result, you won and the other team lost. However, winning can lead to complacency, and to the warped perspective that the victory equates to perfection.

許多學生害怕在教育中冒險，因為在結果導向的教育中，從糟糕的成績挫折中恢復的空間很狹小。由於大家的分數中只有一小部份將學生劃分為「最高分」，任何微小的風險都可能導致平均績點的下降，從而導致班級排名的下降。學生們不願冒險去追求好奇心或挑戰某種假設，因為他們擔心冒險的代價不值得。這實在讓人惋惜。生活中的偉大發明之所以能夠實現，是因為人們的好奇心達到頂峰，人們願意承擔風險。根據「數據」，對結果進行評估，好奇心可能會加深，並承擔額外的風險。失敗並不會讓學習停止。它只是塑造和完善著學習的過程。

So many students are afraid of taking risks in education because in results-driven education, there is little room to recover from a poor grade setback. With just a fraction of a grade separating students for the "top spots", any slight risk could cause a drop in grade point average and therefore a drop in the class ranking. Students are hesitant to take a risk to pursue curiosity or challenge an assumption, for fear the risk is not worth the result. That is a shame. Great inventions in life were only achieved because curiosity was piqued, and risks were taken. Based on the "data", results were evaluated, curiosity was likely deepened, and additional risks were taken. Failure did not stop the learning. It simply shaped and refined it.

作為教育者，我們應該讓學生體驗參與式學習。我們不應該簡單地把答案背下來，然後在考試時再現它們。那不是教育！相反，我們必須促進一種氛圍，在這種氛圍中，課堂上的冒險是健康的。我們希望學生挑戰假設、質疑內容、驗證他們的理論，以確保他們在學習。然後，我們可以對學生和其學習進行公平的評估。評估之後，我們可以幫助他們應對學習中的成功和失敗，透過建設性的評估達到更深層次的理解。

As educators, we should want students to experience engaged learning. We should not simply give them the answers to memorize and give back on an exam. That is not education! Rather, we must promote an atmosphere where it is healthy to take risks in the classroom. We want them to challenge assumptions, question content, and test their theories to ensure that they are learning. Then, we can assess them and evaluate their learning fairly. After the assessment, we can help them process the success and failure of their learning to reach even deeper depths of understanding through constructive evaluation.

學校、班級和學生之間總是會有競爭。無論如何，成績最好的學生將被視為最優秀的學生，但這就意味著大多數學生都是失敗者的假設。這不是我們應該傳遞的訊息。事實上，要成功，你不是非得成為第一。成功有很多層次。要鼓勵學生別害怕失敗，因為在失敗中，學習也是可以發生的。我們應該教導學生永不失敗就意味著永不嘗試。這顯然是一種不現實的人生觀和生活方式。生活將充滿失敗，未來的失敗可以帶來未來的成功。失敗可以提供不同的視角和學習。然而，學校、校長、教師、學生和家長的態度目前並不承認失敗的好處。無論如何，我們必須改變對失敗的看法，這樣人們才能對這種不可避免的、往往是有益的情況抱以一種更為健康的態度。

There will always be competition in schools, classes and among students. No matter what, the top students will be heralded as the best, but that leaves the assumption that the majority are failures. That is not the message to send. In fact, you don't have to be number one to be successful. There are many levels of success. Encourage students to not fear failure because in failure, learning can happen. We should teach students that to never fail is to never try. This is obviously an unrealistic outlook and approach on their life. Life will be full of failures and future failures can produce future success. Failure can provide perspective and learning. However, the attitudes of schools, principals, teachers, students, and parents are not currently acknowledging the virtues of failure. Somehow, we have to change the narrative about failure, so people can adopt a healthier attitude toward this inevitable, and often beneficial, circumstance.

我們如何讓學生做好失敗的準備？
How Can We Prepare Our Students to Fail?

做好心態上的準備。教導學生每一次失敗的經驗都是一次豐富的學習機會。失敗提供了勝利所不能提供的視角。只有當我們親身體驗某件事時，我們才能對它有一個真切的看法。我不知道膝蓋手術後的恢復會是什麼樣子，直到我自己經歷了這一切。一個人不可能知道經歷癌症治療是什麼感覺，除非他目睹或近距離感受。大多數人不願意忍受消極的經歷，但是生活中需要的心態和情商只能透過經歷來培養。當失敗發生時，預設的心態不僅是生存的重要工具，也是個人成長的重要工具。失敗本身並不一定反映出一個人的身份。它只是成長過程的一部份。為失敗做準備的方式是擁抱這樣一種心態：從不經歷失敗實則會剝奪我們深入和真實的個人成長機會。

Prepare the Mindset. Teach students that each new experience of failure is a rich opportunity to learn. Failure provides perspective that winning does not. We can only gain a true perspective of something when we experience it for ourselves. I did not know what recovery from knee surgery would be like until I went through it on my own. One cannot know what it feels like to go through cancer treatment unless it has been seen or felt close up. Most people do not want to endure a negative experience, but the mindset and emotional intelligence needed in life is only developed through experience. A pre-determined MINDSET, when failure happens, is an important tool for not only survival, but for personal growth as well. The failure, itself, does not have to reflect the personal identity. It is just part of the growth process. Preparation for failure takes the form of accepting the mindset that to never experience failure robs us from the opportunity for deep and authentic personal growth.

預先確定反應。「心態」是我們想要的態度。而反應則是所採取的行動。它支持「行勝於言」的說法。一家業內領先的移動電話公司最近為商店搶劫實施了一項「虛擬現實模擬培訓」。儘管企業高管們知道這種情況可能比較少見，但他們選擇了積極的虛擬現實培訓，而不是靜態的幻燈片培訓。最後，他們花了很多錢聘請了一家虛擬現實公司來創造多種生動的現實場景，這樣員工們就能更好地準備好做出訓練有素的反應。他們知道，如果事情真的發生了，在它發生之前演練一種反應，會讓人們做出更好的回應。這也是消防隊員、警察和軍事人員花費大量時間進行演習訓練的原因。他們希望這種反應是預先計劃好的肌肉反應，而不是毫無計劃的情緒反應。人類可以預先思考和演練一個反應，這樣一來，當失敗發生時，他們便可以依靠他們的訓練來減輕衝擊和改善反應。教師可以幫助學生設想和演練各種冒險帶來的不願看到的結果。實踐可以為難以避免的不幸事件提供虛擬現實訓練。

Pre-determine the response. "Mindset" is the attitude we want to have. The response is the action taken. It supports the saying that "Actions speak louder than words". One major cell phone company recently implemented a "virtual reality simulation training" for store holdups. Even though corporate executives know these may be rare events, they opted for active virtual reality training instead of a static PPT training. They ended up spending a lot of money hiring a virtual reality firm to create multiple vivid reality scenarios so that employees felt better prepared to give a trained response. They know that practicing a response before it happens creates a better human reaction, should the event take place. This is the same reason firefighters, police officers, and military personnel spend so much time in drill training. They want the response to be a pre-planned muscle-response, not an unplanned emotional response. Humans can pre-meditate and rehearse a response, so that when failure happens, they can rely on their training to ease the shock and improve the response and reaction. Teachers can help students visualize and rehearse various scenarios where the risk-taking brings about undesired results. The practice can provide virtual reality training for the inevitable unfortunate occurrence.

建立應對機制。做好**萬一**失敗的準備是很重要的，但是做好失敗**發生時**的準備更有用，因為生活中難免會有挑戰。機制則是應用的工具。當失敗發生時，我們需要「求助」於一個應對機制。在危機時刻，許多人求助於他們喜歡的機制工具，即推卸責任或編造藉口。我像大多數人一樣犯過這種錯！儘管我很努力，但我對失敗的第一反應往往是尋找讓我失望的人或事。通常，在思考後，我找時間更誠實地評估實際情況，然後我便可以接受那可能是我自己的錯，也可能不是我自己的錯。

Develop A Coping Mechanism. It is important to Be prepared **IF** failure happens, but it is even better to be prepared for **WHEN** it happens, because life is inevitably challenging. A mechanism is a tool to apply. We need a "go to" coping mechanism when failure happens. In times of crisis, many people reach for their favored mechanism tool - cast blame or create an excuse. Like most, I am guilty of that! As hard as I try, my first response to failure is often to look for who or what I can blame for letting me down. Usually, after some reflection, I find time to evaluate the situation with more honesty, and I can, then, accept what may or may not have been my fault.

許多人沒有應對機制，因此，當失敗發生時，他們會進入情緒恐慌模式或在壓力下走向崩潰。擁有優秀情商的人在遭遇失敗時能建立起良好的應對機制。像麥可.喬丹這樣的人並不比其他人更享受失敗。只不過當失敗發生時，他們運用了更強的應對機制。我像他一樣，想比任何人都更擅長於失敗！善於失敗意味著我知道如何接受它，並比別人更好地處理它。我的機制必須很強大。

Many people have no coping mechanism and therefore, when failure happens, they go into an emotional panic mode or simply crumble under the pressure. Individuals with exceptional emotional intelligence are those who develop excellent coping mechanisms when failure finds them. People like Michael Jordan don't enjoy failure more than anyone else. They simply apply stronger coping mechanisms to the situation when failure happens. Like him, I want to fail better than anyone else! Being good at failure means that I know how to accept it and handle it better than others. My mechanisms must be strong.

開發健康的手段來處理失敗是很重要的。有些人會向比自己聰明的人請教，以此幫助他們處理事件和情緒。老師和家長通常是提供建議和觀點的好資源。有些人把閱讀作為一種處理失敗的工具，而另一些人則把寫日記作為一種健康的方式來處理他們的失敗。還有一些人則會進行一些極具攻擊性的活動來「發洩」和反思。關鍵是找到一種工具來採取行動，公認為健康而富有成效的反應的行動。許多人會發展出一些破壞性的工具，如責備、藥物治療或抑鬱。健康的工具是建設性而非破壞性的。

It is important to develop healthy tools for dealing with failure. Some turn to counsel with someone wiser than they to help process events and emotions. Teachers and parents are often great resources for advice and perspective. Some turn to reading as a tool to process, while others turn to writing in a journal as a healthy way to deal with their lack of success. Still others turn to highly aggressive activity to "burn off steam" and reflect. The key is to find a tool to put into action that is known as a healthy and productive response. Many people develop destructive tools such as blame, medication, or depression. Healthy tools are constructive, not destructive.

分析應對方式。精神上做好準備，然後積極應對是很重要的，但是需要不斷評估這些「手段」的有效性。這就像一場賽後新聞發佈會，教練必須在球隊輸球之後進行復盤。教練進入新聞發佈室時，知道他／她將回答記者關於發生了什麼以及為什麼球隊失敗等方面的問題。教練將會對比賽指令、球員執行、比賽策略和決策進行分析。分析情況並形成對逆境的應對方式，有助於確定所採用的應對手段是健康還是不健康。

Analyze the Response. Mentally preparing, and then actively responding, are important, but these "tools" need to be constantly evaluated for effectiveness. This is like a post-game press conference that a coach must deal with after a team loss. The coach enters the press room knowing he/she will field questions from the reporters as to what happened and why the team failed. The coach is expected to give an analysis for play calling, player execution, game strategy and decisions. Analyzing the situation and formulating a response to adversity help one determine whether the coping tools applied are healthy or unhealthy.

健康的分析練習需要對所有情況和個人反應進行清晰的回顧。這是有可能獨立做到的，在導師的指導和客觀性的幫助下做這件事也是很有幫助的。進行分析的時間會有所不同，但重要的是它要發生。以層層深入的方式，找出難題，尋求真理。反應的有效性、反作用和結果將變得越加清晰。這將導致更好的自我理解和反應手段的強化。

A healthy analytical exercise requires a clear-minded review of all circumstances and personal reactions. It is possible to do this independently, or it may be helpful to do it with the guidance and objectivity of a mentor or someone who gives good counsel. The timing of when this analysis takes place will vary, but what is important is that it happens. Peel back the layers, ask the difficult questions, and seek the truth. The effectiveness of the response, reaction, and results will become clear. This will lead to greater self-understanding and the sharpening of the response tools.

尋找最佳療法。失敗可能會帶來創傷，但不一定會使人衰弱。失敗往往會帶來不安全感和尷尬。當這種情況發生時，一些人傾向於躲到一個私人的、通常是黑暗的地方，而不是尋求有助於恢復信心和治癒的療法。我們都時不時地需要療癒，有些人的需求更甚於其他人！

Seek the Best Therapy. Failure can be traumatic, but it does not have to be debilitating. Failure often produces insecurity and embarrassment. When this happens, some tend to retreat into a private and often dark place, instead of seeking the therapy that will help restore confidence and provide healing. We all need therapy from time to time, and some of us more than others!

要選擇高效的療法。許多人尋求不同形式的治療方案。有些人向知己尋求建議，而有些人則選擇求助該領域的專家。有些人想獲得保證和肯定，而另一些人則希望獲得誠實的客觀性。尋求治療是重要的，知道需要治療的水平也同樣重要。當我們犯錯時，一個有害的傾向是向那些使我們感覺更好的人尋求肯定。在這種時刻，我們想要的不是判斷或建議，而是在尋求支持和肯定，以減輕自我傷害的感覺。雖然我們在絕望的時候都需要安慰，但任何一種治療都只有在以溫和誠實的方式揭示真相時才具有價值。有益的治療應該「實事求是」，而非僅僅告訴我們想聽的話。

Choose productive therapy. Many seek therapeutic solutions in different forms. Some seek the advice of confidants, while some choose experts in the field. Some want reassurance and affirmation, while others want honest objectivity. The act of seeking therapy is important and knowing the level of therapy needed is equally important. One detrimental tendency, when a mistake is made, is to seek affirmation from those who make us feel better. In this moment, we don't want judgment or advice. We are looking for support and affirmation to mitigate hurt feelings. Though we all need comfort in our times of despair, therapy of any kind is only valuable when there is a revelation of truth offered with a gentle dose of honesty. Helpful therapy should "tell it like it is" and not just tell us what we want to hear.

教師和家長可以是很好的治療選擇，前提是他們可以先傾聽，然後給出建議。一個好的治療師會專注地傾聽，不僅仔細衡量患者的解釋或話語，而且要管理他們自己的情緒，這樣他們才能在回應時保持客觀。當一個治療師得知你的失敗時，若他開始哭泣或大笑，你便會對他失去信心。一個好的治療師須保持情感上的抽離，這樣他們可以在沒有情感依賴的情況下給出分析和建議。學生們常常覺得沒有人聽他們說話。許多父母都不會傾聽，他們只是自作主張地給出建議。太多的老師也不傾聽，他們只是告訴學生要「加倍努力」。如果你的課堂是一個人們可以安心失敗的地方，那麼你的學生可能也會覺得你是一個有同情心而且公平的人，這樣一來，他們便會在需要好的治療時向你尋求幫助。

Teachers and parents can be great therapy options, provided they can listen first and advise second. A good therapist listens intently, carefully measuring not only the individual's explanation or words, but also managing their own emotions so that they can remain objective in their response. One would lose confidence in a therapist who started crying or laughing when they learn of your failure. A good therapist remains emotionally disconnected so that they can be analytical and advise without emotional attachment. Students often feel they have no one to listen to them. Many parents do not listen. They simply give unsolicited advice. Too many teachers do not listen. They just tell their students to "work harder". If your classroom is a safe place to fail, then your students may also feel that you are an empathetic and fair person for them to seek out when good therapy is needed.

重新設定方向。最終,如果人們從失敗中學到東西,也能做出改變,那麼失敗相對而言是無關緊要的。不要讓失敗獲得永久居留權。坦承失敗、感受和原因,然後重新設定你的方向。生活充滿了方向性的重置,我們要不斷地調整以適應眼前的環境。

Reset the Course. Ultimately, failure is relatively inconsequential if learning occurs, and changes can be made. Don't let failure take up permanent residency. Acknowledge the failure, the feeling, the causes, and then reset your course for a new direction. Life is full of directional resets, as we constantly adjust to the circumstances presented to us.

讓我們想像一個水手,他研究天氣、風、潮汐和水圖,以確定最佳和最安全的航行路線。然後,經過分析,他確定了最好的航線。他把儀器調校到正確的位置,只有在所有這些設置和關鍵步驟都完成之後,他才會走開。即使在所有這些預防措施都做好之後,有時水手也會根據情況的變化而做出調整。簡單地根據第一組數據「保持航向」可能會使船隻陷入一場猛烈的風暴。

Consider the sailor who studies the weather, wind, tide and water charts to ascertain the best and safest course of travel. Then, after analysis, he decides the best course. He sets his instruments to the correct alignment and will only then depart on the trip, once all those settings and crucial steps have been completed. Even after all these preparatory precautions, there are times when the sailor makes adjustments based on the changing conditions. To simply "stay the course" based on the first set of data could lead the boat into a fierce storm.

在制訂海洋航線時,航海儀器要根據新的數據進行調整。這些調整常常意味著為了支持新的計劃而放棄原來的計劃。失敗不在於計劃的重新調整,而在於缺乏在需要時進行調整／改變的敏感性。有了正確的心態，從失敗中學習，從而揭示新的訊息，這樣我們就可以重新規劃我們的方向。重新制訂我們的航向算不上失敗，但不學習使用新數據進行必要的調整則潛藏著巨大的失敗。

In plotting a course in the ocean, adjustments to the navigational instruments are made based on new data. These adjustments often dictate the abandonment of the original plan to support the new one. The failure is not in the realignment of the plan, but rather in the failure to not have the sensibility to adapt/change when needed. With the right mindset, learning through failure reveals new data so we can re-chart our direction. There is no failure in re-charting our direction, but there is significant potential failure in NOT learning to use new data to make needed adjustments.

考慮風險DNA。我相信，對於失敗的恐懼與對於風險的承受能力密切相關。有些人似乎反感於風險帶來的暴露感，而另一些人則完全被風險所削弱。最近，我看了國家地理頻道的紀錄片《徒手攀岩》，該片講述了極限登山者亞歷斯.霍諾德的故事。他試圖徒手攀登北美最令人恐懼的花崗岩面——酋長岩。值得注意的是，對於一個徒手攀岩者來說，失敗就意味著死亡。他們在攀登岩面時不使用繩索或安全措施。如果霍諾德失敗了，他就會死。

Consider the Risk DNA. I believe the fear of failure is closely connected to the tolerance for risk. There are those individuals who seem to be slightly averse to the feeling of exposure that risk can offer, while others are completely debilitated by it. I recently watched the National Geographic documentary entitled, *"Free Solo"*, featuring extreme mountain climber Alex Honnold, who attempts to free climb the most feared granite face in North America - El Capitan. It is important to note that for a free-climber, failure means death. Free-climbers climb rock faces without the use of ropes or safety measures. If Honnold fails, he dies.

我不是個攀岩者，因為我恐高。在整部電影中，當我試圖理解霍諾德是如何應對摔死的恐懼，以及如何保持克服這種恐懼所需的精神毅力時，我本人被恐懼所籠罩。就像喬丹比大多數人更能應對失敗一樣，霍諾德也比大多數人更能應對恐懼。他承認有時恐懼是很強烈的，他堅稱自己並沒有求死之心或想要早點結束生命的願望。然而，霍諾德似乎有一種特殊的能力，能將常見的恐懼和失敗的感覺轉化為強烈的專注和決心。他減輕了自己的恐懼，提升了自己的專注和動力。大多數人則恰恰相反。通常情況下，恐懼使人喪失行動能力，使他們無法行動或至少無法清醒地思考，但對霍諾德而言，恐懼只是一種被他掌控、可識別而受尊敬的力量。因此，他並沒有忽視恐懼，只是比普通人更好地控制它。

I am not a climber because I am fearful of heights. Throughout the movie, I was gripped with fear as I tried to understand how Honnold dealt with the fear of falling and sustained the mental stamina required to manage that fear. Like Jordan, who can handle failure better than most, Honnold is able to manage his fear better than most. He acknowledges times when fear is intense and he insists that he does not have a personal death wish or desire to exit life early. However, it seems that Honnold has a special ability to channel and focus common feelings of fear and failure into intense focus and determination. He mitigates his fear to accentuate his focus and drive. Most people are the opposite. Typically, fear incapacitates people and renders them unable to act or at least think clearly, whereas for Honnold, it is simply a recognizable and respected force to be contained and controlled by him. As a result, his fear is not ignored. It is just better controlled than it is for the average person.

大量關於大腦的新研究似乎揭示了強有力的證據，表明風險承受力與選擇無關，而更多地與基因編碼有關。遺傳學家告訴我們，DRD4（即所謂「新奇基因」）附著在第十一號染色體上，它決定了你是一個風險承受者還是一個風險規避者。根據泰勒．特沃倫（風險學創始人，他稱自己為內向者撰寫有關成為偉大領導者的科學和策略的文章）的說法，一個人的風險承受能力實際上是一種寫在遺傳密碼裡的性格特徵。

Plenty of new studies on the brain seem to reveal strong evidence that risk tolerance is less about choice and more about genetic coding. Geneticists tell us that DRD4 (referred to as the "novelty gene") is attached to Chromosome 11, and that it holds the key as to whether or not you are a risk taker or risk avoider. According to Tyler Tervooren (founder of Riskology - who claims he writes for introverts about the science and strategies for becoming a great leader) an individual's risk tolerance is, in fact, a personality trait written in the genetic code.

德拉威大學的研究人員研究了出生時被分開的同卵雙胞胎。他們很好奇，想知道被分開的雙胞胎是否會因為各自的基因而表現出彼此的特徵，或者他們的環境是否影響了他們的基因編碼。研究表明，被分開的雙胞胎表現得更像他們的親生父母，而不是他們的環境父母。這似乎證實了預設遺傳編碼的說法。

Researchers at the University of Delaware studied identical twins that were separated at birth. They were curious to see if the separated twins showed characteristics of the each other because of their genes, or if their environments shaped them regardless of their genetic coding. The study revealed that the separated twins acted like their biological parents more than their environmental parents. This seems to affirm the case for the predetermined genetic code.

是什麼讓一些人能夠冒險而另一些人則不能呢？是什麼讓企業家們敢於冒險？他們在生物學上就是被這樣設計的嗎？企業家似乎能看到機會，在普通人認為不值得冒險和恐懼的地方採取行動。在研究了五百五十位企業家後，研究人員意識到企業家並不認為自己是冒險家。大多數企業家認為自己是風險厭惡者，而非冒險者。特沃倫認為，企業家往往依賴於博學的無知，而不是經過周密計算的風險管理。這並不是說他們更願意承擔風險，而是他們比其他人更願意承擔風險，他們只是能夠以不同的方式看待風險。

What makes some able to take risks and others unable? What makes entrepreneurs risk takers? Are they biologically designed to do so? It seems as if entrepreneurs see opportunity and can act where the average person sees the fear and the risk not worth taking. After studying 550 entrepreneurs, they realized that entrepreneurs do not self-identify as risk takers. Most entrepreneurs identify themselves as risk averse rather than risk takers. Tervooren thinks that entrepreneurs are often dependent on learned ignorance, rather than calculated risk management. It is not that they are more open to taking a risk, but rather more than anyone else, they are just able to view the risk differently.

我有很多朋友是企業家，也有很多朋友不是。我想，我明白特沃倫表達的意思。我的一些企業家朋友把機會視為高風險的東西，然後避開它們，而另一些人則把機會視為挑戰，並傾向於直面它們。成功的企業家之所以出類拔萃，不是因為他們沒有看到其他人所看到的危險，而是因為他們只是以不同的方式應對或管理了這些恐懼。看不到的東西，你是無法逃避的！

I have friends who are entrepreneurs and I have many who are not. I think I see what Tervooren is saying. Some of my entrepreneurial friends see an opportunity as a high level of risk and then avoid it, while others see opportunity and gravitate towards it for the challenge. Successful entrepreneurs excel, not because they fail to see the hazards that others do, but because they simply appease or manage those fears differently. You can't run away from that which you cannot see!

好消息是，雖然你的遺傳密碼可能控制著你的風險承受力，但可能有一些方法可以提高你承擔更多風險的能力。研究人員認為，你可以透過一些集中的練習，簡單地訓練你的大腦繞過杏仁核（大腦中用來遠離危險的部份）。如果你能避開大腦決策的這一部份，你就能創造一個旁路機制，讓你開始看到機會，而不是只感知風險。

The good news is that although your genetic code may claim control over your risk tolerance, there may be some ways to improve your ability to take more risks. Researchers believe that you can simply train your brain to bypass the amygdala (part of the brain designed to keep you away from danger) with some concentrated practice. If you could avoid that part of the decision-making brain, you could create a bypass mechanism, which could then allow you to begin seeing the opportunity more than sensing the risk.

我可能永遠不會跳傘。我為什麼要跳出一架機況完美的飛機？我永遠不會帶著安全繩爬酋長岩，當然沒有安全繩就更不會爬了——這似乎是必死無疑的。我不會體驗自由落體，也不會考慮高空彈跳——這兩種運動對我來說都相當危險。為什麼我不能像看待其他類型的「冒險」行為一樣看待這些活動呢？很明顯，有些人看待它們的風險（或恐懼）程度與我不同。我恐高。我想我對高度的厭惡在很大程度上被第十一號染色體上的東西註定了。然而，總有身邊的人告訴我，我是個冒險家。

I probably will never sky dive. Why would I jump out of a perfectly good plane? I will never climb El Capitan with ropes and certainly not without ropes - that seems like guaranteed death. I will not free fall, nor will I consider bungee jumping - both seem dangerous to me. Why is it that I cannot view these activities in the same way as I do other types of "risky" behavior? Clearly some do not view them with the same level of risk (or fear) that I do. I am afraid of heights. I think my aversion to heights is locked into chromosome #11 in a big way. However, there are those close to me who tell me I am a risk taker.

這可能有助於解釋為什麼有些學生在學校缺乏自信，不敢在課堂上舉手，不敢嘗試擔任領導職務，或不敢參加運動隊。也許他們的基因編碼將競選學生幹部職位和從一架完美的飛機跳下畫上了等號！也許站在同事面前發表演講就像你的腳踝上綁著一根巨大的彈簧繩，然後從橋上被甩下去一樣讓你害怕。也許第十一號染色體對於每個人的影響是不同的，而且是獨特的、難以抗拒的。一種人看到風險，另一種人則看到機會。一種人害怕失敗，另一種人則看到可能性。一種人在恐懼中退縮，而另一種人則似乎信心倍增。它可能不是膽量、天賦或勇氣。它可能只是遺傳編碼使然。

  This may help to explain why some students lack the self-confidence in school to raise their hands in class, try out for leadership positions, or try out for a sports team. Maybe their genetic coding equates running for a student leadership position to jumping out of a perfectly good airplane! Maybe standing in front of peers to give a speech is viewed with the same fear as having an over-sized and super-charged rubber band tied around your ankles and being thrown off a bridge! Maybe the #11 chromosome has a different impact on each person in a unique and compelling way. Where one sees risk, the other sees opportunity. Where one fears failure, the other sees possibilities. Where one retreats in fear, the other surges with seemingly unending confidence. It might not be bravery, talent, or courage. It might just be living out the genetic code.

  教師與學生建立個人關係是很重要的，這樣他們可以更好地幫助學生管理和理解失敗的恐懼。在理想情況下，父母也應該參與到這項任務中來，但由於許多父母忙於工作，孩子們常常被拋在一旁，需要自己去發現這一點。基因編碼在我們對恐懼和失敗的個人看法中起到了作用。幫助學生了解自己將幫助他們更好地駕馭人生，塑造他們面對恐懼和失敗的方式。

  It is important for teachers to build a personal relationship with students so that they can better help students manage and understand fear of failure. Ideally, parents should also participate in this task, but with many parents who are too busy with work life, children are often left to discover this for themselves. Genetic coding contributes to our personal perspective of fear and fear of failure. Helping students learn about themselves will help them better navigate life and shape their approach to fear and failure.

總結
Summary

人們對失敗和恐懼的態度及反應在年輕時就已經形成了。遺傳編碼似乎在風險承受或風險規避方面起到了作用。教師和家長對學生的成長有著不可否認的影響，因此，他們必須認識到自己的責任和使命，從而真正地教授更多的東西，而不僅僅是學科知識。真正的教育要把學業內容和人生管理結合起來。細心的良師益友必須細心地指導他們的學生。要做到這一點，他們必須非常了解學生。

Attitudes and reactions to failure and fear are established at a young age. The genetic code seems to contribute to risk tolerance or risk aversion. Teachers and parents have undeniable influence on the growth of students and, consequently, must recognize their responsibility and mission to truly teach more than just subject content. Real education combines academic content with life management. Attentive mentors, who understand, love, and care, must carefully guide their students. To do that, they must know them well.

麥可.喬丹因為不夠好而被高中籃球隊除名。然而，他的教練很小心地幫助喬丹克服了這次失敗，並將其轉化為一種鼓舞。四年後，他幫助北卡羅萊納大學贏得了大學籃球賽全國冠軍。麥可.喬丹並沒有打算要失敗。事實上，他對失敗恨之入骨。然而，他學會了比大多數人更好地處理失敗。透過失敗，喬丹提高了他的專注力，約束了他的行動，重新下定決心，培養毅力並形成觀點。他擁抱失敗的機會，不是因為他喜歡失敗，而是因為他可以從失敗中吸取教訓。你的課堂裡的失敗文化是這樣的嗎？

　　Michael Jordan was cut from his high school basketball team because he wasn't good enough. However, his coach was careful to help Michael manage that failure, which he turned into inspiration. Four years later, he helped the University of North Carolina win the College Basketball National Championship. Michael Jordan did not set out to fail. In fact, he hated failure with every fiber of his being. However, he learned to handle failure better than most. Through failure, Jordan was able to sharpen his focus, discipline his actions, reset his determination, develop his perseverance and shape his perspective. He embraced the opportunity to fail, not because he loved failure, but for the lessons that could be learned. Is this the culture of failure in your classroom?

　　沒有人想失敗，但是從失敗中獲得的經驗和教訓可能是毀滅性的，也可能是影響深遠，這取決於一個人管理失敗的能力。我們不應該害怕失敗，而應該害怕浪擲失敗可以提供給我們的機會。有了正確的心態、態度、指導和反應，所有人都能學到人生課程並形成未來的經驗。有了決心和努力，學生們就能學會接受失敗的教訓，雖然這常常讓人不安，卻是有必要的。有了耐心、愛心和同理心，老師和家長需要提高警惕，並且意識到教育學生如何正確處理失敗的必要性。

　　No one wants to fail, but the experience and learning that can come through failure can be either devastating or impactful, depending on one's ability to manage it. We should not fear failure, but we should fear not having the opportunity that failure can provide. With the proper mindset, attitude, guidance, and response, all humans can learn life lessons and shape future experiences. With determination and hard work, students can learn to embrace the often uncomfortable, but necessary, lessons of failure. With patience, love, and empathy, teachers and parents need to be vigilant and aware of the need for teaching students how to properly fail.

學校需要智商，人生需要情商
IQ for School – But EQ for Life

Image credit: Greater Zurich Area

年幼的孩子演示了情緒智力發展的最佳圖景。把一組兩歲和三歲的孩子放在同一個房間裡，把玩具數量放得比孩子的數量少，你就會發現誰的情商得到了增強，而誰的情商還有待提高。他們的互動似乎是天生的反應，而不是深思熟慮之後的選擇。我們都知道學校的任務是提高學生的智商，但是誰來負責學生的情商呢？其中哪一個對人生的「成功」更為重要呢？

Young children provide the best picture of what emotional intelligence (EI) development looks like. Put a group of 2 and 3-year old children in a room together with fewer toys than there are children and you will see who has, or who needs increased EQ (Emotional Quotient) enhancements. Their interactions appear to be innate reactions, as opposed to thoughtful choices. We all know schools are charged with increasing the learner IQ, but who is responsible for the student EQ? Which will be more crucial to "success" in life?

下文摘自2013年十二月二十八日的文章《智商是遺傳的嗎？》作者

為IQ-Brain:「智商是先天決定的還是後天環境造就的？長期以來，科學家們一直對智商的起源以及智商是遺傳的抑或環境刺激的結果很感興趣。事實上，如果智商能解釋為環境因素（即養育，而非天性使然），那麼這便驗證了全球數以百萬計的父母的做法，他們相信自己為孩子投入的所有時間、精力和金錢，以及由此創造的環境刺激，將使他們的孩子獲得更高的智商，而更好的教育和智慧將幫助他們的孩子在這個充滿競爭的世界表現得更好。」

According to the December 28, 2013 article, "IS IQ GENETIC?" by IQ-Brain: *"Is IQ genetically pre-determined or is IQ formed and acquired by the environment? Scientists have long been intrigued by the origins of IQ, and whether IQ is genetically inherited or whether a high IQ is the result of a stimulating environment. If IQ is, in fact, explained by environmental factors (i.e. nurture rather than nature) then this provides validation to millions of parents, globally, who would like to believe that all the time, effort, and money that they are investing in creating stimulating environments for their children will pay off with higher IQs, and that greater education and smarts will help their children to do better in a competitive world."*

然而，如果智商被發現是遺傳決定的，那麼這就對許多學校賴以生存的高壓、以結果為導向的學習環境的有效性提出了質疑。可能有一部份學生在這種環境中茁壯成長，因為他們的智商早已被內置，只是在學習中受到了激發。對其他人來說，他們在努力挖掘自身潛力時，被迫感到缺乏安全感和能力。父母和老師要求他們加倍努力地學習。然而，如果智商存在於基因編碼之中，又能有多少變異和改變的可能呢？雖然透過數據得出的結論表明智商主要是由基因編碼決定的，但情商則是由經驗開發和塑造的。哪個對一個人未來的人生有最大的貢獻呢？

However, if IQ is found to be genetic, then this calls into question the usefulness of high pressure, results-driven learning environments in which many schools thrive. There may be some segment of students who thrive in this setting because their IQ is already built in and is simply stimulated. For the others, they are forced to feel insecure and less than capable as they try to work towards their potential. Parents and teachers demand they work harder. However, if IQ is in the genetic coding, how much variation and change is possible? Whereas it seems conclusive through data that suggest IQ is primarily determined through genetic coding, EQ is developed and shaped by experiences. Which will make the greatest contribution to one's future life?

在2016年世界經濟論壇的文章《機器人能做你的工作嗎？》中，創始人克勞斯.施瓦布重申，需要採取「緊急和有針對性的行動」，建立一支具備未來所需技能的勞動力隊伍。人們可能很快就會認為，在這個人工智能創新的時代，「應對未來的技能」可能會集中在高技術和先進的電腦或工程技能上。顯然，這些技能是有需求的，並將繼續保持需求。然而，哈佛大學副教授大衛.戴明強調，分享和談判等技能也將會至關重要！「現代的工作場所中，人們在不同的角色和項目之間轉換，非常類似於幼兒園，我們在那裡學到社會技能，如同情和合作。」事實證明，應對未來技能是我們在學前班就學到了的！具有諷刺意味的是，這些認識不是透過讀書或聽講形成的，而是透過早期簡單的以經驗為基礎的遊戲而形成的。據估計，透過玩耍（十至二十次重覆）形成聯繫的速度要比其他學習方式快四百倍。我們可以從觀察孩子行為中學到很多東西，有證據表明，如果你提供有趣的遊戲體驗，學生的情商會迅速提高。

In a 2016 World Economic Forum article, *"Can a Robot do your job?"*, founder Klaus Schwab iterated that there is an "urgent and targeted action" needed to build a workforce equipped with future-proof skills. One might be quick to assume that, in this AI (Artificial Intelligence) age of innovation, "future proof skills" might be centered on highly technical and advanced computer or engineering skills. Clearly these skills are in demand and will continue to be so. However, associate professor at Harvard University, David Deming, highlights that skills such as sharing and negotiation, will be crucial! "The modern workplace, where people move between different roles and projects, closely resembles pre-school classrooms, where we learn social skills such as empathy and cooperation." It turns out that future-proof skills are those we learned at the pre-school age! Ironically, those realizations were formed not through book reading or attending a lecture, but through simple experience-based play at the earliest age. It is estimated that connections are formed faster through play (10-20 repetitions) versus 400 repetitions for other types of learning. We have much to learn from simply watching children, but evidence suggests that if you provide fun, play experience, a student's EQ increases very rapidly.

EQ（情商）或EI（情緒智力）可以簡單地歸結為理解兩個實體——自我和他人。情商是識別、理解和管理自己情緒的能力，也是識別、理解和影響他人情緒的能力。高情商要求的不僅僅是專注和自我認知。同樣重要的是要有能力看到別人的內在品質。高情商的人通常具有以下特徵：與他人合作融洽、理解團隊的概念（他人第一，自我第二）、有表達同理心的能力。同理心的定義是準確地感知他人感受或表達的情感。如前所述，最純粹的觀察情商發展的形式是觀察一群幼兒玩耍和互動。你能從中觀察到那些已經在構建情商的人以及那些對其提出挑戰的人。觀察是確定情商存在的最好方法。任何學齡前孩子的老師都會告訴你，他們大部份學生行為的重新定向或SEL（社會情感學習）都基於孩子如何對待他人。這就是情商訓練。

EQ (emotional quotient) or EI (Emotional Intelligence) may be broken down to simply understanding two entities - self and others. EQ is the ability to recognize, understand, and manage your emotions, but to also recognize, understand and influence the emotions of others. High EQ requires more than just focus and recognition of self. It is equally important to have the ability to see the intrinsic qualities in others. Characteristics of those with high EQ typically include working well with others, understanding the concept of team (others first, self-second) and having the ability to express empathy. The definition of empathy is accurately perceiving the emotions felt or expressed by others. Again, the purest observable form of blooming EQ is to watch a group of toddlers play and interact. In doing so, you will be able to observe those who are already building EQ and those for whom it is a challenge. Observation is the best way to determine the presence of EQ. Any preschool teacher will tell you that much of their student behavior redirection, or SEL (Social Emotional Learning), centers on how children treat others. This is EQ training.

可能智商的最好定義是在專門測試智力的標準化評估中獲得的評估分數。簡而言之，智商是對所學訊息的認知推理和回憶，是將這些知識應用於技能的能力。智商較高的人可以抽象地思考，並且可以進行邏輯或技術上的聯繫，以簡化歸納。智商高的人具有學習複雜訊息、進行整理的能力，然後他們可以回憶並將其應用於現實生活中。

IQ might be best defined as an evaluated score received from standardized assessments designed to specifically test intelligence. Simply put, IQ is the cognitive reasoning and recall of information learned, and the ability to apply that knowledge to skill sets. People with higher IQ's can think in the abstract and supposedly make logical or technical connections to make generalizations easier. Those with high IQ possess the ability to learn complex information, sort it out, and can then recall and apply that knowledge to real life situations.

許多人認為智商中位數為100（偏差約為15）。有多種智商測試表格可用於建立智商分數。韋克斯勒成人智力量表和史丹佛—比奈測驗等熱門測驗顯示，平均分數介於90到109之間。在這些相同的測試中，落在110和119之間的分數被認為是較高的平均IQ分數。80到89之間的分數則被歸入低平均水平。

Many believe the IQ median score is 100 (with a deviation of about 15). There are various IQ test forms used to establish an IQ score. Popular tests such as Wechsler Adult Intelligence Scale and the Stanford-Binet test, reveal that the average scores fall between a range 90 and 109. On these same tests, scores that fall between 110 and 119 are considered high average IQ scores. Scores between 80 and 89 are classified as low average.

晶態智力是指人類運用和利用知識、技能和經驗的能力。晶態智力依賴於從長期存儲中檢索到的訊息。它就像人一生中獲得知識的主要存儲庫一樣。人們相信，隨著經驗的積累，晶態智力會隨著時間的推移而改善，從而進一步促進知識的增長。這裡傳達的簡單訊息是充份生活，以嘗試積累盡可能多的經驗。你會因此變得更聰明！晶態智力擴展了我們的知識存儲，但也被認為在七十歲左右或沒有使用時就會開始下降。還是那句話，要積極活躍地充實你的大腦，因為「如果不使用它，你就會失去它」。保持好奇心並繼續學習新事物，以使你的晶態智力變得敏銳並積極投入。

Crystallized intelligence refers to the human ability to apply and utilize knowledge, skills, and experience. Crystallized intelligence relies on information retrieved from long-term memory storage. It is like the main storage vault of knowledge obtained and acquired throughout an individual's lifetime. Crystallized intelligence is believed to improve over time, as experience is added, and would therefore contribute further to the growth of one's knowledge. The simple message here is to live life fully in an attempt to add as much experience as possible. You will be smarter because of it! Crystallized intelligence expands our knowledge storage, but it is also thought to begin declining at about age 70 or without usage. Again, live an active and full life to engage your brain because, "if you don't use it, you lose it." Stay curious and continue learning new things to keep your crystallized intelligence sharp and actively engaged.

流體智力容易被認為是個人利用理性解決新遇到的問題或情況的能力。流體智力高的人可以輕鬆應對新問題或新情況，並創建合乎邏輯的解決方案。它需要歸納和演繹推理，邏輯思維過程以及數學、科學和／或對技術數據的回憶。流體智力也被定義為一個人的天生學習能力。流體智力是一個人腳踏實地思考、處理訊息並做出適當反應的能力。

Fluid intelligence may be easily thought of as an individual's capability to utilize reason to solve newly encountered problems or situations. A person with a high fluid intelligence can comfortably approach new problems or situations and create logical solutions to use in their response and reaction. It requires both inductive and deductive reasoning, a logical thought process, and the recall of mathematical, scientific, and/or technical data. Fluid intelligence is also defined as a person's innate ability to learn. Fluid intelligence is a person's ability to think on his/her feet, process information, and come up with an appropriate response.

流體智力是一個人從以往的經驗中得出的道理，合乎邏輯地處理新情況和解決問題的能力。流體智力不是透過書籍或記憶學來的，而是透過識別模式和空間關係來習得的。它使用已學到的知識和技能來解決任何以前獲得的知識之外的新問題（非常適合填寫空白的測試問題或確定單詞量，例如詞彙測試題）。

Fluid intelligence is a person's ability to logically deal with new situations and solve problems using reason drawn from previous experiences. Fluid intelligence is not learned through books or memorization, but rather from identifying patterns and spatial relationships. It uses learned knowledge and skills to resolve new problems outside of any previously acquired knowledge (great for fill-in-the blank test questions or defining words such as vocabulary tests).

在許多以學生考試成績為中心的學校裡，我看到的是對事實記憶的狹隘關注，而對「經驗」或課堂知識應用的忽視。重覆學習有其價值，但是學生也非常需要體驗可以挑戰流體智力的新場景。看重事實性知識的課堂常常忽視過程對產品的價值。如果學生在考試中得分不高，則會被認為沒有進行有效的學習。許多專家認為，過份強調測試結果的學校會向學生傳遞錯誤的訊息，因為這種策略贊成獲得晶態智力，而這往往是以犧牲流體智力為代價的。也許學校可以更好地平衡對流體學習和晶態學習的重視程度。我認為這將鼓勵教師改變他們的教學風格和方法，以便學生能夠不斷地適應和全面鍛煉他們的智商。

What I see in many schools where the focus is on student testing results is a narrow focus on factual memorization and less about "experiences" or application of knowledge in the classroom. There is value to repetition in learning, but students also have a significant need to experience new scenarios in which they can challenge their fluid intelligence. The factual classroom often disregards the value of process over the product. If the student does not score well on a test, the assumption is that the student has not learned effectively. Many experts believe that schools which over-emphasize testing results send the wrong message to students, because this strategy endorses gaining crystallized intelligence, often at the expense of fluid intelligence. Perhaps schools could do a better job of balancing their emphasis on fluid versus crystallized learning. I think this would encourage teachers to vary their teaching styles and methods, so that the learners would be able to continually adapt and exercise their full IQ.

研究發現，儘管基因在決定智力方面確實發揮了作用，但環境因素也是很關鍵的。數據表明，提高平均智商得分的因素還可能包括教師素質、學習環境、學生的健康和營養水平、社會經濟狀況、測試偏見以及學生群體作為少數團體的狀況等。智商測試也無法解決諸如學生對整個世界的好奇程度等考量指標。教育環境不能單單迫使每個學生進入「學習模板／模型」並試圖瘋狂地產出高智商的「克隆人」。促進因素非常重要，而且它們無法均等控制或輕易得出。因此，那些只講一種基本方法而不理會差異化的教學方式的學校就將它們所服務的大量學生排除在外了。他們沒有教育每個孩子，而是只教一種智力風格，並最終無視其他風格。

Research has found that while genes do play a role in determining intelligence, environmental factors are also key contributors. Data indicates that factors that enhance the average IQ scores may also include teacher quality, learning environment, the health and nutrition of the student, socioeconomic status, and testing bias, as well as the minority status of the student population. IQ tests also fail to address considerations like how curious the student is about the world in general. The education environment cannot simply force each student into a "learning template/mold" and attempt to frantically produce high-IQ clones. The contributing factors are significant and cannot be equally controlled or easily reasoned away. As such, those schools that simply teach one basic way and disregard differentiated teaching and learning styles exclude a significant population of the students they serve. Instead of teaching each individual child, they teach to one intellectual style of child and ultimately disregard the others.

麻省理工學院的神經科學家與哈佛大學和布朗大學的教育研究人員合作，在2013年的一項研究中得出結論，學業成績優異的學生不一定能改善流體智力。有趣的是，在標準化考試成績中獲得最高成績的學生在流體智力方面並未有同等表現。實際上，那些在晶態智力測試中得分較高的學校也並未看到學生在流體智力技能（記憶容量和回憶能力、訊息處理速度以及解決抽象問題的能力）測試中的表現有所提高。麻省理工學院的神經科學家和腦與認知科學教授 約翰.加布里列說道：「**這些技能（流體智力）看起來並不像你想像的那樣能輕易獲得，關鍵只在於大量學習和做一名好學生。**」

Massachusetts Institute of Technology neuroscientists, working with education researchers at Harvard University and Brown University, concluded in a 2013 study that students at academically high-performing schools did not necessarily have improved fluid intelligence. Interestingly, students who had the highest gains on standardized test scores did not show equal gains in their fluid intelligence. In fact, those schools which recorded higher scores on crystallized intelligence tests failed to show an increase in student performance on tests of fluid intelligence skills: memory capacity and recall, speed of information processing, and the ability to solve abstract problems. *"It doesn't seem like you get these skills (Fluid Intelligence) for free in the way that you might hope, just by doing a lot of studying and being a good student,"* says John Gabrieli (neuroscientist and professor of brain and cognitive sciences at MIT).

維吉尼亞大學心理學教授丹尼爾.威靈厄姆（不屬於上述研究團隊的成員）說：**「我們通常主要關注在校成績，但潛在的機制也很重要。」**這為教育過程提供了支持，而不僅僅是針對產品或最終結果的教育。在全球範圍內，學校花費大量時間專注於提高晶態智力，但卻犧牲了流體智力。威靈厄姆希望最近和將來的發現將鼓勵教育者和決策者重新考慮當前的「最佳教育實踐」，以設計一種可以增強學習者廣泛認知技能的教育模式。這類研究表明，學生的流體認知能力確實會影響他們的整體學習成績，並為他們人生中的成功做出更大的貢獻。 但是，以結果為導向的教育很少能提出這樣的主張。

Daniel Willingham, a professor of psychology at the University of Virginia (who was not part of above-mentioned research team) said, *"We're usually primarily concerned with outcomes in schools, but the underlying mechanisms are also important."* This gives support to the *process* of education, not just the product or end results-focused education. Globally, schools spend much of the time and focus on improving crystallized abilities, but at the sacrifice of fluid intelligence. Willingham hopes recent and future findings will encourage educators and policymakers to reconsider current "best practices" to emphasize designing an education model that enhances a broad range of cognitive skills for learners. Studies like this reinforce that students' fluid cognitive skills do influence their overall academic performance and contribute more to their life success. However, results-driven education rarely can make this same claim.

在這一點上，我要表彰《運動員之道》的作者克里斯多佛.伯格蘭在大腦方面的研究工作。我鼓勵你在《今日心理學》中查找其於2013年的文章，也可以在下列鏈接找到。他在這方面的成就傑出，總結了我在成長型教育期間對自我智商的看法，。

　　At this point I want to credit Christopher Bergland (author of ***The Athlete's Way***) for his research work on the brain. I encourage you to seek out his 2013 article in "PSCHOLOGY TODAY" which you can find below. Better than anyone else, he summarized what I personally felt about my own IQ during my formative education years.
https://www.psychologytoday.com/us/blog/the-athletes-way/201312/too-much-crystallized-thinking-lowers-fluid-intelligence

我高中學習成績頂多算中等。我知道自己並不笨，但是在某些學科領域，我就是感到自己學不進去。我從小就知道自己的個性，可以輕鬆地結交朋友並和他們相處。我很受歡迎，人們喜歡我，認為我很有趣，很多人很高興有我陪伴。我一直很喜歡周圍有朋友，這一點一直保持至今。同樣，我知道那些不喜歡我的個性風格的人。我很容易理解他們提出的社交暗示，即我不成熟且令人討厭（對此我不表示反對）。同樣的不成熟行為使我被踢出了西班牙語班和樂隊。（我在此對兩位老師深表歉意。）本來應該把美術課加進去，但是我的美術老師是我父親的教堂的教眾之一，我想她很可憐我是傳教士的兒子。我以全班排名第二十五的成績結束了高中生涯。聽起來好像不錯，但如果知道我所在的班級一共就二十九名學生，這比較就讓人難過了！

My high school academic performance was mediocre at best. I knew I wasn't dumb, but in certain subject areas, I felt out of my league. I knew at an early age that I had a personality, and it was easy for me to both make and manage friends. I was well liked, popular, considered funny and many people were happy to share in my company. I always liked having friends around me, and that remains constant to this day. Likewise, I was aware of those who did not prefer my personality style. I could easily read the social cue that was cast by them that I was immature and annoying (and I would not disagree with them one bit). That same immature behavior got me kicked out of Spanish class and Band. (My apologies to both teachers.) Art class would have been added to that list, but my art teacher went to my dad's church, and I think she took pity on my being the preacher's son. I ended my high school career ranked 25th in my class. That may sound good, but knowing my class was comprised of a total of 29 students puts that into a painful perspective!

像SAT這樣的標準化測試結果似乎為我的平庸學業表現提供了證明。老實說，我不記得我的確切分數，但是肯定比平均分數低。這些結果使我感到「善於書本知識」好像與我無關。幸運的是，我的舒適區域是體育運動方面。我擅長任何與體育有關的事情。不是說我是「最好的」，而是我有能力，因此很有信心。我可以快速學會技能，有高於水平的表現，更重要的是，我覺得體育似乎是我排名順數第四，而不是倒數第四的領域。我在運動場上獲得的成功幫助我發展了影響力技能，包括領導能力、決心、時間管理、接受指導、閱讀社交線索、溝通、解決問題等諸多技能。有些同學的科學或數學得分最優，而在體育領域，我卻是全班排名最高的。最終，體育將成為一種使我收獲成功和成就感的職業。我選擇了二十年的職業生涯，教體育課以及擔任運動教練。

My lackluster academics were seemingly supported by my standardized test results such as the SAT. I honestly do not recall my exact score, but it was certainly less than average. These results made me feel as if "book smarts" was not my thing. Fortunately, my comfort zone was in the area of athletics. I excelled in anything that involved sports. Not that I was "the best", but I was competent and therefore confident. I could learn skills quickly, perform at a high level, and more importantly, I felt as if sports were a place where I was ranked 4th from the top, as opposed to 4th from the bottom. The success I experienced in the sports arena helped me develop my impact skills that included leadership skills, determination, time-management, accepting instruction, reading social cues, communication, problem-solving, and many more such skills. Whereas some classmates scored straight A's in Science or Math, in the area of sports, I was near the top of my class. Eventually, sports would become a vocation that made me feel successful and fulfilled. I chose to teach PE and coach sports for a 20-year career.

在教室裡的時候，我目睹事實性知識被灌進學生的大腦，等待考試時使用。我發現所學的書本知識與未來生活所需的訊息之間沒有任何聯繫。但是，經驗方面的流體智力啟發了我，最終使我對更大的晶態智力產生了興趣。我很幸運，因為我就職的小型私立學校對我很有耐心，許多學校卻不是這樣。後者通常給我這樣的學生的訊息是「你不夠好」，直到你獲得更高的成績為止。

While in the classroom, I saw the facts that were being crammed into my brain as simply facts to be recalled for a test to take. I saw no connection between the book facts being learned and the information I would need in future life. However, the fluid intelligence of experience was inspiring to me, and it drove me to an eventual interest in greater crystallized intelligence. I was fortunate in that my small private school was patient, but many schools are not. Too often, the message to students like me is that "you are not good enough" until you get higher grades.

在一位有影響力的老師（感謝唐.馬丁代爾）的指導下，我確定自己的情商比智商高，正是我的情商驅動了我在人生中獲得成功。當然，他鼓勵我努力學習和工作，但是有限潛力的鏈條給我的動力，遠比投入更多時間研究無聊且不切實際的訊息要多。他讓我知道，儘管我的學習成績很差，但我已經足夠好了。他幫助我在某些領域感受到成功，所以我得以提高自己的晶態智力。

One influential teacher (thank you Don Martindale) guided me to a self-assurance that my EQ was higher than my IQ, and that it would be my EQ that would drive my success in life. Of course, he encouraged me to study and work harder, but the chains of limited potential provided me with far more motivation than investing more hours into studying data that I found boring and impractical. He let me know that despite my weak academic performance, I was good enough already. Because he helped me feel successful in some areas, I was able to improve my crystallized intelligence too.

經過努力和老天爺可能的眷顧，我不僅成功地從大學畢業，而且連研究生學習也平安度過了。我非常感謝他（和其他人）對我的情商進行的大量投入，這在我的一生中一直培養並保持著我的好奇心和企業家精神。如今，我挑戰自我，去體驗對我的智商和情商都有幫助的新事物。其中蘊含著教育的力量：透過激勵，幫助學生發揮他們的潛力，而不是讓他們灰心喪氣，僅僅根據他們的學業成績而讓他們向命運低頭。要讓學生知道他們已經足夠好了。他們可能只是在過程中與其他人不在同一個地方。不要讓他們的學業成績成為他們是誰或成為什麼樣的人的唯一標識符。要提高他們的情商，使他們信心滿滿。

With effort and probably some grace, I managed to not only graduate from a university, but then survived graduate school as well. How grateful I am that he (and others) invested heavily in my EQ, which has nurtured and sustained my curiosity and entrepreneurial spirit throughout my life.

Nowadays, I challenge myself to experience new things that will contribute to my IQ as well as my EQ. Therein lies the power of education: to help students reach their potential through empowerment, not by discouraging them and relegating them to a destiny based solely on their academic results. Let students know they are good enough already. They may simply be at a different place in the process than others. Do not let their academic results be the sole identifier of who they are or what they will become. Sharpen their EQ so the confidence may lead them to a place of fulfillment and confidence.

現在有新證據證明SEL（社會情感學習）技能是可以教授和衡量的。SEL能促進積極發展、幫助減少有問題的行為，並提高學生的學業成績、社交技能以及身心健康。這些是更可能預測學術、生活和職業成就的特徵，也是在全球教育中需要更好地平衡的素質。SEL的實施取決於老師，但是我們需要政策和決策者擺脫自己的方式，並允許開展真正有意義的學習。

New evidence now confirms that SEL (Social Emotional Learning) skills can be taught and measured. SEL promotes positive development and helps reduce problematic behaviors while improving students' academic performance, social skills, and mental and physical health. These are the characteristics that are more likely to predict academic, life, and career success. These are the qualities that need to be better balanced in global education. The implementation of SEL rests with the teachers, but we need policy and decision makers to get out of their own way and allow true meaningful learning to take place.

金伯莉.A.舒納德—賴克爾在她的《社會、情感學習與教師》一文中分享了維吉尼亞大學的帕特里夏.詹寧斯和賓夕法尼亞州立大學的馬克.格林伯格等研究人員的發現。「**師生關係的質量，學生和課堂的管理，以及有效的社交和情感學習計劃的實施，都可以調節課堂和學生的學習**

成果。具有良好師生關係的課堂可促進學生的深度學習:與老師和同齡人相處融洽的孩子們更樂於應對具有挑戰性的材料並堅持艱苦的學習任務。相反,當教師對教學中的社交和情感要求管理不善時,學生表現出較低的學業表現和任務行為。顯然,我們需要幫助教師建立自己的社交情感能力,優化教師的課堂表現,以及他們在學生中促進SEL的能力。」

In her article, ***Social and Emotional Learning and Teachers***, Kimberly A. Schonert-Reichl shares findings from researchers Patricia Jennings of the University of Virginia and Mark Greenberg of Pennsylvania State University. *"The quality of teacher-student relationships, student and classroom management, and effective social and emotional learning program implementation all mediate classroom and student outcomes. Classrooms with warm teacher-child relationships promote deep learning among students: children who feel comfortable with their teachers and peers are more willing to grapple with challenging material and persist at difficult learning tasks. Conversely, when teachers poorly manage the social and emotional demands of teaching, students demonstrate lower performance and on-task behavior. Clearly, we need to optimize teachers' classroom performance and their ability to promote SEL in their students by helping them build their own social-emotional competence."*

做出改變人生決定的學校行政人員、校長、教育局和任何其他高等教育官員應首先接受SEL支持培訓。也許到那時,他們會接受教育改革並優化教師的影響力。太多的官員,要嘛離開教室太久了,要嘛根本沒上過課,他們正在迫使老師和學生陷入高壓倦怠的狀態。才華橫溢的教師成為決策者們無知的犧牲品,這些決策者們決定將學生獲得較高的考試成績作為「讚揚勳章」,用來別在他們的衣領上。這些榮譽是以有才能的老師和學生的犧牲為代價的。真正學習和享受人生的職業和機會被用作實現個人認可(職位爬升)的典當品。

School administrators, principals, headmasters, education bureaus and any other higher education officials who make life-altering decisions should be the first ones to receive SEL support training. Maybe then they would embrace education reform and optimize the impact teachers can have. Too many officials, who either have been out of the classroom too long or never in it at all, are driving both teachers and students to high-pressure burnout. Talented teachers fall prey to the ignorance of policy makers who have decided that achieving high student test scores should be used as "pins of praise" to be placed on their lapels. These honors come at the expense of talented teachers and students. Careers and opportunities for true learning and life enjoyment are used as pawns for personal recognition.

我與許多老師交談過，他們坦率地透露，儘管他們同意教導學生情商，但那是不可能的，因為雇用他們的人首先需要優異的考試結果。實際上，許多人發現自己陷入了與同一所學校中其他老師的競爭，因為他們希望能夠聲稱自己的學生是最好的，從而獲得升職。學生的福祉應該始終如一地放在教育的中心。遺憾的是，在某些學習場合中，對於學生福祉的重視甚至毫無蹤影！

I have spoken to many teachers who frankly reveal that, as much as they agree with teaching their students EQ, it is impossible because those who employ them demand strong test results first. In fact, many find themselves competing against other teachers in the same school, as they hope to be able to claim their students are the best, thereby earning themselves a promotion. The student's best interest should always be at the center of education. I am sorry to say that, in some places of learning, it doesn't even seem to be found anywhere in the equation!

向學生施壓以使其適應相同的學習成績模型是一個危險且錯位的概念。它惡化了教育的哲學概念，後者是建立在管理生活和維護社會所需要的知識和經驗的基礎上的。不幸的是，許多國家正在培養一群智商高的人,他們的大腦充滿了知識、事實和算法,但是其中許多人缺乏如何在現實生活中使用或吸收其知識的常識。當然,他們可以記住和吸收很多訊息,甚至可以回憶起來,但是這樣做有什麼好處?他們缺乏合作、團隊協作和溝通等面向未來的技能,這使他們無法接受全面的教育,並無法在工作場所和人生中取得成功。

Pressuring students to fit in to the same academic performance mold is a dangerous and misaligned concept. It deteriorates the philosophical concept of education, which is to build a base of knowledge and experience that will be needed for the management of life and the maintenance of society. Unfortunately, many countries are producing a segment of HIGH IQ individuals who have a brain full of knowledge, facts, and algorithms, but many of these people lack common sense regarding how to use or assimilate their knowledge in a real-life concept. Granted, they can memorize and absorb lots of information, and maybe even recall it, but for what benefit? They lack the future-proof skills of cooperation, teamwork, and communication, which round out a complete education and lead to success in the workplace and in life.

我知道,對於不符合高學業成績標準的學生,許多文化和社會對他們並不表示公開支持或誇耀。我最近拜訪了中國山東省的一所學校。到目前為止,我可能已經拜訪了中國的六十所學校,但這是我有幸拜訪的第一所「職業」學校。在參觀期間的某一時刻,我停下了腳步,告訴副校長,牆上掛著的學生和老師的照片令我震驚,因為照片中的所有人都在笑!她問我這話是什麼意思?我告訴她,在中國(和美國)有如此多的學校,學生們承受著巨大的學習壓力。在那些學校裡,我很少見到像她的學校那樣保持微笑的學生。這是說得通的,因為她的學生不必參加高考。對於她的學生來說,他們不會為可怕的期末考試而心生懼怕,他們也為此感到高興。他們確實承受著家庭和社會的恥辱,也許不像傳統教育體系那樣「聰明」,但我相信職業學校的學生非常聰明和勇敢。他們可能是冒險者，他們將在各種領域中從事有價值的工作，也將是冒險創業的人。他們可能並不是讀書的料，但他們非常聰明。許多人的情商也很高。

  I know many cultures and societies do not always openly support or boast about their population of students who do not fit in the standard "academic" mold of high academic performers. I recently visited a school in Shandong Province, China. At this point, I have probably visited more than 60 schools throughout China, but this was the first "vocational" school I had the pleasure of touring. At one point on the tour, I stopped and mentioned to the Vice Principal how noticeable it was to me that the photos of the students and the teachers posted on the walls were striking because all were smiling! She asked me what I meant? I shared with her that so many schools throughout China (and the US) have students who are under tremendous academic pressure to perform. In those schools, I rarely see as many smiling students as I did at her school. It makes sense because her students will not take the Gaokao examination. For her students, they do not feel the fear of the dreaded final examination, and as a result, they seem quite happy because of it. They do bear the family and social stigma of maybe not being as "smart" as those in the traditional educational system, but I believe the vocational students are quite bright and bold. They will likely be the risk takers who will work valuable jobs in all sorts of business areas and will also be those taking the risk to launch a business. They may not be book smart, but they are very intelligent; many with high EQ's as well.

  在教育全人時，我們必須認識到每個學生獨特的學習風格和興趣。教師經常堅持要求所有學生必須對數學和科學有很高的理解，認為只有那樣才能過上成功的生活。為什麼？我經營著幾家公司，我的數學技能十分有限，但我適應得很好，仍然獲得了成功。我的商務學位不是從學校或大學獲得的，而是來自生活這所學校。當我陷入困境，並需要比我所知或能自我學習的更高的知識水平時，我都只會交由會計師處理。我現在從事的各種工作與我接受的正規科學教育幾乎沒有關係。為什麼我要花時間學習週期表，或者混合一些老師們試圖說是至關重要的化合物呢？我倒希望我的理科老師能教我完美的配方，讓我煮出完美的咖啡。那對我的日常生活要有用得多，而且利潤頗豐！生活中的基本技能是基礎更廣泛的實踐技能，比測試學生的大多數事實性知識要重要得多。

In teaching the whole child, we must recognize the unique learning style and interests of each student. Teachers often insist that all students must have a high level of Math and Science understanding for success in life. Why? I run several businesses, and I have learned to adapt my limited Math skills and still be successful. My business degree was not from a school or university, but from the school of life. When I am stumped and need a higher level of knowledge than I can either learn on my own or recall, I simply refer it to my accountant. The various jobs that I do now have little, if anything at all, to do with the formal Science education I received. Why did I spend time learning the periodic table chart, or mixing certain compounds that my teacher tried to convince me was so crucial? I wish my Science teacher had taught me the perfect compound combination so I could make the perfect cup of coffee. That would have been far more useful to my everyday life, and quite lucrative as well! Essential skills in life are more broad-based practical skills that are far more significant than most of the facts that students are being tested on.

當老師和學生了解學習的成果收益時，在老師和學生之間建立聯繫就更加具有意義。我知道新知識將是生活中必不可少的實用知識，就能學得更加專心和滿懷興趣。我認為學生也是一樣。如果他們知道學習的原因，以及學習方法能如何惠及他們的現實生活，他們將變得更加積極主動。這就是企業主從經驗中學習的原因，因為一旦他們發現自己不了解的知識，便會嘗試去學習，以便為下一次做好準備。

Making a connection between teacher and student is so much more meaningful when the teacher and student understand the outcome benefit for learning. I am always more attentive and interested in new knowledge when I know it is going to be essential and practical learning. I think students are the same way. If they know the reason for their learning, and how it will benefit their real life, the more motivated and attentive they will be. It is why business owners learn from experience, because once they learn what they don't know, they then try to learn it for the next time.

總結
Summary

　　成功與學生建立牢固聯繫的老師們將走上正確的道路，提供超越考試成績的真正教育收益。很少有學校會放棄將考試作為對學生進行排名和評估的一種手段，但是真正的社交情感學習不僅可以培養同理心，而且可以教人如何處理壓力。

　　Teachers who successfully build strong connections with their students are on the right path to providing true educational benefits that extend beyond the examination results. Very few schools will ever abandon exams as a means for ranking and assessing students, but true social emotional learning teaches not only empathy, but also how to manage the stress.

　　真誠地教育整個班級、教育全人以及每個孩子，這是老師面臨的最大挑戰。對於大多數人來說，本能似乎是自然的，但是他們發現自己所處的「系統」傳達的是不同的訊息。對於許多滿懷善意的老師來說，在這樣的環境中進行教學意味著他們必須達到一種艱難的平衡。

　　Making a sincere effort to teach the whole class, the whole child, and each individual child is the single greatest challenge facing teachers. For most, the instinct seems natural, but the "system" they find themselves in preaches a different message. It is a difficult balance for many well-meaning, well-intended teachers to teach in these environments.

根據研究，我們的智商可能是受到基因編碼左右，可能無法改變，但是研究表明，新的經驗以及不斷追求好奇心會對整體智商產生積極影響。排在倒數第四位的學生的流體智力可能的確是中等偏下的水平。但是，同一位學習者也可能極有動力且非常努力，而這可能導致晶態智力的提高。好奇心真的是無可替代的東西，因為它會導致積極的努力。

According to research, our IQ may be genetically coded and may be unable to change, but research is suggesting that new experiences, and the continued pursuit of curiosity, can positively impact overall IQ. It is likely that the student ranked 4th from the bottom may indeed have low to moderate fluid intelligence. However, that same learner may also be extremely motivated and hardworking, which can lead to an increase in crystallized IQ. There really is no substitute for curiosity that leads to motivated hard work.

發揮最大潛力是一個值得追求的目標。為什麼有些人似乎「充份利用了自己的智慧」，而另一些人卻似乎永遠無法發揮自己的潛力？我感到自己在生活中取得了成功。我有一個美滿的家庭，兒孫滿堂。我並不總是過著經濟寬裕的生活，但我的狀況比許多人要好。我已經創業，從事令人滿足且充實的職業，曾在中國各地廣泛開展教師培訓，並有許多有趣而寶貴的生活經歷。我認為，我在自身性格優缺點的範圍之內生活和學習，因此提高了我的智商。我不把成功定義為物質財富的積累，而是定義為一個人將所做的事情視為對自己和他人有意義的事情。就我的標準化測試結果而言，我覺得自己的表現已經超標了。我不確定自己這種「感覺」有多少是基於遺傳編碼或因為生活經歷而有所提升。但我確實知道的一件事是，有一位老師曾讓我覺得自己已經足夠好了，我對新奇事物的追求都要歸功於他的同理心，這些新事物激發了我的智商和情商的發展。

Reaching maximum potential is a worthy pursuit. Why do some

individuals seem to "make the most of their intelligence" and others seem to never reach their potential? I feel successful in life. I have a beautiful family of children and grandchildren. I haven't always lived a financially comfortable life, but I feel better off than many. I have started businesses, worked a satisfying and fulfilling career as teacher, traveled extensively in China training teachers, and have had many other intriguing and valuable life-experiences. I think I have sharpened my IQ as a result of living and learning within my personality strengths and weaknesses. I do not define success as an accumulation of material goods, but rather as doing things that I feel are meaningful to self and to others. Based on my standardized test results, I feel that I have over-achieved. I am not sure how much of what I "feel" was genetically coded or elevated based on my life experiences. But one thing I do know is that a teacher made me feel that I was good enough already, and I credit his empathy to my pursuit of new curiosities that inspired my IQ and EQ development.

當然，智商對學校很重要，對生活而言，情商則絕對是至關重要。我個人認為，我的成功有百分之八十五來自情商，而百分之十五與智商有關。我認為我的運動和生活經歷提高了我的流體智力和好奇心，進而激發了我晶態智力。我認為毅力、艱苦的工作和較高的情商使我得以在這個星球上有目的和有意義地存在。我感謝那些曾讓我相信自己已經足夠好的老師們，他們耐心地使我對看得見的優勢領域充滿信心，而不是專注於我明顯的智商劣勢領域。當我的學業成績容易使我陷入不安時，他們的指導喚起了我的自尊和自信。也許我的表現已經超標，又或許我只是按照我的計劃去實現了自己的遺傳編碼。無論如何，我要感謝那些耐心而慈悲的人，他們奉獻自己，讓我成為了後來的我。永遠不要低估你在領導生涯中能對至少一名學生（可能更多）產生的影響。

Sure, IQ is important for school and absolutely EQ is essential for life. I personally feel 85% of my success is a result of my EQ and 15% is related to my IQ. I think my athletic & life experiences have sharpened my fluid IQ and my curiosity, which in turn, inspired my crystallized IQ. I think grit, hard work, and a high EQ combined to give me a purposeful and meaningful existence on this planet. I am grateful to the teachers who helped me believe I was good enough already and then patiently empowered me with confidence in visible areas of strength, instead of focusing on my clear IQ areas of weakness. Their guidance kept my self-esteem and self-confidence alive when my academic results could have easily driven me into insecurity. Maybe I have over-achieved or maybe I have simply lived out my genetic code as I was designed to do. Whatever is the case, I am grateful for those who patiently and lovingly gave of themselves to make me who I am. Never underestimate the influence you can have on at least one student, probably more, over the course of your leadership career.

訊息點：與老師和同學相處融洽的孩子，更願意面對有挑戰性的材料，並堅持完成困難的學習任務。

Point of Information: Children who feel comfortable with their teachers and peers are more willing to grapple with challenging material and persist at difficult learning tasks.

- 肯德拉.切里，流體智力 vs. 晶態智力，更新日期2019年三月十五日。

Kendra Cherry, Fluid Intelligence vs. Crystallized Intelligence, Updated March 15, 2019. (https://www.verywellmind.com/kendra-cherry-2794702)

- 肯德拉.切里，平均智商意味著或者暗示著什麼，更新日期2019年三月十三日。

Kendra Cherry, What an Average IQ Means and Indicates, Updated

March 13, 2019. (https://www.verywellmind.com/kendra-cherry-2794702)

- EQ vs.IQ, Diffen.com.Diffen LLC, n.d. 2019年四月十三日。
"EQ vs IQ." *Diffen.com.* Diffen LLC, n.d. Web. 13 Apr 2019. (https://www.diffen.com/difference/EQ_vs_IQ)

- 克里斯多佛.伯格蘭，《運動員之道：汗水和生物學祝福》
Christopher Bergland, *The Athlete's Way: Sweat and the Biology of Bliss* (www.theathletesway.com)

- 克里斯多佛.伯格蘭，「體育活動能提高流體智力嗎？」，《今日心理學》，2013年十二月十三日。
Christopher Bergland, *The Athlete's Way: Sweat and the Biology of Bliss* (www.theathletesway.com)

- 金伯莉.A.舒納德—賴克爾，《社會、情感學習和老師》，VOL. 27/NO.1/2017年春。
Kimberly A. Schonert-Reichl, *Social and Emotional Learning and Teachers*, VOL. 27 / NO. 1 / SPRING 2017.

預備，開火，瞄準
Ready, Fire, Aim

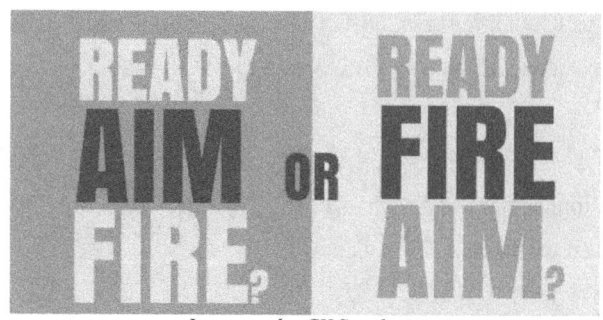

Image credit: CX Simplicity

　　作為「美國內戰」課題的狂熱愛好者，我研究了士兵們在美國內戰的激烈戰鬥中射擊子彈的過程和步驟。士兵的步槍重約七至十磅。再加上攜帶的其他裝備，很明顯，一個典型的士兵很容易在負重四十五至五十磅的情況下為了活命而「奔跑」。如果敵人在你開槍前想先對你開槍的話，揹著這麼重的裝備尤其是個問題。使用當今的武器，熟練的士兵可能會在一分鐘的時間內打中四個目標球。而那時候當士兵朝向敵人或遠離敵人的方向移動時，很容易花費更長時間。然後，考慮到裝填和射擊過程所需的多個步驟，要說士兵在一分鐘內可以實際擊發兩發或三發子彈是現實的。如果給敵人配上一把可以每分鐘射擊十二至十六發子彈的連發步槍（史賓斯連發步槍）將是多麼不公平啊！在生活中，有時候我感覺自己就是那位內戰士兵，盡我所能地用老式步槍「射擊」，而敵人卻似乎擁有無窮無盡的裝彈能力和射擊能力，以及出色的槍法！

　　As a civil war enthusiast, I have studied the process and procedure it took for soldiers to get a rifle shot off during the hectic battles of the American Civil War. A soldier's rifle could weigh anywhere from 7-10 pounds. Couple that with the other gear carried, and it becomes apparent that a typical solider could easily be "running" for his life, burdened with 45-50 pounds of gear. Carrying that much weight is particularly problematic when being chased or shot at by those who would prefer to shoot you before you shoot them. With the weapons of the day, a skilled solider could possibly get 4 aimed shots off in a 1-minute timespan. That time proficiency would easily be lengthened as that soldier moves towards or away from the enemy. Then, factor in the multiple steps required in the loading and firing process, and it is not unrealistic to say a soldier may realistically get 2 or 3 shots off in one minute. How unfair it would be to introduce a repeating rifle (Spencer Repeating Rifle) to the enemy who could now shoot 12-16 shots per minute! There are times in life when I feel as if I am that civil war soldier trying my best to "get shots off" with the old rifle, while the enemy seems to have endless reload and firing capabilities to go with their excellent marksmanship!

常見的槍法訓練命令可能是「預備，瞄準，開火！」當他覺得瞄準了的時候，聽話的士兵會穩定自己、瞄準並自信地扣下扳機。但是，在業務和領導過程中，我經常發現自己使用的是「預備，開火，瞄準」，而不是「預備，瞄準，開火」。我很想說，在我停下腳步，穩定自己並朝著既定目標邁進之前，我的業務和個人計劃始終將「目標」放在明確的位置，但事實完全不是這樣。這到底是我在競爭中處於十字準線的反應，還是由於缺乏規劃和設計呢？可能兩者兼而有之吧！

Common marksmanship training commands would likely follow with "ready, aim, fire!" The obedient solider steadies himself, takes aim, and confidently squeezes the trigger when he feels the shot is a good one. However, in business and in leadership, I often find myself using "ready, fire, aim", as opposed to "ready, aim, fire". I would like to say that my business and personal plans always have the "target" in clear site before I stop, steady myself, and fire towards the intended goal, but that simply isn't true. Is this a reactionary response because I am in the crosshairs of competition, or is it due to lack of planning and design? Probably a combination of both!

　　在擔任中學老師的那些年裡，我感到自己經常還沒瞄準就開火了，並借助學生們的反應來幫助自己瞄準。許多課堂活動的想法起初只是一個簡單的點子，而沒有經過深思熟慮。在這種時候，我「扣動扳機」以了解學生的反應。看到反應之後，我調整目標，並以比最初嘗試更高的精確度調整或重新定位目標。我覺得我最初的目標對最終的成功並不重要，反而是先開火並對子彈行進或著陸的位置進行衡量更加重要。有時候，我命中的點離靶心很遠，但有的時候，我打得比想像的要準得多。

　　In my years spent as a middle school teacher, I felt I was constantly firing without clear aim, and I let the reaction of my students help improve my aim based on their response. Many classroom activity ideas started out as a short thought or idea without deep planning. In these times, I "pulled the trigger" to see what the student response and reaction would be. Once I saw the reaction, I adjusted my aim and refined or repositioned my target with a greater degree of accuracy than what I achieved in my original effort. I felt as though my initial aim was not as significant to the eventual success as was simply firing and getting an immediate gauge as to where the bullet traveled or landed. Sometimes, I was way off, and other times, I was far more accurate than I had imagined.

　　我不建議對所有事物都使用這種「命中或脫靶」的方法，但我確實認為它具有一定的價值。也許我認同「行動勝過無所作為」的口頭禪，或者是你透過說的話或做的事「要嘛影響要嘛感染」他人的想法，但是我發現這就是我的風格，而且「預備，開火，瞄準」對我而言比這組詞的常規順序更加好用。作為一名老師，我想冒險，嘗試一些我認為可能會吸引或啟發學生的想法。一旦我嘗試並評估了學生的反應，就可以修正或停止。這兩種反應似乎都很有價值，因為回饋表明會揭示成功或失敗。如果我正在投資，並且繼續觀察資產下跌的價值，那麼我有兩種選擇——等它回升或停止投資。

I do not recommend this "hit or miss" method for everything, but I do think there is some value to it. Maybe I am fixated on the mantra that "action always beats inaction", or the idea that you either "affect or infect" people by what you say or do, but I have found that this is my style, and that "ready, fire, aim" works better for me than does the more common order of the phrase. As a teacher, I wanted to take risks and try ideas that I thought might appeal or inspire my students. Once I tried and evaluated the reaction of students, I could either revise or discontinue. Either response seemed valuable because feedback revealed success or failure. If I am investing, and I continue to watch the value of an asset drop, I have two choices - wait it out or discontinue the investment.

總結
Summary

教育傾向於預備，瞄準，開火。教育喜歡清晰的目標，精心計劃和明確的預定標靶。但是，教育中的許多「士兵」更喜歡現成的目標。我認識的許多老師都是最靈活的那種人。他們可以快速適應和調整，因為許多老師每天都在這樣做。但是，對於許多人來說，這種靈活性是一種掙扎，因為他們的性格類型要求控制和秩序。

Education tends to be ready, aim, fire. Education likes clear goals, careful planning, and clear intended targets. However, many of the "soldiers" in education prefer ready, fire, aim. Many teachers are among the most flexible people I know. They can adapt and adjust quickly because many teachers do that on a daily basis. However, there are many for whom this flexibility is a struggle because their personality types demand control and order.

學生經常缺乏靈活性，因為老師或體制缺乏靈活性。作為一種人為創造，一致性使教學工作變得容易開展。但是在某些情況下，有些學習者被整合和秩序所吞噬,他們天生的好奇心遭到削弱,因為這被視為違逆常規的表現。

Students often lack flexibility because the teacher or the system also lacks flexibility. Conformity, as a construct, makes teaching easy. But in some instances, there are learners who are swallowed up in the conformity and order, and their natural curiosity is diminished because it is seen as rogue.

要成為在每個獨特的學生中尋找優點和缺點的老師。嘗試去滿足每個學生的需求,同時管理整個班級的需求。這是巨大的教學挑戰。許多人也認為他們應該「教育全人」,卻沒有得到這樣做的支持。課程決定教學流程,考試時間表也決定教學流程。結果是弱小的「士兵」們試圖順應預備、瞄準、開火的順序,但實際上,他們太害羞了,根本無法扣下扳機。缺乏自信使他們感到憂慮和不安,這幾乎確保了他們即使選擇開火也無法命中目標。

Be the teacher who looks for the strengths and weaknesses in each unique learner. Try to meet the needs of each student, while you also manage the needs of the entire class. This is the great teaching challenge. Many believe they should "teach the whole child" but are not given the support to do so. The curriculum dictates progress and the examination schedule dictates process. The results are weak "soldiers" who try to conform to ready, aim, fire, but in reality, they are too shy to pull the trigger at all. Lack of self-confidence has rendered them apprehensive and insecure, which almost ensures that they will not hit the target, even if they do choose to fire.

應該鼓勵師生們冒險。擁有「扣下扳機」的信心會產生顯著而未知的結果。整合更易於管理和操縱,但結果往往只照顧到很小的一部份,而忽略了自由思考、有好奇心的學生。教師應樹立創造力和靈活性的榜樣。教師應該承認自己的學習目標,但也不要害怕在脫靶時對目標進行調整。靈活性可以激發好奇心,而這將繼續激發學習的熱情。

Teachers and students should be encouraged to take risks. Having the confidence to "pull the trigger" can produce remarkable and unknown results. Conformity is easier to manage and maneuver, but the results are too often directed to a very small percentage, while ignoring the freethinking, curious learner. Teachers should model creativity and flexibility. Teachers should acknowledge their intended targets for learning, but also not be afraid to adjust the target when the shot fired misses the intended target. Flexibility can breed curiosity, which will continue to inspire learning.

你打算什麼時候挑戰自己？
When Are You Going to Challenge Yourself?

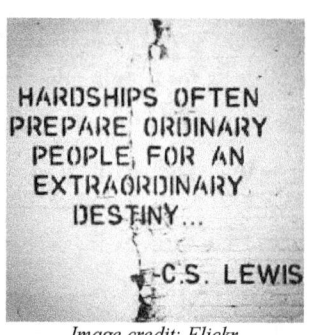

Image credit: Flickr

我認為體育運動之所以如此吸引人我的原因之一就是它們帶來的挑戰。對於許多運動員來說，嘗試學習或掌握一項技能可以滿足他們接受挑戰的無限需求。這一挑戰為競爭者提供了一個「試試看能不能」的機會，也為一小部份人提供「證明我能」的機會。

I think one of the reasons sports were so appealing and even inviting for me was the challenge they provided. For many athletes, trying to learn or master a skill fills an insatiable need to accept a challenge. This challenge presents an opportunity for the competitor to "see if I can" or, for a smaller number, "prove that I can".

也許我對運動挑戰的渴望是學業掙扎的結果，這些掙扎使我在傳統的學習環境中感覺「缺乏裝備」，但是在體育領域，我感覺自己比大多數人都要精通。對於運動員來說，練習是為實際比賽進行準備所需的時間。在實踐中，我們完善比賽策略，發展自律，演練時間管理，加強團隊溝通，並聽取教練的指導。實際比賽是對練習期間是否進行學習的即時回饋評估。這種學習流程是實用的，因此對我來說很有意義。我發現體育運動是我樂於接受的挑戰。我不怕失敗。實際上，在這種情況下，我只怕自己不去冒險。

Maybe my thirst for the athletic challenge was a result of some academic struggles that made me feel ill-equipped in the traditional learning environment, but in the sports realm, I felt better equipped than most. For athletes, practice was time taken for actual game preparation. In practice, we perfected our game strategy, developed self-discipline, rehearsed time-management, enhanced team communication, and listened to coach's instruction. The actual game competition became the instant feedback assessment as to whether or not learning took place during the practice. That flow of learning was practical and therefore made sense to me. I found sports to be a challenge that I loved to accept. I did not fear failure. In fact, in this case, I feared not taking the risk.

是什麼讓你不敢思考當前的挑戰是否值得呢？你是否害怕失敗的可能性，還是害怕連在挑戰中失敗的機會都沒有？為什麼有些人將挑戰視為可怕的障礙，而另一些人卻僅僅將其視為人生道路上的減速帶呢？這些問題的答案可以對我們最深層的感受提出挑戰。

What holds you back from seeing if the current challenge is one worth taking? Do you fear the possibility of failure or do you fear never having the opportunity to fail at a challenge? Why do some people view a challenge as a fearful obstacle, yet others see it as a mere speed bump in the road of life Answers to these questions are those that can challenge our deepest feelings.

父母可能負責孩子的最初遺傳連結，而老師則似乎對於重塑學生對挑戰的看法有很大作用。回顧我的求學時代，我發現有些老師比其他老師更能夠提出有助於塑造我觀點的挑戰。最好的老師說服了我，儘管過程將十分艱難，但結果將是對我有益的，值得我去奮鬥。這些老師讓我相信，教育過程更多的是關於整個過程中的成長，而不僅僅是考試的結果。他們告訴我，成長存在於過程中，而不僅僅存在於最終的產品中。

Whereas parents may be responsible for the initial genetic wiring of children, teachers seem to have a lot to do with the re-wiring of the student's mind regarding their perspective on a challenge. Looking back on my education, I found some teachers were more able than others to present the challenge in a way that helped shape my perspective. The best teachers convinced me that although the process will be difficult, the result and benefit would be beneficial and worth my struggle. These teachers made me believe the education process was more about growth through the process than it was about the results of the examination. They taught me that growth was in the process, not just in the product.

我記得曾教過八年級學生有關歷史研究論文寫作的過程。我們曾花費幾個星期的時間開展這項工作，在痛苦的研究寫作過程中，有條不紊地逐步加強學生的學習。對於大多數學生來說，這是他們首次嘗試完成此類項目。我告訴他們，我從以前的學生那裡聽到最多的話是：「感謝你讓我寫出八年級的研究論文！」儘管他們讀八年級的時候感到痛苦，但他們發現挑戰的結果在他們進入高中之後證明是非常值得的。

I remember teaching my 8th graders about the history research paper writing process. We would devote several weeks of class time to this endeavor, methodically stepping and scaffolding student learning through the painful research writing process. For most, this was their first attempt at completing such a project. I would tell them that one of the things I heard most from former students was "Thank you for making me do the 8th grade research paper!" As painful as the process was when they were 8th graders, they found the result of that challenge to be well worth it when they arrived in high school.

如果教師能夠說服學生知識或技能的實用性，那麼學生就可以看到為了長期獲益而承受暫時痛苦的價值。這可能是學校有些科目對我無用的原因，因為我不相信我在將來的生活中會隨時需要用到這些知識。例如，在我追求體育和歷史學位時，記憶元素週期表似乎是一項完全沒用的任務（請不要透過電子郵件向我表達反對意見或試圖說服我接受相反的觀點）。同樣，有些數學概念被吹捧為對考試至關重要，但由於我不知道它們對生活有何用處，學習過程也十分折磨。結果是我的大腦拒絕吸收它們。學習材料的挑戰並沒有讓我有興趣接受這一挑戰。這到底是因為材料本身、挑戰提出的方式、還是我與提出挑戰的老師「脫節」導致的呢？

If teachers can convince students of the usefulness and application of the knowledge or skill, then students can see the value in enduring the temporary pain for the sake of long-term gain. It may be the reason why some subjects in school felt useless to me, because I could not believe I was ever going to need that knowledge at any point in my future life. For example, memorizing the periodic table seemed like a completely useless task (please do not email me with your disagreement trying to convince me otherwise) in my pursuit of a Physical Education and History degree. Likewise, there were Math concepts that were touted as crucial for the test, but sheer torture to learn because I had no idea how they would be crucial for life. As a result, my brain refused to absorb them. The challenge of learning that material did not present itself as a challenge I was interested in accepting. Was it the material, the way the challenge was presented, or was it my "disconnect" with the teacher's presentation of the challenge?

老師和領導者是否可以幫助塑造學生及受領導者的態度，以讓後者擁抱任務？有沒有辦法說服學習者，告訴他們，現在要求他們進行的努力對以後的生活或學習極具價值？如果教師和領導者可以將過程的好處與最終結果的必要性聯繫起來，則可以變得更加有效。如果老師可以說服學生，現在他們難以忍受的這個過程將會帶來不小的好處，那麼這過程就是有可能做到的。

Can teachers and leaders help shape the attitude of students and those they lead in such a way that the task can be embraced? Is it possible to convince the learner that the required effort will be later viewed as invaluable to life or future learning? Teachers and leaders can be far more effective if they can connect the process benefits to the necessity of the end result. If a teacher can convince the student that the displeasure of enduring the process now will pay dividends down the road, then it may be possible.

有時候，我們可以清楚地看到自己經歷的痛苦最終是值得的。我自身的例子是，我在演唱會的現場表演中，在舞台上撕裂了自己的膝蓋前交叉韌帶。那是我們的告別演唱會，再唱三首歌就結束了。我希望這場表演給我們自己和觀眾都留下深刻印象，這願望顯然也成了真。我們總是將最後四或五首歌曲安排為我們組合中最勁爆的歌曲。作為主唱，我認為我的工作是嘗試唱出正確的音符，但更重要的是，使觀眾瘋狂，這樣他們才能在音樂會結束時感受到樂隊的能量，並透過雷鳴般的掌聲表達他們的認可。

There are times when we can clearly see the pain endured to be worth it in the end. My physical example of this is when I tore my ACL (anterior cruciate ligament in the knee) live on stage during a concert performance. My band was 3 songs from the end of what was to be our final farewell concert. I wanted the show to be memorable to us and to the audience, and I certainly got my wish. We always saved the last 4 or 5 songs to be among the strongest and most lively songs in our set. As the lead singer, I saw my job as to try to hit the right notes, but more importantly, to work the audience into a frenzy so that they would feel the energy of the band at the end of the concert and hopefully acknowledge us with affectionate applause.

我的嗓音是我的樂器，而我在舞台上的動作和能量是我真正與觀眾聯繫的方式。對我而言，與他們的聯繫非常緊密，因為我的能量是直接的，並且是對他們能量的回饋。我試圖在每次表演中都帶來高能量，有時候觀眾卻沒有同樣的回饋。在那些節目中，我的精力在前幾首歌之後就下降了。我記得自己好像是唯一享受我們的音樂的人。但是，當觀眾精力充沛時，我的精力也會提升，我的腎上腺素會飆升，飆高音或記住所有歌詞並不像我所展示的精力那麼重要。

Whereas my voice was my instrument, my movement and energy on stage were my real modes of connection to those who watched. The connection to them was intense for me because my energy was direct, and it was a reciprocal feed to their energy. I tried to bring high energy during every performance, but there were times when the crowd didn't have it. In those shows, my energy dropped after the first few songs. I remember feeling as if I were the only one enjoying our work. However, when the audience energy was high, mine would increase as well, my adrenaline would spike, and singing on pitch or remembering all the lyrics were not as important as the energy I displayed.

在最後的一場演出中，能量非常高，與觀眾之間的聯繫被點燃了！用眾多敲擊音響、大型吉他和弦和長久持續最後一個音符來結束每一首歌，實在是好玩極了。為了結束這首特別的歌曲，樂隊一直專注於我的滑稽動作，直到我給他們發出大結局的信號。那一刻到來了。為了發出信號，我高高躍起，一拳伸過頭頂。和往常一樣，樂隊按照我的提示完美結束！但是當我落地時，右膝蓋前交叉韌帶過度伸展而斷裂了。我倒在地上，感受到劇烈疼痛。不確定發生了什麼事，我跛著腳走下台，想知道自己為什麼站不直。可以想像，那短暫的停頓幾乎把整個房間裡的空氣和能量都吸走了，因為觀眾不知道發生了什麼事。有些人以為我們的表演結束了，開始喝采鼓掌，大喊安可。我們決定表演完最後的曲目，我用一條腿跳來跳去，試圖重新找回我們之前擁有的能量。

In this one final show, the energy was at a very high level and the audience connection was right on! Ending the songs with lots of clanging symbols, big guitar chords and holding out the final instrumental notes was so much fun. To end this particular song, the band was focused on my movement antics until I gave them the signal for the big ending. The moment came. To initiate the signal, I jumped high into the air with fist stretched up high over my head. As usual, they ended perfectly on my cue! But as I landed, my right ACL ligament hyperextended and shredded into pieces inside my knee. I collapsed to the floor, feeling the intense pain. Unsure of what had just happened, I hobbled off the stage wondering why I could not stand up. As you can imagine, the short break pretty much sucked the air and energy out of the room because the audience had no idea what had happened. Some thought we were done and were applauding for an encore. We decided to finish the final songs with me hopping on one leg trying to regain the energy we once had.

即將進行的手術使我的腿在六週內無法動彈，而前三週是不能負重的。醫生告訴我，破壞疤痕組織會很痛苦，但必須確保充份癒合並恢復所有活動能力。他是對的。這是該過程中最痛苦的部份。但是這種痛苦是可以忍受的，因為我有清晰的目標，那就是膝蓋完全恢復，讓我對它有完全的信心並回歸積極的生活方式。他無需說服我，這樣做是為了讓我能繼續做我以前喜歡的所有事情。作為我的「老師」，他幫助我重新進行了思考，明白了康復的痛苦最終是值得的，因為我最終會在無需裝設支架或帶著恐懼的情況下恢復全部活動能力。

The impending surgery had my leg immobilized for 6 weeks and the first 3 were non-weight bearing. The doctor told me that breaking up the scar tissue would be painful but necessary to ensure full healing and to resume the full range of activities. He was right. It was the most painful part of the process. But that pain felt bearable because my desire to resume an active lifestyle with full confidence in my knee was my clear goal. He didn't have to convince me that I wanted to continue to do all the things that I previously enjoyed. As my "teacher", he helped rewire my thinking to know that the pains of rehabilitation would be worth it in the end when I could resume full activities without a brace or fear.

接受這一考驗中遇到的挑戰需要正確的心態。關於我們如何看待挑戰的一些參數可能已預先植入我們的DNA中，但是老師、父母和領導者可以幫助我們重新思考，讓我們雖然可以將挑戰視為痛苦的過程，卻能明白它將帶來積極的成長與變化。所有領導者（老師也是領導者）都必須謹慎對待並計算如何向學生或團隊提出挑戰。擺出清晰的視野，同時列出可能會遇到的經歷和感受，這可能很困難，但有助於塑造他們的思維方式。如果將其視為癒合和恢復過程的一部份，則可以忍受恢復過程中伴隨的疼痛。

Accepting the challenges encountered in this ordeal required the proper mindset. It is possible that some parameters regarding how we view the challenges are precast in our DNA, but teachers, parents, and leaders can help re-wire our thinking so that we can view challenges as a painful, process but one that will bring about positive growth and change. All leaders (and teachers are leaders) need to be cautious and calculated in how challenges are presented to students or teams. Casting a clear vision, while laying out the likely experiences and emotions that will be encountered, may be difficult but beneficial to helping shape their mindset. Pain in recovery can be endured when it is seen as part of the healing and restoration process.

如果人們可以理解，在將來的人生經歷或工作中，雙語能力將是必不可少的救命技能，那麼持久的語言學習之苦是可以是值得經歷的。如果我們能夠說服學生，他們有一天可能需要掌握化學特性知識來製造藥物，那麼學習元素週期表甚至可能就會很有價值。要指出的是，領導者和教師可以鑄就清晰的願景，但願景鑄就並不是全部。領導者是否可以拋棄願景，在情感和心理上讓追隨者做好準備，以面對那終將對他們有益而目前卻痛苦的學習過程？那些被領導的人是否可以因為相信結果終將帶來的好處而接受過程中的痛苦和不適？沒有遠見的領導者當然無法有效領導，但是，不能準確傳達痛苦過程和最終結果都有其價值的訊息的領導者也無法有效領導。

  The pain of enduring language learning can be seen as worthwhile preparation if it is understood that one day, in an immersion experience or job, the bilingual abilities will be life-saving or essential. Learning the periodic table may even be valuable, if we can convince those who may one day need to have that chemical property knowledge to make medicine. The point to be made is that leaders and teachers can cast a clear vision, but vision casting is not the whole story. Can the leader cast the vision, but also emotionally and mentally prepare the follower for the painful learning process that will benefit them personally? Can those being led embrace the pain and discomfort of the process because they believe the result will be good for them? Leaders without vision certainly cannot be effective, but neither can leaders who cannot accurately communicate the message that there is value in the painful process, as much as in the result.

  許多人有「遺願清單」，列舉了他們在生命中想完成的挑戰。「遺願清單」是他們在「踢桶」之前想有的體驗或要做的事。（「踢桶」是英語用語，委婉語，意為「去世」。）遺願清單可能包含極端挑戰（例如高空彈跳、跳傘或駕駛飛機）或造訪某些特定地點（阿爾卑斯山、萬里長城或艾菲爾鐵塔）。坦白說，我們所有人都應該有一個遺願清單，因為它代表了我們設定的終生目標。達成目標時，清單可以為我們提供動力、決心以及滿足感和成就感。我們將為實現我們認為值得努力和犧牲的目標而更加努力。

  Many people have a "bucket list" of challenges they intend or desire to complete in life. A "bucket list" is a set of experiences or things they want to do before they "kick the bucket". (To kick the bucket is an English idiomatic expression, considered a euphemistic slang term meaning "to die".) A bucket list may contain an extreme challenge (such as bungee jumping, sky diving, or flying an airplane) or a visit to some desired location (the Alps, the Great Wall, or the Eiffel Tower). Truthfully, we should all have a bucket list because it represents lifetime goals we set with great intention. A bucket list can provide us with motivation, determination, and a feeling of satisfaction and accomplishment when the objectives are achieved. We will work harder for the goals that we determine are worth the effort and sacrifice.

總結
Summary

你打算什麼時候挑戰自己？ 人們很容易陷入常規。我們以一定程度的一致性開展工作，這可能會帶來舒適感，但也會讓你感到自滿。曾經被視為我們「知道如何做好自己的工作」的事物迅速變成了我們難以擺脫的例行工作。為此，我們需要重新思考並集中精力，開始制定一項計劃，該計劃將為自己提出挑戰，以新的緊迫感和重要性重新努力工作。

When are you going to challenge yourself? It is easy to fall into the rut-routine. We go about our work with a level of consistency that may yield comfort but can also give way to complacency. What was once seen as us "knowing how to do our job well" quickly morphs into us performing our job in a rut routine that is difficult to steer out of. To do so, we need to renew our minds and focus and begin to enact a plan that will challenge ourselves to work back towards taking our job with a renewed sense of urgency and significance.

偏離常規需要付出努力和耐心。保持自滿要容易得多，因為它比起打破常規所需的精力少得多。我的建議是從微小而可衡量的事情做起，但也不要害怕大膽的夢想。

Steering out of the rut will require effort and endurance. It is far easier to stay complacent which requires far less energy than breaking the routine does. My advice is to start small and measurable but do not be afraid to dream big and bold.

嘗試任何事情時，起初幾次不要指望立即收獲大的變化。可能需要一些時間才能將變化融入你所從事的工作文化以及班級或團隊的文化。所有相關人員都需要時間進行調整和做出反應。重要的是，你要盡力而為。

When trying anything for the first few times, do not expect massive change right away. It may take some time to build the change into the culture of what you have been doing and the class or group has been experiencing. All involved need time to adjust and react. The important thing is that you try and make the sincere effort.

選擇你認為可以實現的一兩個關鍵事項，這將為你的領導方式和你領導的人造成改變。如果是老師，且你覺得自己的課程呆板，那就花點時間每週做一堂課，一堂令人難忘且有意義的重點課。這節課將具有更深層次的學生參與度，其設計與之前的課程都不同。請評估這一節課，然後在下週考慮第二節課。當你養成新習慣時，這種節奏就可能會持續下去。

Pick one or two key things that you think you could implement that would make a difference in how you lead and to who you lead. If a teacher, and you feel like you are in the rut routine with your lessons, spend time making 1 lesson per week a M & M focus lesson (Memorable & Meaningful). This lesson has a deeper level of student engagement and is designed differently than your previous lessons. Evaluate this one lesson and then consider a second lesson the following week. This pace may be something able to sustain as you build in your new habits.

如果你真誠地希望與自己的學生或團隊建立更深的聯繫，那麼請承諾做出改變並對結果進行回應。變革總是困難的，但是過程和結果對自己和他人都會有益。隨著你越來越多地實踐變化，挑戰變得越加容易，變化的目標也變得越加大膽。突然之間，你會發現自己已經脫離常規，走上了一條新的道路，充滿活力，並準備好應對你的「遺願清單」中的其他挑戰。

If it is your sincere desire to build a deeper connection with your students or a group, then commit to change and respond to the results. Change is always difficult, but the process and results are rewarding to self and to others. As you practice change more and more, the challenge becomes easier and the goals for change become more even more bold. Suddenly you will find yourself out of the rut routine and on a new path, feeling energized and ready to tackle other such challenges in your bucket list.

結論
Conclusion

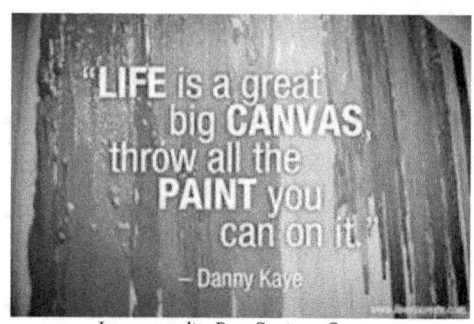

Image credit: Best Sayings Quotes

　　生活的畫布剛開始都是空白的，等待著被稱為經驗的藝術家添加大而明亮的色塊以逐漸形成圖像。隨著我們的生活不斷向前，這幅畫從未處於完好無損的狀態，痛苦和令人愉悅的時刻不斷添加到畫面中。有時我們能控制藝術家，而其他時候則不能。除了經驗豐富的藝術家之外，我們還從許多幫助我們繪圖的人那裡收穫寶貴的貢獻。個體的每次互動都會留下一個印記，聯繫越緊密，這些顏色在畫布上的顯示就越多。透過經驗和個人相遇可以使人感受到人生的豐富性。

　　The canvas of life starts out blank and colorless waiting for the artist known as experience to begin adding both bold and bright colors to slowly form an image. The picture is never quite finished as we live and continue to add to the painting with both painful and pleasurable moments. Sometimes we control the artist and other times we do not. In addition to the experience artist we also find valuable contributions from the many people who help in building our picture. Each personal interaction leaves a mark and the more intimate the connection the more those colors appear on the canvas. The richness of life is felt through experience and personal encounters.

我非常感謝人生中的許多或好或壞的經歷。有許多經歷是我所追求的，而有些經歷我希望它們從未發生，但無論如何，我仍然必須全神貫注。不管是豐富的經驗還是較小的經驗，我都逐漸嘗試去體會每種經驗對我人生的貢獻。這些經驗的最終影響幫助塑造了我對教育和領導能力的看法。在經歷失敗和成功的時間裡，我的觀點被雕刻和塑造出來，形成了我目前的思想和觀念。如果我以正確的心態看待每種體驗，那麼它們都能夠對我有所貢獻。

I am so grateful for the many good and bad experiences in my life. Many of the experiences I have sought after and others I wished had not happened, but all had to be absorbed nonetheless. Whether the experience was profound or minor in comparison, I have grown to try to appreciate the contribution each experience has had in my life. It is the culminating impact of these experiences that have helped shape my thoughts on both education and leadership. Through times of both failure and success my view is chiseled and shaped and forms my immediate thoughts and ideas. Each experience can have something to add if I view it with the right mindset.

為這幅人生畫面做出深刻貢獻的另一個群體是我生命中的人們。我畫布上顯眼的第一道顏料來自我親密的家人。從家中五個孩子之一的人成長到到自己擁有五個孩子的人，每種關係對我都有著重要的意義，而且永遠都無法取代。老實說，我對生命中的人的重視程度超過了對經驗教訓的重視。由於大多數經驗無論如何都會有人參與，因此在為我的畫布上塗顏色時，人際關係的畫筆似乎要濃墨重彩得多。感謝我的大家庭為我的人生畫面提供了深層次的基調。

The other profound contribution to this life painting has been the people in my life. The obvious first paint on my canvas came from those in my intimate circle of family. From being a child in a family of five children to having my own family of five children, each relationship has something significant to offer and never replaced. To be truthful, I value the people in my life more than I do the lesson of experience. Since most experiences have people included anyway, relationships seem to have a much thicker paintbrush when applying color to my canvas. Thank you to my big family for providing a deep color base to my life painting.

我有很多朋友，他們也做出了很多貢獻。只是談朋友對我的影響就可以寫一整個章節，但我只想簡單地說，與朋友在一起的生活更加豐富多彩和充滿活力。對我來說，我知道我需要有人在身邊。有些人沒有太多朋友也能活得自在，我卻靠朋友維生。我希望我為他們的生活做出的貢獻與他們對我的人生所做的貢獻一樣。感謝朋友們，正是我們的互動塑造了我這些書頁中分享的想法。願你們在我逐漸成長期間依然對我保持耐心！

I have a lot of friends who have added greatly as well. I think I could write a whole chapter just on the impact friends has had on me, but I will simply state that life is far more colorful and vibrant with friends. For me, I know I need people close to me. Some people may fair well with fewer friends, but I survive on many friends. I hope I contribute to their life as much as they contribute to mine. Thank you friends, it is our interactions that have shaped ideas shared within these pages. May you continue to show patience for me as I slowly grow up!

從廣義上講而重要性絲毫不減的是，許多為我的畫面做出貢獻的是偉大的導師領袖。如果不是他們相信我，我懷疑自己是否會相信自己。也許我的DNA決定了我會成為誰，但我相信我的命運受到那些努力塑造我的人的極大影響。許多無私的老師來到我的身邊，這幫助我找到了我的強項，增強了我的長處，知道了我的弱點，並且知道了面對人生挑戰的益處。我不能說我一直都享受這個挑戰中的痛苦，但是我聽到他們內心深處的聲音說，這一切到最後都是值得的。他們沒有讓學習成績簡單地變成我的自我價值感。他們鼓勵我努力，但又以某種方式使我相信，我的學業成就只是人生圖畫不斷變化過程的一小部份而已。學生的自我價值遠遠超出他們所取得的考試成績，並且在此過程中的成長遠重於結果本身。感謝老師們，你們的藝術貢獻深刻地塑造了我的圖畫。

On a broad level, but not necessarily in a diminished role, has been the many great teacher leaders who have contributed to my painting. Had it not been for their belief in me, I doubt that I would have believed in myself. Maybe my DNA was wired to pre-determine whom I would become, but I believe my destiny was heavily influenced by those who worked so hard to shape me. Many selfless teachers poured into me which helped me find my sweet spot, enhance my strengths, know my weaknesses, and know the benefits of accepting a challenge in life. I can't say I always love the pain in the process, but I hear their voices inside my head saying this, too, will be worth it in the end. They did not let my academic results simply become my sense of self-worth or value. They encouraged me to work hard but somehow helped me believe that my academic results were just a small and temporary part of the changing landscape of the picture being painted. A student's self-worth is far greater than the grade earned, and the growth found in the process is greater than the outcome itself. Thank you to the teachers. My picture was profoundly shaped by your artistic contributions.

在一些非常好的經歷和一些非常好的人啟發下，我寫了這本書。在過去的十年中，我有幸去了中國許多次。訴說這一切如何開始的故事太長，我們只能說是一件事導致了另一件事，而一種關係又導向了另一件事，總之最終的結果是，我在旅途中收獲了很棒的人生經歷，遇見了無數偉大的人。我最初的目的只是參觀我的國際營員生活的地方，最後卻成了在一個令人驚嘆的國家/地區培訓老師和營地負責人的機會。我現在每年都要來回幾次以培訓中國的老師，了解他們的團隊成長過程，以及如何在師生之間建立更個人化的課堂。為什麼？因為我的圖畫正是這些類型的人和經歷描繪出來的。

  I was inspired to write this book because of a some really great experiences and some really great people. I have been fortunate to make many trips to China over the past 10 years. The story of how this started is far too long but let's just say one thing led to another and one relationship invited another and the end result is that I have had great life experience and met nothing but great people on these trips. What turned out to initially be a visit to see where my international campers lived has turned into the opportunity to train teachers and camp leaders in an amazing country. Now, I travel a back and forth a few times each year training Chinese teachers about the Group Growth Process and how to have a more personally connected classroom between teacher and students. Why? Because it has been these types of people and experiences that paint the picture.

  我的希望是激勵人們無私奉獻，我就曾受到這樣的對待，讓學生知道自己的價值遠遠超出他們所取得的成績。他們以某種方式說服我，儘管上學是一種經歷，但這並不是我唯一可以學習的經歷。與我的人生教育相比，我在學校的時間非常短暫。我相信人們在我身上進行了一些重要的投入，並且在學校中曾發生了一些非常重要的領導機會。我認為我的教練和我從事體育運動的經驗，與我曾經擁有的任何基礎經驗同等重要。感謝老師們，特別是唐.馬丁代爾的耐心和堅持。你的貢獻為你的筆刷提供了大量鮮艷的色彩。

  My hope is to inspire someone to do for a student what was selflessly done for me - reach out and let them know they have value far beyond their grade earned. They somehow convinced me that even though school was an experience to be had, it would not be the only experience I would learn from. My time spent in school was brief in comparison to the education I would get living life. I believe there were some significant investments made in me by people and some very important leadership opportunities that happened in school. I consider my coaches and my experience playing sports as to be as vital as any foundational experience I ever had. Thank you to the many teachers, in in particular one - Don Martindale - for the patience and persistence. Your contributions provided massive strokes of bright colors with your brush.

與你信任的家人、朋友、老師和領導相處，你知道他們會想幫助你成為一個更好的人。擁抱生活為人生圖畫增添的色彩。有時，顏色是柔和且有意添加進去的，但有時候又似乎是一種飛濺的顏料，使你在畫筆每次刷動時都發出驚嘆。請吸收它，從中學習，並嘗試將其視為正在進行但尚未完成的藝術品的一部份。

Surround yourself with good family, friends, teachers, and leaders who you trust, and who you know want to help make you a better person. Embrace the color that life adds to the painting. Sometimes the color is added softly and with great intention and other times it seems as if it is a splatter paint that leaves you gasping at each flick of the brush. Absorb it, learn from it and try to appreciate it as being part of an ongoing, yet unfinished work of art.

團隊成長過程涉及經驗和人員。二者緊密相連，不可分割。你處於領導者的位置（例如老師）時，請意識到你班上的學生就像我一樣，排在倒數第四位而努力想找到作為學生的價值。請確保你不會忽視那些學生，或錯誤地讓他們覺得自己沒有在未來做出貢獻的價值。相反地，你應該認識到，作為有影響力的人生領導者，你有能力透過在圖畫中添加色彩來改變某人的人生軌跡。他們的回報可能不是立竿見影的，或許要等到他們將來寫書時才會出現，但無論如何，還是請你無私地傾注，讓他們感到自己受到關愛和珍惜，且在你握住畫筆的短暫一刻，為他們畫上鮮豔愉悅且主導他們生命那一刻的色彩。教師為每個學生的生活增添色彩，這種色彩比任何給定的知識都能持續更長的時間。這才是真正的教育。

The Group Growth Process involves both experience and people. They are intimately connected and unable to be separated. When placed in a position of leadership, such as a teacher is, please realize that in your class is a student just like me. Ranked fourth from the bottom and struggling to feel value as a student. Make sure you do not overlook that student or mistakenly make him/her feel as if they may have nothing of value to contribute in the future. Instead, recognize that as an influential life leader you have the power to change the course of someone's life by adding your color touches to their painting. Their payback may not be immediate, or it may come when that student writes a book in the future, but nonetheless, pour selflessly into them so they feel loved and valued for that temporary time that you hold the paintbrush in your hands and hopefully apply bright and happy colors that dominate the picture for that time in their life. Teachers apply color to the life of each student which will last longer than any content knowledge given. This is true teaching.

額外材料
Bonus Material

Facilitating the Group Growth Process
引導團隊成長過程

成為有意識的「建築師」，為團隊設定方向和目標
*Become the intentional architect
of the direction and destination of your group*

Image credit: Ray Chong

聯繫活動
Connection Activities

這個額外部份旨在透過為引導者配備一些簡單的遊戲和活動來提高他們的能力，他們可以利用這些遊戲和活動來塑造通往預定目的地的過程。這些活動可能並不總是能將你的團隊帶到所需的**目的地**，但是它們至少可以幫助你按照希望的**方向**帶領你的團隊。

This bonus section is designed to empower facilitators by equipping them with some simple games and activities, which they can utilize to shape the process of moving towards an intended destination. The activities may not always take your group to the desired d**estination,** but they can at least help guide the group in the **direction** you want them to go.

了解團隊成長過程
Understanding the Group Growth Process

每當一群人第一次（或頭幾次）聚在一起時，成長過程就會啟動。這種成長不僅發生在當下的個體中，而且還發生在整個群體中。編寫本手冊的目的是為引導者配備工具，使他們能夠帶領團隊朝預期的方向前進。這樣可以確保更有效地實現你的目標或團隊目標。

Anytime a group of individuals comes together for the first time (or first few times), a growth process is initiated. The growth occurs not only in the individuals present, but also in the group as a whole. This booklet is written to equip the facilitator with tools that empower the facilitator to move the group in the intended direction. This ensures that your objective or destination for the group can be more effectively achieved.

重要的是要了解，無論是否存在有意的設計，團隊的成長過程都會發生。作為領導者，努力成為過程中有意識的建築師，以便實現想要的結果。

It is important to understand that the group growth process is going to happen with or without your intentional design. As a leader, strive to be the intentional architect of the design process so you can achieve your desired results.

有許多因素可能會阻礙團隊的方向和成長。這些因素包括：目的、團隊規模、社群的感覺、引導者的經驗、引導者與團隊必須共處時間的長短，甚至包括團隊成員的個性等。良好的領導能力和團隊管理的關鍵是要認識到這一過程中的力量，並意識到透過利用它，引導者／領導者是可以指導和激發團隊成長過程的建築師。

There are many factors that may impede the direction and growth of a group. These include: purpose, group size, the feeling of the community, the experience of the facilitator, the length of time the facilitator must work with the group, and even the personalities of those within the group. A key to good leadership and group management is to recognize the power in this process and to realize that by harnessing it, the facilitator/leader is the architect that can guide and inspire the group growth process.

許多人發現團隊的成長經歷很難堪，在社交上讓人不舒服。社交上充滿自信和外向的參與者最終承擔了大部份的社交風險，而害羞和內向的人則感到這種社交實驗令他們很痛苦。強有力的引導者可以識別團隊中的不同個性，觀察解社會規範的形成，並設計活動以幫助引導團隊朝著預期的方向前進。這便是引導的藝術。透過利用有目的性、參與性和趣味性的活動，團隊成長過程的有效性可以牢牢掌握在引導者的手中，而不會是偶發事件。

Many people find the group growth experience to be awkward and socially uncomfortable. Participants who are socially confident and outgoing end up taking most of the social risks, while the shy and reserved find this type of social experiment painful. The strong facilitator can recognize the personalities in the group, see the social norms forming, and design activities to help guide the direction of the group towards the intended destination. This is the art of facilitation. By utilizing purposeful, engaging, and fun activities, the effectiveness of the group growth process can be firmly in the hands of the facilitator and not left to chance.

方向與目的地
Direction vs. Destination

Image credit: Lundbeck.com

了解你希望團隊到達的目的地至關重要，這樣你才能知道前進的方向。

It is crucial to know where you want the group to end up so you can know the direction to take.

為了這些目的，「團隊」這個詞用於表示出於某個目的或目標而聚集在一起的人的集合。無論是一次聚會還是重覆聚會，大多數團隊都會有聚會的目的。它可能是一班聚集學習的學生，或者是為設計學習目的而進行交流的教師或系部。也可能是一群在工作場所聚集在一起訓練的同事。無論何種情況，「團隊」都因為某個目的地（結果或目的）而結合在一起。

For these purposes, the term "group" is used to refer to the collection of individuals brought together for a purpose or objective. Whether it is for a one-time gathering or for repeated gatherings, most groups will have an objective or purpose for meeting. It may be a class of students gathering to learn, or a faculty or department of teachers who communicate together for the purpose of designing the learning. It could also be a group of colleagues in the workplace who gather to train. Whatever the occasion, the "group" has come together with a destination (result or purpose) in mind.

作為引導者，你將充當建築師，設計團隊成長過程的方式。你的領導角色至關重要，它將決定過程的成敗。如果你控制過度，團隊可能會拒絕你的指導。而如果你太被動，你可能會被團隊中更為強大的領導者所取代。有效的引導需要自信、領導經驗、具有吸引力的性格、創建清晰願景的能力，以及閱讀和操縱各種個性特徵的能力。一旦成功，引導者將提高團隊的互動關係，並在整個過程中為團隊的成功做出貢獻。

As a facilitator, you serve as the architect who will design how the group growth process will unfold. Your leadership role is crucial and can make or break the process. If you are too controlling, the group may resist your guidance. If you are too passive, you may lose control to stronger leaders within the group. Effective facilitation requires self-confidence, leadership experience, an engaging personality, the ability to cast a clear vision and the ability to read and manipulate various personality characteristics. When successful, the facilitator increases the efficiency of the group dynamic and contributes to the success of the group throughout the process.

> 「你不能在一夜之間更改目的地，但你可以在一夜之間改變方向。」
> ― 吉姆. 羅恩
> "You cannot change your destination overnight, but you can change your direction overnight." – Jim Rohn

成為好引導者的五個簡單要點
Five Simple Keys to Being a Good Facilitator

除了死之外，人們最害怕的就是公開演講！我說的不是在一大群人面前講話，我說的是那些連在十五個、十個、甚至五個人面前講話都成問題的人。要成為一名良好的引導者，必須在各種規模的團隊面前表現自如。引導者需要意識到，每個團隊的引導機會中都有一個表演要素。為了提高效率，引導者必須表現得很自在，並與一群參與者一起工作。對於那些感到恐懼的人，我有個好消息。這種引導的信心和技巧是可以透過練習來培養的！對於已經熟悉此過程的人員，你已經清除了團隊引導的第一大障礙。

Second to dying, people are most afraid of public speaking! I am not just talking about speaking in front of large crowds. I'm talking about those who feel incapacitated to speak in front of only 15, 10 or even just 5 people. To be a good facilitator, one must be comfortable in front of groups of various sizes. Facilitators need to realize that there is an element of performance in each group facilitation opportunity. To be effective, the facilitator must appear comfortable speaking and working with a group of participants. For those who find this fearful, there is good news. This facilitation confidence and skill can be developed through practice! For those already comfortable with the process, you have cleared the first hurdle in group facilitation.

1. 擁抱表現——爭取在他人面前站立或講話的經驗。為了舒展你自己，請先寫一些事前準備的內容（最好是你感興趣的話題），然後簡單地閱讀你準備的內容。這可能在學生和教職員工面前進行，或者你可能是加入讀書俱樂部這樣的安全場所，讓你可以在一個團隊中表達自己。這是第一個障礙。如果你不能在別人面前表現出自信，那麼你可能很難帶領或引導一個團隊實現預定的目標。

1, Embrace the performance - Gain experience standing or speaking in front of others. To stretch yourself, start with something pre-written (preferably a topic you are interested in) and simply read what you have prepared. This could be in front of students, faculty, or maybe you join a book club as a safe place to express yourself in a small group. This is the first hurdle. If you cannot gain confidence performing in front of others, you will likely struggle to lead or facilitate a group towards an intended goal.

2. 設計你的過程——理想情況下，每個團隊或會議都應有明確的目的。作為引導者，你要確定自己知道原因。了解聚會目的可以幫助你設計預期成果的活動。引導者可能會被派到一個功能失調的團隊中，或帶領一個成員互不相識的團隊。了解你帶領的團隊的目的地，以便精心設計指導過程。

2. Design your process - Ideally, each group or meeting should have a defined purpose for gathering. As a facilitator, you want to make sure you know the reason for the gathering. Knowing the purpose for meeting helps you design the activities for the intended outcome. A facilitator may be brought into a dysfunctional group or lead a group where members may not know each other. Know your group destination so you can carefully design the process of direction.

3. 超額準備，以便超額完成——成為一個好的引導者需要經驗和實踐。作為引導者，你應該具有良好的語言和表達能力。你應該具有吸引人的個性，以贏得團隊的關注和信心。熟悉你手上的資料，使自己顯得知識淵博且能夠自如地傳遞內容。在設計團隊時間時，請多做準備，以便超額完成。這也使你可以在整個過程中解讀你的團隊，並在必要時更輕鬆地進行改變。

3. Over prepare so you over deliver - Being a good facilitator takes experience and practice. As facilitator, you are expected to use good language and presentation skills. You should have an appealing personality to gain the attention and confidence of the group. Know your material so that you appear knowledgeable and comfortable delivering the content. As you design your group time, over-prepare so you can over-deliver. This will also allow you to read the group throughout the process, and it will allow you to make changes more easily when needed.

4. 成為將要發生的團隊成長過程的一部份——經驗豐富的引導者通常對團隊可能會最終到達的目的地很了解，但是由於團隊成員的個性，最終目標的路徑（方向）總是各不相同。敬業的引導者會為他引導的團隊準備替代活動。團隊成員將顯示不同的個性。會有一些人只是坐著，聽著，然後按照你的要求去做。其他人會坐著，不聽，實際上也不會按照你的要求去做。你可能會遇到領導者性格，有人甚至可能試圖（有意或無意）劫持你的團隊，或至少控制引導者的時間和精力。引導者不僅是流程的建築師，而且還是貢獻者。你如何「利用」你的個性來進行引導非常重要。你應該保持足夠的警醒，以適應房間中的各種個性，並在需要引導時足夠靈活以幫助引導團隊。有時，當需要這種視角時，引導者只需要坐下來觀察。

4. Be part of the Group Growth Process that will take place - An experienced facilitator usually has a good idea where the group will likely end up, but the path (direction) to the end goal is always different because of the personalities of those in the group. Engaged facilitators are prepared to propose alternate activities as they read the pulse of the group. Group members will display different personalities. There will be those who simply sit, listen, and do what you ask them to do. Others will sit, not listen, and really not do what they are being asked to do. You may encounter leader personalities who may even try to (knowingly or unknowingly) hijack the group, or at least dominate the time and attention of the facilitator. The facilitator is not just the architect of the process, but also a contributing member. How you "use" your personality to facilitate is very important. You should be alert enough to embrace the various personalities in the room and flexible enough to help steer the group, when it needs to be steered. Sometimes, a facilitator just needs to sit back and observe, when that perspective is needed.

5. 平易近人——許多小組成員會因為性格或不安全感有關的多種原因而害怕與引導者建立聯繫。也有其他人會積極接觸引導者來佔用你的時間和注意力。作為引導者，你必須平易近人。一個好的引導者將在活動中、休息時間或會議前後和參與者積極互動。這對於你與正在共處的人建立聯繫是非常寶貴的時間。平易近人包括具有良好的社交能力，例如：進行眼神交流、微笑、展示出聆聽的能力、以適當的身體觸摸（握手，擁抱，擊掌）表現出舒適感、語氣柔和宜人、表現出提問探究的能力，或提供誠實的答案等。最重要的是，一個好的引導者必須具備謙遜的品質。

5. Be approachable - Many group members will be fearful to approach the facilitator for any number of reasons related to personality or insecurity. There will also be others who will actively seek out the facilitator to control your time and attention. As a facilitator, you must be approachable. A good facilitator will actively engage with the participants during activities, during breaks, or before and after meetings. This is extremely valuable time for you to connect with those you are working with. Being approachable involves having good social skills such as: making eye contact, wearing an inviting smile, demonstrating the ability to listen, showing a comfort level with appropriate physical touch (handshake, hug, high-five), having a soft and welcoming tone of voice, showing the ability to ask probing questions or provide honest answers. Above all, a good facilitator must be humble.

使用遊戲和活動建立連結
Building a Connection Using Games & Activities

Image credit: Inc.com

建立團隊之間的聯繫（在課堂、在辦公室、在教職員之間等）對於最終取得成功至關重要。為此，你需要花費時間和精力進行仔細的計劃和設計。作為建築師，引導者必須對團隊的最終目標有清晰的認識，以便制定有效的計劃，提升成功的機率。不管有沒有你的存在，團隊的成長過程都會發生，但若要成功，引導者就需要明智地指導成長過程。

Building connection within your group (classroom, office, faculty, etc.) is imperative for ultimate success. To do so requires the intentional investment of your time and energy into careful planning and design. As the architect, the facilitator must have a clear vision of where the group should end up so that an effective plan can be created to increase the chances of success. The Group Growth Process will happen with or without you, but to be successful, the facilitator needs to wisely guide the growth process.

以下十項活動可用於補充你的引導技巧，並幫助你制定計劃，以最佳方式指導團隊的成長過程。如何使用它們以及何時使用它們取決於你的直覺、舒適度以及團隊的期望方向。有些活動可以直接導致或支持你想要的設計，而另一些活動可能只是「打破常規」的活動，用於有趣的過渡或當你需要從內容中解放出來時。作為目標建築師，你可以自行決定何時何地使用它們。可以對它們進行修改，以適應各種標準、團隊目標或時間分配。冒險並嘗試其中的一些吧！

　　The following 10 activities can be used to complement your facilitation skills and help you design plans for how to best direct the group growth process. How you use them, and when you use them, depends upon your instincts, comfort level, and desired direction for the group. Some activities can directly lead to, or support, your intended program design, while others may simply be "break the script" activities for when you just need a fun transition or brain relief from the content. As the intentional architect, you decide when and where to use them. Activities like these can be easily modified to accommodate various criteria, group objectives, or time allotted. Take a risk and try some of them out!

　　在進行每項活動時，你必須考慮自己的個性、引導力量以及每個團隊的動態感覺。你可能會覺得有必要進行修改，這些修改對於你的團隊目標、過程或團隊的方向性成長很重要或很恰當。你儘可隨意修改。這些活動只具引導性，不是必須遵行的腳本。任何活動要產生影響，關鍵都在於引導者。練習你的引導技巧，以便發揚你的長處，而你的弱點也不至於阻礙整個團隊的成長過程。

　　With each activity, you must consider your personality, facilitation strengths, and the perceived dynamics of each group. You may feel the need to create modifications you see as important or appropriate to the group objectives, process, or directional growth of the group. Feel free to do so. They serve as a guide to use, not a script to follow. The key to any impactful activity rests predominantly with the facilitator. Practice your facilitation skills so that your strengths develop and so your weaknesses do not hinder the overall group growth process.

　　1. 名字遊戲——大家圍成一圈，參加者花點時間思考他們名字的首字。我們的任務是想一個正面的形容詞（不要用自我貶低的形容詞），該形容詞與其名字的首字相同；這可能還會使其他人洞悉與他們的性格有關的特徵或他們希望別人如何看待他們。

例如，「嗨，我叫爵士簡，因為我喜歡演奏爵士樂。」或，「嗨，我叫謹慎卡爾，因為我在新的社交環境中表現得比較害羞。」（譯註：為了適合中文名字，可以考慮這兩個例子：「嗨，我叫張美宣，因為我擅長美術宣傳。」「嗨，我叫劉志勤，因為我的志向是保持勤儉。」）

1. **NAME GAME** - With each person sitting in a circle, the participants to take a moment to think about the first letter of their first name. The task is to think of a positive-sounding (no self-putdowns) adjective that begins with the same letter of their first name; one that might also give others insight into characteristics related to their personality or how they want others to perceive them.

For example, "Hi my name is Jazzy Jane because I like to play Jazz music." Or, "Hi, my name is Cautious Carl because I am usually shy in new social situations.

2. **溝通隊列**——首先，讓參與者排成兩條平行的隊列，這樣每個人對面都有一個伙伴，兩個隊列距離約為一米。目的是「強迫」對話並營造一種氛圍，讓參與者可以感受並處理他們的脆弱性。主持人透過提供「交流話題」來指導活動，雙方可以在給定的時間內討論和分享。交流主題可以從愜意的幽默環境到有關主題數據、內容、感覺或公司的使命和價值觀的問題等。可能性是無止境的。

例如，「與你的伙伴討論你小時候做過的夢？」或「與你的伙伴分享你想共進晚餐的名人，以及原因。」或者，如果你希望它與主題內容或數據有關，請說出這個問題，以便學生互相討論自己學到的知識。活動的目標可以進行改變，以滿足你的需求。

你可以決定讓大家保留相同的伙伴，也可以在每個問題後讓其中一個隊列向前移動一個位置。

2. LINES OF COMMUNICATION - Begin by having participants form two parallel lines so each person is facing a partner with about one meter of space separating the lines. The object is to "force" conversation and create an atmosphere where vulnerability is felt and dealt with by the participants. The facilitator guides the activity by offering "communication topics" which both individuals can discuss and share for a given length of time. Communication topics can vary from random humorous circumstances to questions about subject data, content, feelings, or the mission and values of a company. The possibilities are endless.

For example, "Discuss with your partner a popular dream you had as a child?" or, "Share with your partner the name of a famous person you would love to have dinner with and why?" Or, if you want it to be about subject content or data, phrase the questions so students are discussing what they have learned with one another. The objective for the activity can change to meet your needs.

You can decide to keep the same partners or have 1 line move down 1 space after each question.

3. 思考 / 配對 / 分享——這是一種簡單但有效的團隊活動，可用於分享想法、感覺、情感，甚至評估學習或發現學習內容的差距。首先是結對。一種簡單的方法是讓團隊成員找到在身高上最接近他們的伙伴（或使用你想要的任何配對條件）。目標是快速而有效地為活動創建配對，並避免朋友或熟人為了舒適而結成對。然而，事實上，這些結成的對子將隨著每個主題而變化，因此在整個活動中，人們最終都將轉移到一個新的伙伴上。

配對後，引導者可以向整個班級介紹討論的話題（與內容有關或與內容無關）。鼓勵兩人輪流分享和回應。一個人發言時，另一人應記下他所講的內容。演講者說完他們關心的所有內容後，聽眾就會「重述」前者所說的內容，保證其清晰度和含義。切換角色。完成所有人的工作後，想出一種創新的方式來切換伙伴。

3. THINK/PAIR/SHARE - This is a simple but effective group activity that can be used to share ideas, feelings, emotions, or even assess learning or reveal gaps in content learned. Begin by creating partner pairs. One simple way is to ask group members to find a partner who is closest to them in height (or use any matching criteria you want). The goal is to quickly and effectively create pairs for the activity and to possibly avoid friends or acquaintances pairing up for comfort sake. However, the truth is, these pairs will change with each topic, so they will end up moving to a new partner quite a bit throughout this activity.

Once pairs are made, the facilitator can present the entire class with the discussion topic (content or non-content related). Encourage the pair to take turns sharing and responding. While one is speaking, the other should take notes on what is said. Once the speaker has said all they care to, the listener "restates" what was said to ensure clarity and meaning. Switch roles. Once everyone is done, come up with a creative way to switch partners.

4. 公車站——該活動是一種揭示性的冒險活動。要求參與者用椅子排成兩個單獨的隊列。（如果團隊人數為十五人或更少，則排成一列。如果人數超過十五，可排成兩列，以便所有人都能聽到你的指令。）排成列後，要求每個人坐下。說明他們都在公車上，且公車將沿著路線在不同站點停靠。至於下車，只需根據他們想給的答案站在他們的椅子的左邊或右邊即可。

每個公車「停靠站」都是引導者給出的一對詞語。聆聽然後對給出的單詞做出反應將確定團隊成員站到隊列的哪一側。如果坐車的人識別或喜歡第一個單詞，他們可以站在椅子的「右」側「離開公共汽車」。如果他們認同或偏愛第二個單詞，他們可以站在椅子的「左」側「離開公共汽車」。如果他們一個詞都不喜歡或沒有意見，則可以繼續坐在公共汽車上。

可以考慮從簡單的選擇開始。 根據你何時進行此活動，建議從一些非常基本的概念配對開始，例如：早餐或晚餐。如果他們喜歡早餐，他們會「下車」並站在椅子的右側。如果晚餐是優選的選擇，那麼他們會站起來並站到左側。如果他們沒有偏好，則可以繼續坐在車上。

該活動可以塑造為你的團隊目標，包括主題內容，術語和定義，數學問題的答案或揭示對環境的情感反應。單詞配對也可以用來建立社群和娛樂。以下是可能的例子：炎熱或寒冷的天氣；水果或糖果，咖啡或茶，麵食或大米，冰淇淋或糖果，跑步或散步，自行車或摩托車。

4. BUS STOP - This activity is a revealing, risk-taking activity. Ask participants to form one or two single file lines using their chairs. (If you have a group of 15 or fewer, 1 line is preferred. If you have more than 15, form 2 lines so all can hear your instructions). Once the line is formed, ask each person to be seated. Explain the scenario that they are all on the BUS and the bus is going to stop at different stops along the route. Getting off the bus is accomplished by simply standing to the LEFT or RIGHT of their chair, depending on the answer they want to give.

Each bus "stop" is a pair of words given by the facilitator. Listening and then reacting to the words given will determine which side of the bus they exit on. If the rider identifies with or prefers the first word, they "exit the bus" by standing on the "RIGHT" side of their chair. If they identify with or prefer the second word, they "exit the bus" by standing on the "LEFT" side of their chair. If they do not prefer either word or have no opinion, they may remain seated on the bus.

Consider starting with simple choices. Depending on when you present this activity, it may be advisable to start with a few very basic concept pairings such as: BREAKFAST or DINNER. If they prefer Breakfast they would "exit" and stand on the RIGHT side of their chair. If dinner is the preferred choice, they rise and stand on the LEFT side. If they have no preference, they can remain on the bus.

The activity can be molded to your group objective, including subject content, terms and definitions, answers to math problems, or to reveal emotional responses to circumstances. Word pairings can also be used to build community and fun. Examples might include: HOT or COLD weather; FRUIT or CANDY, COFFEE or TEA, NOODLE or RICE, ICE CREAM or CANDY, RUNNING or WALKING, or BICYCLE or MOTORCYCLE.

5. 快速餅乾——快速餅乾是一項有趣的活動，其中兩個團隊在主題內容範圍內或僅為娛樂而選擇的主題上互相競爭。首先創建兩條平行的參與者隊列，相互之間的距離為五英尺（主持人可以沿著這些線的中間走動）。目的是在五秒鐘內對已宣佈的主題給出正確的（且不重覆的）答案。如果回答正確，則轉至另一隊，後者有機會提供新的、正確的和未給出的答案。如果一個團隊犯了錯誤（重覆已經說過的答案、給出錯誤答案或根本沒有給出答案），則另一個團隊將獲得一分，並有權選擇一個新類別。遊戲從另一個類別繼續進行。

例如，給定的主題類別是：水果。第一個排隊的第一人必須提供準確的答案，才能「傳遞」給另一個團隊。他們大聲說：「蘋果。」現在輪到另一支隊伍，第一人說「梨」；答題的嘗試繼續在團隊之間來回移動，直到有人給出錯誤或重覆的答案（或五秒鐘內給不出答案）為止。這是一項輕鬆的活動，其中可包含主題內容訊息。

5. FAST COOKIE - Fast cookie is a fun activity where 2 teams compete against each other in subject content areas or topics selected just for fun. Begin by creating two parallel lines of participants separated by 5 feet (enough for the facilitator to walk down the middle of the lines). The object is to give the correct (AND UNREPEATED) answers within 5 seconds to the announced topic. If answered correctly, the turn moves to the other team who is given the chance to provide a new, correct and UNREPEATED answer. If a team makes a mistake (by repeating an already stated answer, answering incorrectly, or not having an answer at all) a point shall be awarded to the other team and a new category is chosen. The game continues from where it left off with another category.

For example, the topic category given is: FRUITS. The first person in line one must provide an accurate answer in order to "pass" the attempt to the other team. They loudly say, "Apple." The turn now moves to the other team and their first person says, "PEAR." The answer attempt continues moving back and forth between the teams and down the line until such time as an incorrect or repeated answer is given (or no answer at all after 5 seconds). This is an easy activity in which to include subject content data.

6. 互動之輪——對於這項活動，你需要足夠的空間來圍成一個大圓圈，並在外部圓圈的內部形成一個較小的圓圈。讓一半的參與者形成一個內圈，並排站立，但面對外圈。其餘所有參與者將面對「內圈」的一個人。擁有相等的數字很重要，因此每個人都必須與圈子中的另一個人配對。如果參與者的數量為奇數，則你可以考慮加入，以形成偶數。

告訴團隊，你將給他們一個單獨的話題。他們將與面對的伙伴一起輪流進行響應。根據你的目標，建議每個人的響應時間限制為六十或九十秒。彼此分享後，請伙伴們在繼續前進之前提出一些離開的手勢（擊掌、握手、握拳）。讓他們知道，在你執行「旋轉」命令時，輪子的外圓將向左移動一個位置（如果你想的話，也可以向右移動）。輪子的內圈不旋轉。它保持不動。當大家有了「新」伙伴時，他們應該進行簡單的自我介紹，並詢問對方的名字、生日和最喜歡的電影（或發起對話的內容），以增進彼此的了解。他們這樣做之後，請在與以前相同的時限內提供一個新的討論主題。重覆此過程，以便他們與團隊中的五個或更多的人進行有關選定主題的互動對話。

6. WHEEL OF INTERACTION - For this activity, you need enough room space to form a large circle with a smaller circle inside of the outer one. Ask half of the participants to form an inner circle, standing shoulder to shoulder but facing toward what will become the outer circle. All remaining participants will stand facing ONE person on the "inner circle." It is important to have equal numbers, so each person is paired up opposite another person on the circle. If the number of participants is odd, you might consider joining in to even the numbers.

Instruct that you will be giving the entire group a single topic of conversation. Together, with the partner they are facing, they will take turns responding to the topic prompt. Depending on your objectives, it may be advised to say each person will be limited to a 60-90 second response time. After both have shared with one another, ask the partners to come up with some sort of departing gestures (high five, handshake, fist pump) before moving on. Let them know that on your command to "ROTATE," the outer circle of the wheel will move one space to the LEFT (or right if you prefer). The inner circle of the wheel does NOT rotate. It remains fixed. When they have their "new" partner, they should conduct a simple personal introduction and greeting of name, birth month, and favorite movie (or something to initiate the conversation) to help get to know one another. Once they have done so, provide a new topic for discussion with the same time limits as before. Repeat the process so they get to experience engaged conversation on selected topics with 5 or more people in the group.

7. 排隊——分成兩組參與者，每組人數相同。告訴大家，這是一個合作團隊活動，第一個正確完成任務的團隊將成為獲勝者。提醒他們必須正確完成任務，並要根據你可能對小組施加的任何條件（例如不講話）完成任務。

引導者將調出命令「按姓氏開頭字母順序排列」。第一個這樣做的人便「贏得」了這一點。你可以決定添加一些條件，例如「不允許任何人講話」或「某些人（可能是最大聲的人）不許講話」。更改條件或限制可以幫助創建有趣的團隊動態。

排隊的點子：

- 根據的出生月份和日期排列
- 按姓的字順序排列（譯註：中文名字可用注音符號或漢語拼音）
- 按名的字順序排列（譯註：中文名字可用注音符號或漢語拼音）
- 按出生那個月的日期（一號至三十一號）排隊
- 根據鞋子的尺寸排列
- 按年齡排列——從大到小
- 按高中畢業年份排隊
- 按出生體重排隊

活動問題可以進行調整，以滿足許多團隊的成長目標。

7. LINE UP - Form 2 groups of participants with the same numbers in each group. Reveal that this is a cooperative group activity, and the first group to finish the task correctly will be declared the winner. Remind them that the task must be done correctly and according to any conditions you may put on the group (such as no speaking).

The facilitator will call out the command, "Line up in alphabetical order according to last name." The first group to do so "wins" the point. You may decide to add conditions, such as "no one is permitted to speak" or "certain people (those who may be the loudest) are not permitted to speak." Changing the conditions or restrictions can help create interesting group dynamics.

Line Up Ideas:
- Line up according to your birth month and day.
- Line up in alphabetical order by last name.
- Line up in alphabetical order by first name.
- Line up by the day of the month you were born (1st-31st)
- Line up by shoe size.
- Line up by age - oldest to youngest
- Line up by high school graduation year.
- Line up by birth weight

Activity questions can be adapted to meet many group growth objectives.

8. 驕傲起立——當試圖了解一個團隊時，這是個很好的初始活動。你發現的內容可以導致更深入的對話、聯繫和理解。對於此活動，不需要進行特殊設置。無論房間的設置或設計如何，都可以提問。主持人只是問一些問題，「如果」適用，參與者只需要站起來。

例如：如果你曾經去過美國，請驕傲地站起來

如果你很容易尷尬，請驕傲地站起來

如果你曾經獲得過一等獎，請驕傲地站起來

如果你喜歡麵條，請驕傲地站起來

如果你喜歡籃球，請驕傲地站起來

如果你在學校沒有通過考試，請驕傲地站起來

如果你觸犯法律並被抓住，請驕傲地站起來

8. STAND UP PROUD - This is a good initial activity when trying to get to know a group. What you discover can lead to deeper conversations, connections, and understanding. For this activity there is no special set up needed. Questions can be asked regardless of the room set up or design. The facilitator simply asks questions and, "if" the question applies, the participants simply stand to their feet.

For example: Stand proud if you have ever travelled to the United States?

Stand proud if you embarrass easily?

Stand proud if you have ever won a first-place award?

Stand proud if you love noodles?

Stand proud if you love basketball?

Stand proud if you ever flunked a test in school?

Stand proud if you ever broke the law…and got caught.

9. 八種握手——這是一項很好的活動，可以幫助參與者安頓下來並建立彼此之間的聯繫。首先要求參與者排成兩條平行隊列（相距約三英尺），以便每個人都有一個伙伴。在每條平行線後的五到六英尺處創建一條「清晰的線」。（清晰的線只是為了下一次握手之前返回與各自的伙伴見面的地方）。

參與者將創造八個特殊的握手方式，當所有握手方式放在一起時，將成為一組獨一無二的握手方式，只有他們兩個人自己知道。鼓勵創造力，使他們的創造力與其他人有所不同。

一次創建一個「握手」方式。在創建、練習和掌握了握手的每個部份之後，每個伙伴將轉身退到在其後五至六英尺處創建的那條線。每個參與者只需回到自己的「空白線」，然後回到面對對方的原始位置。當合作伙伴聚集在一起時，他們將進行已建立的握手的所有部份，然後再添加下一個部份。重覆這個過程，直到每對都集齊八個獨特的握手部份並向團隊進行展示。

9. 8-PART HANDSHAKE - This is a good activity to help participants settle in and forge connections with each other. Begin by asking participants to form two parallel lines (about 3 feet apart) so each person has a partner. Create a "clear line" 5-6 feet behind each of the parallel lines. (The clear line is simply a place to go before returning to meet your partner when adding the next handshake).

Participants will be creating 8 special HANDSHAKES that, when all put together, will be a UNIQUE set of handshakes that only the 2 of them will know. Encourage creativity so theirs is different from what others may come up with.

Each handshake "segment" is created one at a time. After each segment of the handshake is created, practiced and mastered, each partner will turn and retreat to the line that was created 5-6 feet behind them. Each participant simply touches their "clear line" before returning to their original spot facing their partner. When the partners come together, they do any and all segments of the handshake already established before adding the next segment. This process is repeated until each pair has 8 unique handshake parts to show to the group.

10. 向下看／向上看——這是一個有趣且簡單的「打破常規」遊戲。形成小圈子的參與者（每六至八人為一組，站在一起）。每個小組都將玩同一個遊戲，但是當某個人「離開」時，他們將離開該小組並加入另一個小組。告訴參與者，儘管小組中沒有領導者，但仍需要有人負責進行口頭指示。

該活動從站立在圓圈上的成員之一發出的簡單口頭命令開始：「向下看，（暫停）向上看！」在「向下看」命令上，所有人的頭和眼睛都低頭看著地板。當發出「向上看」的指令時，所有參與者都將抬起頭，看著圈子中其他人的眼睛。如果兩個人碰巧彼此直接看向對方，那麼他們兩個都「出局」，離開小組並加入另外的圈子。（大家不可以移開視線，改變正在看的人）。

根據你有多少個圈子，一個圈子可能會減少到只有兩個人。他們可以選擇玩遊戲，或者只是等待邀請其他圈子中的人加入他們的行列。

10. LOOK DOWN/LOOK UP - This is a fun and simple "break the script" activity game. Form small circles of participants (6-8 standing in each group). Each group will be playing the same game, but when someone is "out" they will leave that group and join one of the others. Instruct participants that although there is no leader in the groups, someone will need to take charge to give the verbal directions.

The activity begins with simple verbal commands given by one of the members standing on the circle, "**Look down, (pause) Look up!**" On the "Look down" command, all heads and eyes look down at the floor. When the command, "Look up" is given, all participants will raise their heads and look at the eyes of someone else on the circle. If two individuals happen to be looking directly at one another, they are both "out" and they leave and go join different circles. (You may not look away or change the person you are looking at).

Depending how many circles you have, it is possible for a circle to get down to 2 people. They can choose to play or simply wait to invite someone who gets out in another circle to join them.

額外活動
Bonus Activities

額外活動 #1 把他們整合起來——這是一個非常有趣的活動,可在團隊第一次聚在一起時使用。(你要有足夠的身體空間供團隊移動,因此請確保沒有椅子、書桌或其他可能妨礙安全移動的障礙物。)

告訴團隊,作為引導者,你會拍手,你拍手的次數等於他們必須盡快形成的小組人數。例如,如果你拍手四次,參與者要迅速組成四人小組,彼此牽手抱成一團。

被「排除在外」的參加者被視為「出局」。但是,他們有機會在下次拍手時加入。

(注意:停下來並指出人類行為是很有趣的,例如他們意識到多出一個或兩個成員時而予以「推擠」時,或者他們意識到缺少一個或兩個人而從另一個群體「竊取」。)

Bonus #1 GROUP 'EM - This is a fun activity to be used the very first time a group is together. (You will want to ensure you have enough physical space for the group to move about, so make sure there are no chairs, desks, tables or other obstacles that could prevent safe movement.)

Instruct the group that, as facilitator, you will be clapping your hands. The number of claps you do is equal to the size of the group they must form as quickly as possible. For example, clap 4 times and participants quickly form groups of 4 people huddled and holding on to one another.

Participants who are "left out" of a group are considered "out." However, they have a chance to get back in on the next clapping number.

(Note: It is quite funny to stop and point out the human behavior you will see as groups "push out" a member when they realize they have 1 or 2 too many, or when they "steal" from another group when they realize they are short 1 or 2.)

額外活動 #2 如果你曾……就跟我動起來吧——這是一項有趣的活動，可以幫助發現有關團隊成員的一些有趣事實，或者透過查找團隊成員的共同點來建立更牢固的聯繫。這項活動需要足夠的空間，讓團隊站立成一個大的圓圈，每個人與兩側的人大概保持一臂的距離。每個參與者還需要某種位置標記，例如可以在圓圈上站立的塑膠貼點。如果在室內且空間不多，請使用膠帶甚或紙盤（不會輕易移動的東西）在圓圈上確定每個人的地點。

首先（圈子形成，且每人都有一個清晰的點位），引導者站在圈子中間，告訴大家，圈子上沒有額外的點位，但每個人都要得到一個 。如果點位被引導者成功搶走，別人可能最終將站在中間。中間的人以這句話開頭：「如果你曾……就跟我動起來吧。」中間的人用其認為可能適用於多個成員的詞來完成該語句，使他們離開圓圈點位。你可以規定中間的人必須完成他/她說的話，或不予執行，具體取決於你如何運作該活動。如果說的內容確實適用於圓圈中的任何人，那麼所應用的對象必須離開他們的位置並移至圈子中的另一個空點位。同時，在中心的人要試圖佔據一個空點位，迫使某人失去點位。在圓圈上沒有搶到點位的人將去到中心位置。

例如，「如果你曾經乘飛機，就跟我動起來吧！」則無論誰乘過飛機，都要離開他們的位置去佔據新的位置。你不能去佔領緊鄰你左邊或右邊的空位。你與原點位之間的距離至少應隔開一個位置。

Bonus #2 MOVE WITH ME...IF YOU EVER - This is a fun activity that can help uncover some interesting facts about members of the group or create stronger connections as a result of finding what group members have in common. This activity requires enough space for the group to stand in one large circle with about 1 arm length separating them from the person on either side of them. Each participant will also need some sort of place marker, like a rubber "poly-spot" on which to stand on the circle. If indoors, and you don't have poly-spots, use masking tape or even a paper plate (something that won't move too easily) to establish each person's spot on the circle.

To begin, (once the circle is formed and each person has a clear spot marked) the facilitator stands in the middle of the circle noting to the group that they do NOT have a spot on the circle, but that they would like to get one. If successful, someone else will end up standing in the middle. Whoever is in the middle is the person who starts with the same phrase: "Move with me if you ever…" The person in the middle completes the phrase with something that they think might apply to multiple members and get them moving off their spot on the circle. You can stipulate that the person in the middle has to have done what he/she says, or not, depending on how you want to run the activity. If what is said does apply to anyone on the circle, those to whom it applies must leave their spot and move to another open spot on the circle. At the same time, the person who was in the center is trying to occupy an open spot, forcing someone to be without a spot. Whoever is left without a place on the circle, takes over the center spot.

For example, "Move with me if you ever have flown on an airplane!" Whoever has flown on a plane is obligated to leave their spot to occupy a new spot. You may not take a spot that opens up on your immediate right or left. There must be at least 1 spot between you and the place from which you originated.

額外活動 #3 ZIP, ZAP, ZOOM——對於這個遊戲，團隊成員圍成六至八個參與者組成的小圈子。（較大的團隊也可以用，但效果不佳。）

該遊戲類似於「往下看，往上看」，沒有「領導者」，但需要一個人來啟動遊戲並保持下去。

該遊戲有一個模式，它總是以相同的Zip－Zap－Zoom模式進行 。

該模式中的每個單詞都伴隨著手勢：

——「ZIP」是將左手或右手抬到額頭處敬禮。ZIP（敬禮）手指指向的方向決定了圓圈中的誰必須用下一個手勢做出響應。

——「ZAP」要求將手抬至胸部敬禮（不是在額頭處）。同樣，這是用右手或左手完成的。手指指向的方向確定了該模式的第三個單詞也是最後一個單詞的響應對象。

——「ZOOM」是將雙手的手掌放在一起，手臂伸直，向前並指向圓圈中的其他人的響應。指向誰，誰就使用ZIP（敬禮）重新開始該模式。

當某人按順序犯任何錯誤時，他們「出局」，離開圈子。去參加正在進行的另一場比賽。

更改單詞：如果不用Zip, Zap, Zoom，可以改用：滴，答，砰，或你好，再見，我愛你。

Bonus #3　ZIP, ZAP, ZOOM - For this game, group members stand in small circles of 6-8 participants. (Larger groups can work, but not as effectively.)

This game, similar to "Look down, Look up", has no "leader" but needs a person to start the game and keep it going.

This game has a PATTERN and it always goes in the same pattern of Zip – Zap - Zoom.

There are hand motions that accompany each word in the pattern:

- "ZIP" is a salute with either the right hand or the left hand up to forehead. The direction that the ZIP (salute) fingers are pointing determines who in the circle must respond with the next hand gesture.

- "ZAP" requires a hand motion that is a chest high salute (not at the forehead). Again, this is done with the right or left hand. The direction the fingers point determines who is next to respond for the third and final word of the pattern.

- "ZOOM" is a response in which the palms of both hands are placed together, with the arms stretched out, forward, and pointing to someone else on the circle. Whoever is being pointed at starts the pattern over again, with ZIP (and the salute).

When someone makes a mistake, of any kind, in the sequence, they are "out", and they leave the circle. They must go and join another game in progress.

Change the words: Instead of Zip, Zap, Zoom, insert: Tick, Tock, Bang, or: Hello, Good-bye, I Love You.

關於作者
About the Author

　　史蒂夫.海恩斯是一名教育家、引導師、營地設計師兼指導員，在領導和引導學生和成人的團隊成長過程方面擁有二十五年以上的經驗。他用這二十五年時間教授中學歷史、衛生和體育課程，以及設計和指導兒童夏令營項目。這些豐富的經驗幫助他發展和提高了他作為團隊引導者和培訓負責人的技能。透過他的引導經歷，他注意到所有團隊都會經歷團隊成長的過程。**「我曾經與之合作的每一組學生，夏令營工作人員或領導團隊都經歷了類似的成長過程。有時候，這種成長會朝著預期的方向發展，但是有時候它會達到我沒有想像或不一定希望的地方。」** 史蒂夫認為，團隊成長的過程儘管每個團隊各不相同，但應以引導者的有意設計為指導。史蒂夫並沒有讓團隊的成長成為「偶發事件」，而是向他的研討會參與者介紹了成為過程中有意識的「建築師」的重要性。他認為，這是透過創造性的設計和理解人群在團隊環境中的行為方式和參與方式來實現的。

　　Steve Haines is an educator, facilitator, camp designer and director with more than 25 years of experience leading and facilitating the Group Growth Process with both students and adults. He spent 25 years teaching middle school History, Health, and Physical Education, as well as designing and directing summer camp programs for children. These varied experiences helped develop and sharpen his skills as a group facilitator and training leader. Through his facilitation experience, he noticed that all groups go through a group growth process. *"Each class of students, summer camp staff, or leadership team I have ever worked with goes through a similar growth process. Sometimes that growth goes in the intended direction, but occasionally, it goes to a place where I did not imagine or necessarily desire."* Steve believes that the group growth process, although uniquely different with each group, should be guided by the intentional design of the facilitator. Instead of letting the group growth just "happen," Steve educates his workshop participants about the importance of being the intentional "architect" of the process. He believes that this is accomplished through creative design and by understanding how groups of people behave and engage when in a group setting.

本手冊旨在透過為引導者配備一些簡單的遊戲和活動來增強他們的能力，他們可以利用這些遊戲和活動來指導他們的團隊成長過程，以達到預期的目標。這些活動可能並不總是能將團隊帶到期望的目的地，但是它們總是可以幫助將團隊帶向期望的方向。

This booklet is designed to empower facilitators by equipping them with some simple games and activities, which they can utilize to guide their group growth process toward their intended destination. The activities may not always take the group to the desired destination, but they can always help lead the group in the desired direction.

史蒂夫.海恩斯是Camp Concepts和Advantage-USA的總裁兼首席執行官。Camp Concepts在賓西法尼亞州的亞德利地區設計並指導多個夏日日間營。Advantage-USA則開展國際業務，包括國際教育諮詢，以幫助國際高中生和大學生在美國找到「合適的」學校。海恩斯先生就其工作的許多方面進行演講和培訓，特別是與領導力、營地管理、遊戲和活動以及引導技能有關的主題。

  Steve Haines is the President & CEO of Camp Concepts and Advantage-USA. Camp Concepts designs and directs multiple summer day camps in Yardley, Pennsylvania. Advantage-USA handles his international initiatives, including international education consulting, which helps international high school and university students find the "right fit" schools in the United States. Mr. Haines does speeches and trainings on many aspects of his work, particularly on topics related to leadership, camp management, games & activities, and facilitation skills.

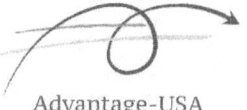

諮詢，演說或培訓聯絡
Contact for Consulting, Speaking, or Training

有關教育諮詢、團隊、老師、員工或領導力培訓，請透過以下聯繫方式與史蒂夫聯繫：

For educational consulting, team, teacher, staff, or leadership training, please contact Steve through the following contact methods:

www.CampConcepts.org
www.Advantage-USA.org
www.ImmeriveEducationAssociates.com
email: CampConcepts@comcast.net
email: Advantage-USA@comcast.net
email: info@immersiveeducationassociates.com

© 2018版權歸屬於史蒂夫.海恩斯，Camp Concepts公司。版權所有。根據美國1976年版權法案，任何未經書面同意地複製、發表或複印都是嚴格禁止的。封面照片版權人：雷.鐘，菁果國際教育，2017。

© 2018 by Steve Haines, Camp Concepts, Inc. All rights reserved. Reproduction, publication, or reprinting without written consent is strictly prohibited under the U.S. Copyright Act of 1976. Cover photo credits: Ray Chong, Jingle International Education, 2017.

附加值獎勵：耐心計劃
Added Bonus: The Patience Plan

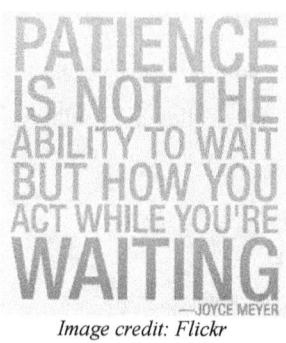

Image credit: Flickr

本部份針對希望在課堂內學習更多有關衝突解決管理的老師。其中某些部分很容易運用於工作場所，但它是從教育者的角度編寫的。

This section is specifically for the teacher who wants to learn more about conflict resolution management inside the classroom. Some of it could easily be adapted to the workplace, but it is written from an educator perspective.

本部份主要是為經驗不足的老師設計的，經驗更豐富的資深老師也可能在這裡找到一些新想法，或者能重溫以前已經理解的概念，從而獲益。如果你具有完善的課堂規則和穩定的課堂文化，則可跳過此部份。如果你是一位新手老師，那麼你可能想更仔細地閱讀這個部份。要認識到這並不是一個可以簡單照搬的模板。這是一個計劃的想法，可以根據你的個性、學生年級水平和領導風格進行修改或調整。

This section is primarily designed for less experienced teachers, though even more seasoned, veteran teachers may find some new ideas herein, or at least benefit from revisiting previously understood concepts. If you have well-established classroom rules and an established classroom culture, you may want to skip this section. If you are a new teacher, then you may want to read it a bit more closely. Recognize that it is not a template to simply put in place. It is a plan idea that can be modified or adjusted to fit your personality, student grade level and your leadership style.

「耐心計劃」旨在使你成為一名教師領導者，表現出強大的情商，並始終控制住自己的情緒，即使在面對叛逆和不聽話的學生時亦然。即使對於最有經驗的老師來說，具有挑戰性行為的學生也可能讓你在課程或職業中耗盡精力和激情。了解如何建立教師主導的課堂並為其奠定基調，可能會幫助你管理課程並保持耐心和理智。

A "Patience Plan" is designed to empower you as a teacher leader to exemplify strong EQ and remain in control of your emotions at all times, even amid disruptive and disobedient students. Even for the most experienced teacher, behaviorally challenging students can drain the energy and passion from your lesson or your career. Understanding how to establish, and set the tone for, a teacher led classroom may help you manage your class and keep your patience and sanity.

「耐心計劃」與教師的管理紀律無關，而與教師如何透過讓學生參與設計並同意明確的行為期望有關，進而使學生能夠採取適當的行動。告訴學生做什麼和什麼時候做是一回事，你能讓他們做則是另一回事，因為他們認為這是履行他們作為你的課堂參與者所做出的承諾。我相信「耐心計劃」消除了許多情況下的主觀性，並將紀律負擔從教師轉移到學生身上。畢竟，這是他們表示了同意的事情。

A "Patience Plan" is less about the teacher administering discipline and more about how the teacher can empower students to act appropriately by engaging them in the process of designing and agreeing to clear and desired behavioral expectations. It is one thing to tell a student what to do and when to do it, but it is a different level of influence when you can get them to do it because they see it as fulfilling an agreement to which they contributed as a participant in your class. I believe the "Patience Plan" takes much of the subjectivity out of many situations and transfers the discipline burden from the teacher to the student. After all, they agreed to it.

我在教書的時候就開始了「耐心計劃」。 我沒有用這個名字來稱呼它，但是多年以來，我逐漸了解自己所使用的過程，並且自此以後就為我的全球教師培訓創造了這個術語。我發現，無論我在哪裡旅行，總會出現一個普遍的問題：「如何控制學生的行為？」實施起來很容易，但是否需要強大的教師引導技能來讓學生「認可」？請與你的個性和引導技巧相結合，使用、調整和更改這些想法。我希望它們可以成為你的工具，並使你保持耐心。好了，請允許我向你介紹「耐心計劃」。

I started the "Patience Plan" back when I was teaching. I did not call it by that name, but over the years, I have come to understand the process I was using and have since coined this phrase for purposes of my global teacher trainings. I find that no matter where I travel, one universal question always arises, "How do I control student behavior?" Implementation is easy, but does take strong teacher facilitation skills to set the appropriate tone for student "buy-in". Feel free to use, modify and alter these ideas to blend in with your personality and facilitation skills. I hope they can be tools that equip you, as well as preserve your patience. Let me introduce you to the "Patience Plan".

設定成功的基調
Setting the Tone for Success

我相信大多數學生都希望在學校學習並感受到成功。儘管學生可能在第一天以積極的態度和新鮮的狀態走進你的教室，許多新老師從陳述學生的學業和行為要求開始，於是那些寄予厚望的學生突然陷入低谷。

許多學生很難理解每個老師的教學風格不一樣。在不同的老師那裡，授課方式、學業期望和個性都有所不同。中小學生經常認為，所有教師都是從同一個老師的模範中復刻出來的，因此，他們的舉止都是一樣的。直到高中，學生才開始意識到教育的一部份正是弄清每位老師的風格，以便他們學會如何適應，以滿足每位老師的具體要求。

I believe most students want to enjoy and feel successful in school. Whereas students may enter your classroom on day 1 with a positive attitude and a fresh "clean slate", many new teachers begin by stating the academic and behavioral demands of the students, and, with that, those high hopes suddenly sink to low depths. It is difficult for many students to understand that every teacher has a different style of teaching. Delivery methods, academic expectations, and personalities all vary within different teachers. Primary and middle school students often think that all teachers are cut from the same teacher mold and, therefore, all act the same. It is not until high school that students begin to comprehend that part of the education game is trying to figure out each teacher's style, so they can learn how to adapt their work to meet the specific requirements of each teacher.

我認為，重要的是要盡早確定教師與學生相處的方式。為此，老師可以選擇分享一些個人的故事，例如有關其家庭、愛好或經歷的訊息。這很容易讓你決定為了什麼而授課、你的教學理念、以及你可以或無法容忍的各種行為。你的初期課程應精心設計，以展現你作為老師和作為個人的身份。這樣做可以將猜測排除在學生的腦海之外，從而為你和學生之間的成功定下基調。這很可能決定著他們是否將你作為教育者而接受你。

I think it is important to set an early tone regarding how personable the teacher intends to be with the students. To do this, the teacher may choose to share something personal such as information about the teacher's family, hobbies, or experiences. This can easily lead into an explanation of why you decided to teach, your teaching philosophy, and which behaviors you will tolerate and which you will not. Your initial class should be carefully crafted to reveal YOU as a teacher and as a person. Doing so can keep the guess work out of the student mind and, in turn, set the tone for your success, and that of your students. From this, they will likely form an opinion as to whether or not you may be a teacher they will embrace as an educator.

我更喜歡以輕鬆有趣的方式開始我的第一堂課，因為那是我的一個面，我希望我的學生早點知道這一點。我喜歡大笑，我希望他們會發現我的課堂是一個有趣的學習場所。現在，我認識到，並不是每個班級都能讓人熱鬧和愉快。毫無疑問，必然有一些課程是緩慢而難以令人興奮的，有些必須要教授和學習的知識，學生可能會發現它們跟以前的方法一樣乏味。這是在所難免的。但是，我發現，由於許多課程都很有趣並且包含笑聲，因此大家對無趣的課程的容忍度更高，其發生的頻率也更低。使用幽默可以幫助我在學生心中建立「儲備耐心」庫，以預備各種不那麼有趣或不具啟發性的課程。

  I prefer to start my first class with something fun and light, because that is a side of me that I want my students to learn early. I love to laugh, and my hope is that they will find my classroom experience to be a fun place in which to learn. Now, I recognize that not every class can be hilarious and enjoyable. There will undoubtedly be those slow, less-than-exciting classes where information must be taught and learned, where the students may find the methodology used to be tedious. It will inevitably happen. However, I find that because many classes are fun and include moments of laughter, the uninteresting classes are far more tolerable and less frequent. Using humor helps me to build a reservoir of "reserve patience" in the students for the times that I may not be funny or quite so inspirational.

  以一些有趣的事情開始之後，我喜歡分享我為什麼決定做老師。我的故事是學業失敗、運動和社會成就的其中一樣。我與學生一樣，也經歷過挫折，當我沒有興趣、無法專注時，我經歷了挫折，無法通過數學和科學課程的學習。但是，在籃球場、足球場、棒球場或體育教學區（體育館）裡，我便是一位表現卓越的學生。如果不是一個有愛心和有聯繫的老師建立我的自信和自我價值的話，我不知道我的人生會走上什麼道路。是他讓我知道，我未來的職業計劃可能不會涉及高級數學或科學計算。我也得以看到，我在那些核心學科領域的劣勢可能會使我將來不去涉及這種思維方法的工作和研究領域。但是，這位老師建議我專注於我的領導才能。他幫助我相信，我在體育方面的領導才能以及與人之間的牢固社交關係成為我關注的重點。我帶著那寶貴的禮物，攻讀了大學學位。我最終獲得了碩士學位，並開始了二十五年的教學生涯。有趣的是，我教體育、衛生、歷史，並執教過籃球、足球和網球，這與我的導師完全一樣！老師即是領導者。影響的能力可以改變人生軌跡。我就是活生生的證明！（多謝你，唐.馬丁代爾。）

After starting with something fun, I like to share my philosophy of why I decided to become a teacher. My story is one of academic failure, and athletic and social success. I share the frustration I experienced as a student having to try, but failing miserably, to get through Math and Science concepts when my mind was anything but interested and focused. However, on the basketball court, soccer field, baseball field or in Physical Education (gymnasium), I was a high achieving student. Had it not been for a caring and connecting teacher who made it his mission to build my self-confidence and self-worth, I do not know what path my life may have taken. He let me know that my future vocational plans probably would not involve careers requiring high level Math or Scientific computations. I, too, could see that my weaknesses in those core subject areas would likely keep me from future fields of work and study that involved such methods of thinking. However, this teacher suggested that I focus on my leadership skills instead. He helped me believe that my leadership skills in sports, along with my strong social connections, should be where I focus more attention. I took that precious gift of hope and pursued a college degree in teaching. I eventually earned my master's degree and embarked on a 25-year teaching career. Ironically, I taught Physical Education, Health, History and coached Basketball, Soccer and Tennis – the exact same job that my mentor teacher had! A teacher is a leader. The ability to influence can change the trajectory of a life. I am living proof! (Thank you, Don Martindale.)

我講我的學業掙扎故事是因為，我知道它可以使我在學生面前更像個普通人。對於某些老師來說，這種故事分享似乎是不合適的，因為他們認為老師應該成為學術上的卓越表現的代表。對於另一些人來說，這顯然並不是他們的背景故事，因此，分享它沒有意義。我的意思不是**你要分享的具體內容**，而是**你要分享**。我相信，由於我與學生之間的個人聯繫，我的教學得到了加強。我希望他們了解我當初的掙扎。我認為這可能會使那些不安全的學生放心，從而對他們起到幫助。我希望他們看到自己在學業上的掙扎只是他們也可以克服的整體人生旅程的一部份。

I tell my story of academic struggle because I know it helps humanize me to my students. For some teachers, that reveal seems inappropriate because they think that the teacher should exemplify academic excellence. For others, that clearly isn't their background story and, therefore, sharing it doesn't make sense. My point is not so much WHAT YOU SHARE as much as it is THAT YOU SHARE. I believe my teaching was strengthened because of my personal connection with students. I wanted them to know my struggles. I think it might have helped those insecure students by putting them at ease. My hope was that they saw their own academic struggles to be just a part of their overall journey that they too could overcome.

我認為，作為一名教育工作者，我取得的成功在很大程度上與我的智商無關，而與我的高情商更有關。如果我的高中老師給我進行情商測驗，我相信我會在這方面取得很高的分數。不幸的是，學校似乎並不在乎我的情商，而只在乎我的智商。我希望我那些高情商的學生感受到希望，也希望我那些高智商的學生知道，情商對整個人生是至關重要的。實際上，我相信情商將佔未來人生成功的百分之七十五至八十。因此，嘗試同時提高情商和智商是很有價值的，但是通常其中一個會蓋過另一個。隨著年齡的增長，我一直在努力學習更多並了解自己的情商（EQ）。我認為，對教師進行教育和培訓以更好地了解情商的重要性和價值是非常重要的。

    I think that much of my success as an educator has not been about my IQ, as much as it has been about my high EQ. Had my high school teachers given me an EQ test, I am confident I would have scored very highly on it. Unfortunately, schools did not seem to care about my EQ, just my IQ. I wanted my high EQ students to feel hope and I wanted my high IQ students to know that EQ matters in the overall preparation for life. In fact, I believe EQ will account for 75-80% of future success in life. Therefore, it is valuable to try to sharpen both EQ and IQ, but typically one will dominate over the other. As I have gotten older, I have worked hard to learn more and understand my own emotional intelligence (EQ). I believe it is important for teachers to educate and train their students to better understand the importance and value of EQ.

    分享過去的失敗經歷之後，我還將與他們分享成功的故事。教育是關於過程的，而不是僅僅關注結果。太多的學生發現自己的自我價值僅體現在他們取得的成績上。他們開始分隔自己在自己得以或無法擅長的每個主題中的成功（或失敗）。每個大腦的發展和學習都不相同。老師們談論教育全人，但常常忘記教育每個孩子。如此一來，教師們開始忽略每個孩子學習時經歷的微妙過程。

    Once I share my past failures, I also share with them stories of success. Education is about the process, not just the outcome. Too many students find their self-worth wrapped up only in the grades they achieve. They begin to compartmentalize their success (or failure) in each subject that they may or may not do well in. Each brain develops and learns differently. Teachers talk about teaching the whole child, but often forget to teach every child. In doing so, teachers begin to ignore the delicate process that each child goes through when learning.

至少可以說，我的學業智商學習之路是艱難的。有很多老師讓我認識到我的掙扎是有效且有價值的，其他老師則使我感到自己的職業前景黯淡無光。由於大腦的皮質區域發展較晚，對於許多人而言，直到1920年代後期，人們很可能在學習早期都經歷了學業掙扎，但這只是一種延遲，而不是永久的無能。我是一個後進的學習者。由於學習延遲，我稱自己為愚蠢和無能的人。現在我年歲漸長，已經重新學習了曾經學過的許多概念，而其中的許多概念似乎已經不再那麼難了。小學、初中甚至是高中的學業失敗並不意味著你不會學習，學業成就也不能保證未來的業務或社交上的成功。教師必須具有積極而強大的影響力，並且在這樣做的過程中，請確保不要在學生的學習過程中壓倒他們作為人的精神。它很脆弱！

My academic IQ road was rocky to say the least. I had many teachers who made me recognize that my struggle was valid and valuable, while others made me feel that it would lead me to a bleak vocational future. Because the cortical region of the brain develops late, for many, not until the late 20's, it is quite possible that the academic struggle people experience early in their education is simply a delay, not a permanent disability. I was a late blooming learner. Because of my delayed learning, I labeled myself as stupid and incapable. Now that I am older, I have relearned many of the concepts once taught, and many do not seem so hard anymore. Elementary school, Middle School, or even High School academic failure does not mean you can't learn, nor does academic achievement guarantee future business or social success. Teachers need to be a positive and powerful influence and, in so doing, be sure not to squash the human spirit in their students' learning process. It is fragile!

在學年之初,你要為自己成為某種類型的老師而定下基調。這將幫助學生認識你,並希望你對作為個人和老師的身份感到滿意。它的好處大於缺點。讓學生了解你,將幫你創造有用的影響力,這將幫助你更有效地領導和影響你的學生。

At the start of the year, it is important for you to set the tone as to what type of teacher you will be. This will help students get to know you and hopefully feel comfortable with who you are as a person and as a teacher. The benefits outweigh the negatives. Allowing the students to know you will create useful leverage, which will help you to more effectively lead and influence your students.

建立行為期望
Establishing Behavioral Expectations

在分享對學生的期望之前,我先分享我的個人故事。我展示出我的人性,因此可以請求他們合作。如果你只是從對學生的期望入手,那麼我認為,你避開了與他們建立有價值的、足以建立關係影響力的初始聯繫點。人類是自主的生物。他們天生渴望好玩、有力量、有愛心以及自由。作為老師,我們必須培養人性的這一面,同時向我們的學生表明,課堂上大家也必須達成一致的社會和行為秩序。對於教師而言,這並不是一個很難理解的概念(儘管有時會曲解這一概念的含義!)。我們要意識到規範我們社會行為規矩的存在。我們可能不喜歡被「逮」並面對後果,但在內部,我們了解違反這些既定規則的後果。我相信學生想知道這個界線在哪裡,如果弄清楚了這界線以及可能的後果,那麼他們就可以更好地處理可能出現的結果。這是建立師生關係的價值所在。

I share my personal story before ever sharing my expectations for students. I reveal my humanity, so I can then ask for their human cooperation.

If you simply start with the student expectations, then I think you avoid establishing a valuable initial connection point with them that could potentially build relationship leverage. Humans are autonomous beings. They have an innate desire to be playful, powerful, loving, and free. As teachers, we have to nurture that aspect of human nature, while at the same time, make clear to our students that there must also be an agreed upon social and behavioral order to the classroom. This is not a concept that is difficult to understand for teachers (though sometimes miss the mark on this notion!). We realize there are laws that govern our social behavior. We may not like getting caught and facing the consequence, but inside, we understand the consequences for breaking these established rules. I believe students want to know where the line is and, if it is made clear, along with the possible range of consequences, then they can much better handle the result that may follow. This is the value of relationship building between teacher and student.

我將「耐心計劃」設計成一種「社會契約」，而不是一系列規則。也許這只是一種掩飾，但我認為這是一種成功的方法，可以把學生的選擇在未來產生的後果從你手中移開，並將良好行為的責任重新置於他們自己做出的選擇上。

　　I craft my "Patience Plan" as more of a "social contract" than a list of rules. Maybe I am trying to disguise it, but I think this is a successful way to take the future consequences of the students' choices out of your hands and place the responsibility for good behavior right back on the choices that they make.

　　通常，我會先對全班學生陳述自己對他們的目標。聽起來可能是這樣：**「我受雇教你［插入主題］。以這種方式為你服務是我的榮幸。我熱衷於與你分享我對這一主題的知識和熱愛。希望你能像我一樣愛它。我持續進行的一件事是學習。我認為自己是終生學習者，我對我所知道**

的、認為自己知道的或想知道的事情充滿源源不斷的好奇。由於有更多關於該主題的知識，我希望我的好奇心不會消失。我認識到你們中的一些人對此主題有先入為主的感覺。你們中的許多人可能會喜歡它，而其他人則可能受不了它。儘管我無法讓你喜歡它，但我的建議是尋求對該主題某些領域的更深層次的好奇心，因為如果你發現一件令人好奇的事情，那麼它可能會幫助你激發對我們正在學習的內容的深入研究。它可以幫助你擁抱它，而不是作為你不喜歡的東西而拒絕它。我希望你永遠保持對所有事物的好奇心，因為那些有好奇的人將是終身學習者。」我覺得這樣的話語會讓學生放心，並與他們分享我關於教育價值以及我的學習方法的訊息。

I typically start by stating my goals for them as a class of students. It might sound like this. *"I have been hired to teach you [insert subject]. It is my pleasure to serve you in this way. I am passionate about sharing my knowledge and love of this subject with you. I hope you learn to love it as much as I do. One thing I continue to do is learn. I consider myself a life-long learner, who is continually curious about things I know, think I know or want to know. Because there is so much more to learn about this subject, I hope my curiosity never fades. I recognize some of you here have a pre-conceived feeling about this subject. Many of you may love it, and others perhaps cannot stand it. Whereas I cannot make you love it, my advice would be to seek deeper curiosity into some area of the subject, because if you can find one thing to be curious about, it may help inspire you to dig a little deeper into what we are learning. It may help you embrace it, rather than reject it as a subject you don't like. I hope you never stop being curious in all things because those who are curious will always be life-long learners."* I feel a statement such as this puts learners at ease and shares my message about the value of education, as well as my philosophical approach to learning.

然後，我說明自己希望他們成功的目標。我可以這樣說：「**你的學**

業成績對我很重要,但這並不掩蓋我更深層的願望,即確保你不僅為下一階段的學業做好準備,而且也為人生做好準備。你可能會忘記在這堂課中學到的知識,但好奇心可能會再次出現,並挑戰你繼續追求進一步的知識。我們都應認識到,教師必須評估你的學習,並在評估中附加一個等級來代表你的學習水平。我將對你進行評估,但我還將嘗試提供許多不同類型的評估,以確保教育不同風格的學習者,而不僅僅是成績優異的學習者。如果你有成長型心態,並且意識到自己的態度決定了自己的高度,那麼每個人都可以確定自己的潛力和成功。你的得分可能低於預期,但是你的努力只能由自己決定。最終,你將與你自己而不是周圍的人競爭。如果我們所有人都擁有相同的才能、才華和能力,並且數值相同,那就將與周圍的人競爭。在本課程中,請專注於與自己的競爭。設定可以實現的目標,將自己推出舒適區。如何定義成功將決定你是否達到了目標。我想幫助你取得長期成功,而不僅僅是暫時的好成績。這對你的人生而言更加重要。」

  I then move to my goals for their success. I may say something like this: *"Your academic success is important to me, but it does not overshadow my deeper desire to make sure you are prepared for not only the next academic level but also prepared for life. You may forget the knowledge learned in this class, yet piqued curiosity may come back and challenge you to pursue further knowledge down the road. We all recognize that teachers must assess your learning and, in doing so, attach a grade to represent the level of your learning. I will assess you, but I will also try to provide many different types of assessment to ensure that I teach to all styles of learners, not just those who memorize well. Each of you can determine your own potential and success if you have a growth mindset and realize that your attitude determines your altitude. You may not score as well as you may want to, but your effort can only be determined by you. Ultimately, you compete against yourself and not those sitting around you. If we all had the same gifts, talents, and abilities, and all in the same amounts, then competition would be with the individuals around you. In this class, focus on your competition with yourself. Set attainable goals and goals that will push you beyond your comfort zone. How you define success will determine whether or not you meet your goals. I want to help you achieve long-term success, not just temporary good grades. This is better for your life."*

至此,我已經概述了個人目標的重要性,並要求學生定義個人成功對他們而言是什麼,我現在準備進入行為標準領域了。同樣,我的目標是避免出現正面和負面行為的典型列表。相反,我會懇請他們採納這些「標準」作為所有學習者實現其目標和潛力所必需的內容。這將幫助我們透過團隊「認可」來塑造課堂文化。

Now that I have outlined the importance of personal goals and asked them to define what personal success is to them, I am now prepared to move into the areas of behavioral standards. Again, my goal is to avoid a typical list of positive and negative behaviors. Rather, I will implore them to adopt these "standards" as necessary for all learners to reach their goals and potential. This will help us shape the classroom culture by getting group "buy-in".

班級的每個成員都是學習社群的成員。作為老師,我只是社群的一部份。這樣,為了使這個社群(老師和學生)能夠有效地共同運作,它必須專注於自我改善,以實現提升。所有偉大的社會都有支配成員行為的法律。這些法律闡明了社群的權利和特權,以便讓大家都清楚社群對他們行為的期望。我們的學習社群還將採用一些準則,這些準則將有助於我們保持班級文化,增強我們的社群,並促進每個成員的發展,也進一步促進整個社群的發展。這為學生奠定了基調,使他們意識到他們是掛毯中至關重要的紗線,並且個人和社群都有責任互相幫助,以使整個團隊獲得成功。

Each member of the class is a member of a learning community. As the teacher, I am also only one part of what makes up the community. As such, for this community to function effectively together (teacher and students), the community must be focused only on bettering itself in order to strengthen the community. All great societies have laws that governed behavior. These laws spell out the rights and privileges of the community, so all know what is expected. Our learning community will also adopt guidelines that will help us preserve our class culture, strengthen our community, and seek to further not only each individual member, but the community as a whole. This sets the tone for the students to realize that they are vital threads in the tapestry, and that there is an individual and community responsibility to help each other, in order for the whole group to be successful.

尊重
R-E-S-P-E-C-T

我強調，我們的社群將堅持一個簡單而又複雜的概念———**尊重**。作為一個社群，我們將使用尊重這個標準來反映行為到底恰不恰當。我們都遵守和維護如下四個方面的尊重：

I stress that our community will adhere to 1 simple, yet complex concept - **RESPECT**. As a community, we will use RESPECT as our lens for what is or is not appropriate. There are 4 key areas of respect we all observe and protect:

1. 尊重老師———儘管我認為自己是終身學習社群的一員，但我被公認為領導者，因為這是我受聘從事的工作。因此，社群中的每個成員都必須尊重老師。學生必須認識到老師的職責是以清晰而令人難忘的方式傳授必要的知識。學生將始終獲得老師所能提供的最好的幫助，而老師也期望學生盡最大的努力以為回報。教師尋求真誠的學習努力，而不只是為獲得考試或科目的成績所需的努力。

1. <u>RESPECT THE TEACHER</u> - Although I consider myself a member of the life-long learning community, I am recognized as the leader because it is the job I have been hired to do. As such, it is necessary for each member of the community to respect the teacher. The students must recognize that the teacher is there to present necessary knowledge in a clear and memorable way. Students will always get the best a teacher has to offer, and in turn, the teacher expects the students to give their best effort in return. Teachers seek sincere effort in learning, not just the effort necessary to earn a grade for the exam or subject.

在以下情況下，教師感覺不受尊重：
- 學生未按時完成交代的作業。
- 學生以粗魯或不適當的方式和老師講話。
- 當老師在講話、教學的時候，或在其他不恰當的時候，學生大聲說話或打擾他人。

Teachers do not feel respected when:
- Students do not complete their assigned work on time.
- Students speak to the teacher in a manner that is rude or inappropriate.
- Students speak out or disrupt others when the teacher is speaking, teaching or at other inappropriate times.

　　2. 尊重自己——每個學生都是學習過程中至關重要的部份。該過程涉及成功和失敗。透過強烈的成長心態，學生的自我價值可以遠遠超過獲得的分數或成績。學生必須對自己有足夠的尊重，以了解自己的優點和缺點。我非常贊同這句格言：「熱愛自己，好事自來。」我們不會以相同的步調或時間走向成熟。儘管表現會令人失望，但學會愛自己卻帶來了未來人生中所需要的韌性。

　　2. RESPECT YOURSELF - Each student is a crucial part of the learning process. The process involves success and failure. By having a strong growth mindset, a student's self-worth can be seen as far greater than just an earned score or grade. Students must respect themselves enough to know their strengths and weaknesses. I often espouse the adage, "Love yourself and good things will follow." We do not all mature at the same pace or at the same time. Learning to love oneself, despite a disappointing performance, reveals the resiliency needed for life in the future.

為了尊重自己，學生們應該：
- 盡力嘗試足以擴展和發展自我經驗的新事物。保持好奇。
- 有效地計劃他們的時間，以便按時完成作業，並能反映預期的工作質量。
- 提高努力的水平，以準確反映他們的職業道德和學習承諾。
- 著眼於發展自己的成長型心態，使他們能做到的事情超出自己的想像。

To respect themselves, students should:
- Commit to trying new things that stretch and develop their experience. Always be curious.
- Efficiently budget their time so that they can complete work on time and of a quality that is reflective of their intended effort.
- Allow their level of effort to accurately reflect their work ethic and commitment to learning.
- Focus on developing their growth mindset so that they can do more than they imagine possible.

3. 尊重他人——教導學生尊重和擁抱他人的多樣性將是你課堂文化的重要組成部份。如果你在以結果為導向的教育體系中任教，這是最困難的事情之一，因為該體系會促進學生與學生之間的競爭。當學生專注於和同學競爭時，他們對建立社群並沒有興趣。我竭盡所能表明，我們將共同努力構建一個學習社群，每個學習者都有自己的長處和短處。因為我們都各不相同，所以我們意識到優點和缺點對於每個人中可能都會有不同的表現方式。作為一個社群，我們必須尊重我們的諸多差異，並慶祝我們彼此之間的不同。每個人都有獨特的天賦，把我們塑造成我們自己的樣子。每個社群成員的大腦也都處於不同的發展階段。目前，有些人具有較高的複雜推理能力，而另一些人則具有較強的創造力、社交能力甚至語言習得能力。我們對這種多樣性以及大家當前的發展階段表示歡迎，而不是試圖迫使每個學生進入相同的學業或社會模式。

3. **<u>RESPECT OTHERS</u>** – Teaching students to respect and embrace the diversity in others will be an important component of building the culture in your classroom. It is one of the most difficult things to accomplish if you teach in a results-driven education system because this promotes student-to-student competition. When students focus on competing against their fellow classmates, they are not interested in building community with them. I state as passionately as I can that, together, we seek to be a community of learners, each of whom has individual strengths and weaknesses. Because we are all different, we realize strengths and weaknesses may reveal themselves differently in each person. As a community, we must respect our many differences and celebrate that we are not all alike. Each personality has a unique set of gifts that help shape who we are becoming. Each community member's brain is at different stages of development. At this moment, some have higher complex reasoning skills, while others have stronger creativity, social skills, or even language acquisition skills. We celebrate this diversity, along with the current stage of development, and do not seek to force each student into the same academic or social mold.

我們應該重視每個人與生俱來的天性是需要與其他人建立聯繫，並渴望成為社群的一份子。有時，這些關係會經歷緊張和人際衝突。這是不可避免的。我們將在產生這些意見分歧時進行投入，因為我們相信衝突帶來的技能將使我們更好地掌握必要的人生技能。如果我們作為社群成員能學會更好地管理自己的情緒，那麼我們將能在需要時協助和幫助他人管理自己的情緒。

We should value that each human has an innate need to be connected to other humans and a yearning to be a part of a community. At times, these relationships will experience strain and interpersonal conflict. It is inevitable. We will invest in these times of disagreement because we believe the skills learned as a result of conflict better equip us with necessary life skills. If we, as community members, can learn to better manage our own emotions, then we will be able to assist and help others manage their emotions when needed.

為了尊重他人，我們必須同意：
- 不要急著評斷他人。不要急著假設或判斷他人。
- 允許犯錯、自私和傷害的機會。當別人做錯事時要保持優雅。
- 在必要時以誠實和尊重的態度與他人面對面認真解決衝突。
- 只與自己競爭。記住，總會有人比我們更有才華。如果我們只和他人競爭，一旦更有才華的人出現，我們就會感到不滿。

To Respect others, we must agree to:
- Give others the benefit of the doubt. Be slow to assume or judge others.
- Extend the opportunity to be wrong, selfish, and hurtful. Be graceful when others are wrong.
- Honestly and respectfully confront others when the need arises. Respectfully work out conflicts.
- Compete only against ourselves. Remember, there will always be those who are far more talented than we are. If all we do is compete with others, we only feel satisfied until someone more talented comes along.

4. 尊重學習——尊重學習的概念意味著每個人都可以選擇如何對學習過程做出反應。有些人出於擔心成績差而做出反應，因此最終選擇了糟糕的高中或大學。其他人則擔心成績差將使他們家族蒙羞。獲得分數並不總是能說明每個學生的真實學習狀況或完整的理解水平。實際上，成績可能無法準確反映你對知識的掌握程度。高分只能顯示出參加或通過考試的卓越能力。同樣，低分可能會顯示考試能力缺乏或僅僅是不善於這種評估。其他影響測試結果的因素可能包括評估方式、測試的複雜性、成功或不成功的猜測，甚至是可能一直在「指導測試」的老師的重視程度。個人學習更多是一個人追求自我完善的過程。你作為學習者的成熟程度取決於你自己的步調，並且該步調可能與你周圍的步調不同。對學習的真正尊重意味著對數據、概念、相關性和應用所學材料的欣賞和理解，這可以透過學生的成績進行證明。我知道許多人可以「解決」該問題，但卻對「何時或如何」應用該問題缺乏了解。這個想法是知識定義的重要組成部份。

4. RESPECT LEARNING – Respecting the concept of learning means that each person has a choice in how to respond to the learning process. Some respond and react out of the fear of earning poor grades and, therefore, ending up with poor high school or university options. Others fear poor grades that will bring disrespect on their family name. Earned grades do not always tell the full or complete story about each individual student's true learning or understanding. In fact, grades may not be an accurate reflection of one's mastery of the information. A high grade could simply reveal a superior ability to take or pass a test. Likewise, a low grade may reveal test taking weakness or simply a struggle in that type of assessment. Other factors contributing to testing results may include the assessment style, test complexity, successful or unsuccessful guessing, or even the emphasis of the teacher who may have been "teaching to the test". Personal learning is more about one's quest for self-improvement. Your maturation as a learner is at your pace and that pace may be different than that of those around you. A true respect for learning suggests an appreciation and understanding of the data, the concepts, the relevance and the application of learned material as demonstrated by student achievement. I know many who can "do" the problem, but lack the understanding of "when or how" to apply it. This idea is an important part of the definition of knowledge.

關於尊重學習的訊息包括一些供學生考慮的關鍵點。我在這方面的目標包括幫助學生：

My message about having a respect for learning includes some key points for student consideration. My goals in this area include helping students:

1. 認識到學習的過程不按學業主題或學年劃分。我們經常談論要成為「終身學習者」。這明確地意味著，隨著年齡的增長，我們將繼續尋找新知識，但是我們也必須重新思考以前學習的知識。很多時候，我重新研究我以前學過的東西，卻發現首先要對這個主題有更多的了解。我的（心懷好意的）老師只給了我一小部份知識，因為在那時，我可能無法吸收全部的複雜性或概念。若是基於你從評估中獲得的成績而認定你已經知道某個主題的全部知識，則是一個錯誤。你的分數永遠不能代表你所學學科的全部真實性或全部知識。總會有更多的東西要學習。

1. <u>Recognize that the learning process must not be compartmentalized into 1 academic subject or school year.</u> We talk a lot about being a "life-long learner." This accurately implies that as we grow older, we continue to seek out new knowledge, but we must also reconsider previously learned knowledge, as well. Many times, I have gone back to re-study something I thought I had previously learned, only to find that there was much more to understanding about the subject in the first place. My teacher (well-meaning) only gave me a small piece of the story because, at that level or at that time in my process, I may not have been able to absorb the full complexity or concept. Thinking that you know everything there is to know about a topic, based on what you earn on the assessment, is a mistake. Your score can never represent the full truth or the full knowledge of a subject you study. There is always more to learn.

2. <u>認識並欣賞學習過程中的掙扎。</u>我的高中教練會告訴我，「失敗是成功之母。」我很難理解，因為在那個階段，我認為贏得比賽意味著我的團隊表現優於其他團隊。但是，經驗表明，有時我們的表現很好，卻輸給了技術水平較高的團隊。當我們回過頭來分析比賽時，我們可以看到其間的成功和失敗之處，這成了新的改進練習計劃的基礎。我在數學和科學課程方面苦苦掙扎。有時候，我覺得自己的努力應該獲得更高的成績。個人的掙扎包括額外的學習、與老師一起度過的時間、或接受專精數學的朋友們輔導的過程。額外的學習並不一定總能幫你取得更高的成績，但這是我整個學習過程不可或缺的一部份。最重要的是，它教會了我勤奮工作的價值。

2. <u>Recognize and appreciate the struggles involved in the process of learning.</u> My high school coach would tell me that, "Losing is the backdoor to success." I had a hard time understanding that because, at that stage, I thought winning the game meant that my team executed better than the other team. However, experience revealed that sometimes we executed very well, but lost to a superiorly skilled team. When we would go back and analyze our play, we could see success and failures in our play, which became the basis of a new practice plan for improvement. I struggled badly in Math and Science. There were times I felt as if my effort should have resulted in a much higher grade earned. That personal struggle included a process of additional work and time spent with the teacher or being tutored by my more math-minded friends. The extra work did not always result in higher grades, but it was very much an integral part of my full learning process. Most importantly, it taught me the value of hard work.

3. <u>尊重其他同學的掙扎可能與你有所不同，且是可以接受的。</u>在許多學校中，學生之間的競爭非常激烈。我曾在中國的教室裡，學生們能記住前三十至四十位學生的排名！對更高排名的追求激發了許多人花費更長的時間學習和準備，以提高他們的等級。如果個人對改進的追求不至於引起對「對手」的輕視，那麼我認為外部動機或決心水平就沒有問題。當發生對他人的鄙視時，**對他人的尊重規則**就會失效。我曾看到許多學生在看到「水平高於他們的學生」考差了、排在他們後面而感到高興不已。在別人的失敗中取樂並不代表尊重。

3. <u>Respect that your classmates' struggle may be different from yours and be OK with that.</u> In many schools, the competition between students is fierce. I have been in classrooms in China where students know the ranking of students through the first 30-40 spots! The quest for a higher class rank inspires many to spend longer hours studying and preparing in order to elevate their class rank. I have no problem with that external motivation or level of determination, if the personal quest for improvement does not breed a disdain for the "opponent". When disdain for others occurs, the RESPECT RULE FOR OTHERS is broken. I have seen many students gleam with joy when those "above them" score poorly and therefore elevate the rank of others. Taking joy in someone else's defeat does not model respect.

4. <u>認識到每個學生都在控制自己的努力程度。</u>努力是無法量化的。努力始於一種心態，而努力的效率有許多促成因素。我在大學裡有一個朋友，他似乎能過目不忘。他甚至承認：「由於我的大腦吸收訊息的方式，我不必在這方面付出努力。」我覺得我表現出的真正努力比他要重要得多，但對我們的考試結果進行比較並沒有得出相同的結論。我不得不意識到我的努力只是**我的努力**。我是唯一知道我是否嘗試某件事以及如何努力的人。有些事情對我來說很容易（歷史、體育、衛生……還有午餐！）。在其他科目上，我很難做出同樣的努力。有些老師說我需要付出更多的努力。有時我可以誠實地表示同意，但是有時候，我覺得我當時已經付出了最大的努力。

4. <u>Recognize that each student controls his/her own effort.</u> Effort is not quantifiable. Effort starts with a mindset, and the efficiency of your effort has many contributing factors. I had a friend in college who seemed to have a

photographic memory. He would even admit, "I don't have to try that hard because of the way my mind absorbs information." I felt I displayed true effort far more significantly than he did, but a comparison of our results did not tell the same story. I had to come to realize that my effort is MY EFFORT. I am the only person who knows if and how hard I tried at something. Some things came easily to me (History, PE, Health…and lunch!). In other subjects it was much harder for me to put forth the same effort. I had some teachers say I needed to apply more effort. Sometimes I could honestly agree and yet, other times, I felt as if the effort given at the time was my best.

我希望我的學生尊重**他們自己的**學習過程；無論是苦苦掙扎還是收穫成功。最終，這就是學習者的故事。成績不會定義他們未來的成功或人生。他們表現出的勇氣、努力、毅力和決心將對他們前進有很大的幫助。每個學習者的學習過程都不同。學習者必須確定並欣賞將為自己的學習故事做出什麼樣的努力。擁抱並擁有它。

I want my students to respect THEIR learning process; both the struggle and the success. Ultimately, this is what makes up their story as a learner. Grades will not define their future success or life. It is the grit, effort, perseverance and determination they put forth that will serve them well as they move forward. The learning process is different for each learner. Learners must identify and appreciate what kind of effort will contribute to their story. Embrace it and own it.

要尊重學習，學生們應該同意要：
- 慶祝努力的過程，而不僅僅是獲得的成績。
- 承認只有每個人自己才知道自己所付出的努力水平。
- 專注於個人的學習過程，而不是與他人的競爭。
- 對那些與自己相似或不同的人表現出同理心。了解大多數學生不想得低分。他們的學習過程可能與你不同。要表現出仁慈、關懷和理解，而不是在他們的苦苦掙扎中獲得快樂。

To respect learning, students should agree to:
- Celebrate the effort, not just the earned grade outcome.
- Acknowledge that only the individual can know the level of effort given.
- Focus their attention on the individual learning process and not on the competition with others.
- Show empathy for those who struggle similarly or differently than they. Understand that most students do not want to score poorly. Their learning process may be different from yours. Show kindness, consideration, and understanding, as opposed to finding joy in their struggle.

教授尊重的四個方面需要時間。我通常會在每學年年初給學生重新提及。作為老師，我必須不斷回顧並指出尊重何時被打破，並慶祝那些美好的模範時刻。因為尊重這四個方面是班級文化的核心，所以我會花時間和精力來教學生學會尊重，讓大家都聽清楚，並且知道它將被嚴格執行。建立班級文化不是一蹴而就的事情。就像學習一樣，隨著老師對學生的了解，這是一個必須逐步發展的過程。當然，我們可能會建議和討論許多其他準則，但我會再將其保存下來。我希望保留有關學生行為的討論，以及個人學習過程是如何與**尊重**這樣簡單（但很複雜）的哲學道理相聯繫的。

Teaching the four areas of respect takes time. I typically revisit it often in the early part of the year. As the teacher, I must keep coming back and pointing out when respect has been broken and celebrate clearly when it has been modeled beautifully. Because the 4 areas of respect are at the core of my class culture, I devote time and attention to teaching it, so it is clearly heard and students know that it will be strictly enforced. Building class culture does not happen overnight. Like learning, it is a process that has to develop gradually, as the teacher gets to know the students. Of course, there are many other guidelines that we might suggest and discuss, but I'll save those for another time. I like to keep the main discussion about student behavior, and how the individual learning process is connected to the simple (yet complex) philosophy of RESPECT.

我發現以這種方式開始會奠定積極的班級基調和文化共性，從而影響每個人在我的課堂內的行為和互動方式。它使許多學生感到放心，因為可以實現尊重的文化，並且創造了心理上安全的學習場所。我傳達的訊息並不是要求他們獲得最好的成績，而是我們討論尊重自我和學習時的內在要求。我希望他們努力奮鬥、成功、失敗、並超越他們好奇心的界限。當他們這樣做的時候，我可以將他們塑造成終身學習者，讓他們時刻尋求學習和重新學習所學的知識。

  I have found that starting out this way creates a positive tone and commonality of culture that influences how each person will act and interact inside my classroom. It is reassuring to many students because the culture of respect feels possible to achieve and it creates a psychologically safe place to learn. My message contains no demands for them to get the best grades, but that is built in when we discuss respect of self and of learning. I want them to struggle, succeed, fail, and push the limits of their curiosity. When they do this, I can shape them as life-long learners who always seek to learn and re-learn what is taught.

盡量讓規則保持簡單明瞭。書面規則有助於確保它們保持固定性和強制執行。我相信學生真的很想知道這界線在哪裡。如果規則似乎僅適用於某些人，而不是適用於所有人，則可能削弱學生對公正性以及最終對教師權威的信心。簡明扼要、措辭謹慎、合理執行應成為你的班規。

  Try to keep the rules simple and clear. Rules in writing help to ensure that they remain fixed and enforced. I believe students really want to know where the line is. If rules seem to only apply to certain individuals, and not to all individuals, that can erode student confidence in the impartiality and, ultimately, the authority of the teacher. Simply written, carefully worded, and fairly enforced should be the criteria for your class rules.

解決衝突的哲學
Philosophy of Conflict Resolution

耐心計劃的第二個同樣重要的方面，涉及你在衝突發生時如何回應學生。建立班級文化後，你將如何應對在學校環境中難免出現的衝突？在接下來的討論中，我將繼續使用「衝突解決」一詞。在我教過培訓課程的幾乎每一所學校中，我都被問到一個與教師管理學生行為有關的問題。年輕的老師往往在管理和「控制」學生方面苦苦掙扎，但是我遇到的資深教學工作者，他們仍然沒有掌握真正的課堂管理技能。你計劃的這一部份將需要一種清晰而深思熟慮的哲學，即你將如何與學生互動以及如何期望他們彼此互動，尤其是在發生衝突的時候。如果沒有解決衝突的計劃，衝突將支配你和你所教的學生並使他們感到沮喪。對於某些人來說，這部份的專業準備足以決定你整個學年的成敗，並且也可能嚴重影響學生的學習。它可以是激發靈感的最佳方式，也可以剝奪教室中的活力。

The second, and equally crucial aspect of your Patience Plan involves how you respond to the students when conflicts arise. Once you have established your class culture, how do you deal with the conflicts that inevitably arise in a school setting? I will use the term "conflict resolution" moving forward. In almost every school in which I have ever done a training session, I get asked a question related to teacher control of student behavior. It is often young teachers who struggle with managing and "controlling" their students, but I have met veterans to teaching who still have not grasped true classroom control techniques. This part of your plan will require a clear and well-conceived philosophy of how you will interact with students and how you expect them to interact with one another, especially when the conflicts arise. Go in without a plan for conflict resolution and it will dominate and frustrate you and the students you teach. For some, this area of your professional preparation will either make or break your school year, and it can seriously affect the learning of your students, as well. It can be the single best energizer of inspiration or it can suck the life right out of your classroom.

當我開始我的教學生涯時，我「深思熟慮」的計劃是想成為一個很酷的老師，讓學生感到開心。我相信，如果學生們認為我很酷，他們會更輕鬆地聽課，而且我也不必對他們進行嚴格的管教。但是，我認為的「計劃」根本不是計劃！相反，是一個年輕而幼稚的老師把自己丟進了獅子坑裡。我就像落入水中，而鯊魚伺機而動，毫不留情地奪人性命。我知道經驗沒有捷徑，但是我希望我當時有一個「耐心計劃」且至少能予以實施而獲得支持，進一步用經驗來完善它。與經驗豐富的老師交談（那些能與學生融洽相處，並得到學生相互尊重的老師），並了解他們如何將其融入課堂。我並不是說你需要的是「耐心計劃」，而是根據我的個性和引導技巧，我發現它對我來說非常有效。

When I began my teacher career, my "well-conceived" plan was that I wanted to be the cool teacher with whom the students had fun. I believed that if the students thought I was cool, they would more easily listen, and I wouldn't have to discipline them very much. However, what I thought was a "plan" was not a plan at all! Instead, it was the ill-conceived notion of a young, naïve teacher who was throwing himself into a pit of lions. I was like "chum" in the water, and the sharks circled and moved in for the kill quickly and without mercy. I know there is no shortcut for experience, but I wish I had a "Patience Plan" to at least implement for support as I gained the experience necessary to perfect it. Talk to veteran teachers (who you see has a rapport with, and mutual respect from the students) and find out how they built that into their classroom.

I am not suggesting my "Patience Plan" is all you need, but based on my personality and facilitation skills, I found that it worked very well for me.

我的理念是在多年的夏令營教學、工作和管理中形成的。我對自己學到的東西不會感到理所當然，因為我是在別人的指導、討論和觀察中做到的，他們都做得比我好。我自己對學習的尊重以及我在提高領導才幹方面的能力，部份原因是，我認識到了自己可以從他人的智慧和經驗中學到很多東西。找到你尊重的人。「解讀」他們，與他們談話並徵求他們的意見，以幫助塑造你自己的理念和計劃。

My philosophy was shaped over many years of teaching, working, and administrating my summer camps. I do not take credit for what I learned because I did it with the guidance, discussion, and observations of others who did it better than I did. Part of my own respect for learning and for my ability to grow my leadership skills stems from the recognition that there is much to be learned from the wisdom and experience of others. Find those you respect. "Read" them, interview them and seek their advice, to help shape your philosophy and your plan.

根本上說，我的理念始於考慮人的需求的同時也了解他們所處的狀況。將二者融合在一起後，它為我提供了人類意識的基礎，而這正是我藉以進行觀察的視角。

At the core, my philosophy begins with understanding the human condition while considering human needs. When blended, it provides me with a basis of human awareness, which becomes the lens I look through.

我認為人在基本上和本質上是自私的，在大多數情況下，我們尋求獲得即刻滿足。大多數人在有需要的時候都想立刻得到他們要的東西，並為了獲得它而做出重大妥協。對許多人來說，這些妥協的價值觀之一就是說出真相，而且是全部的真相。多年來，我評斷過無數營員和學生之間的衝突。我認為我已經非常擅長找出真相，這些真相經常揭示出欺騙的方面或至少已經發生的其他情況。最初總是以「他做了某事，或者她說了某句話」開始，通常也是由最初被認定受冤屈的人發起控訴的。透過許多這樣的經歷，我的詢問技巧、對人類反應的理解雖然不是百分之百準確，卻得到了提高。經驗沒有捷徑，我會保持學習。人際衝突的許多根源來自於自私和「我們想要時就能得到」。其他衝突源於口頭、誤會或曲解的傷害性話語。

I think humans are basically and intrinsically selfish, and we seek immediate gratification in most instances. Most humans want what they want, when they want it and make significant compromises in their values to get it. One of those compromised values for many is telling the truth... the whole truth. I have listened to countless camper and student conflicts over the years. I think I have become pretty good at pulling out the nuggets of truth which often reveal aspects of deception or at least alternative circumstances that have taken place. What starts out as a "he did, or she said" usually turns out to have been initiated by the one initially thought to have been wronged. My interrogation skills, understanding of human responses and reactions, though not 100% accurate, have been sharpened through many such experiences. There is no shortcut for experience, and I continually learn as I go. Many sources of interpersonal conflict arise from selfishness and having "wants" when "we want." Other conflicts arise out of hurtful words, either spoken, misunderstood or misinterpreted.

學生或營員發生衝突時，我覺得自己應該用己身經驗幫他們解決，而我也是最適合處理此事的人。但是，我認為有很多情況可以用對等調解來處理。我鼓勵發展學生領導。儘管並不總是那麼完美，但我發現那些願意參與此過程的學生將其視為寶貴的、賦權的領導學習經驗。我認為，花時間發展年輕人本身的技能，使他們能夠創建和運行學生解決會議，對於老師來說是值得的投資。像其他任何事情一樣，初期投資需要時間，但是如果管理和調整得當，這對你的學生領導和（作為老師的）你都是有益的。

There are student or camper conflicts that arise that I feel deserve my experience and that I am best equipped to manage. However, there are many cases that arise which I think could be first handled and dealt with by using a peer mediator. I encourage the development of student leadership opportunities. Whereas not always perfect, I find that those students willing to partake in the process find it as a valuable and empowering leadership learning experience. I think that taking the time to develop the skills in young people that would allow them to create and run Student Solution Sessions would be a worthwhile investment for a teacher. Like anything, the initial investment takes time, but if managed and shaped properly, it can be good for your student leaders and for you as the teacher.

人際衝突過程
Interpersonal Conflict Process

最好以書面形式進行，口頭解釋也行。當「法律」以書面形式出現時，人們對真理和後果的理解程度往往會有所不同。當一個學生覺得自己與另一個學生發生衝突時，立即參考「**尊重他人**」指南，並提出一些問題將大有幫助：

It is good to have this in writing, as well as explained verbally. There tends to be a different level of understood truth and consequences when the "law" is in writing. When a student comes in feeling they conflict with another student, it is helpful to immediately refer to the RESPECT FOR OTHERS guideline by asking a few simple questions:

(1) 你在不尊重這個人的情況下做了什麼？
(2) 你是否嘗試過親自與其交談以向對方解釋你的感受？

(3) 你是否嘗試不輕易評斷他們，並告訴自己，他們的言行不是有意的？

(1) Have you done anything in the situation that has not shown respect to this individual?

(2) Have you tried to speak to this individual personally to explain your feelings?

(3) Have you tried giving them the benefit of the doubt and telling yourself that is not what they intended by their words or actions?

根據上述問題的回應，我們再決定下一步如何進行。作為老師，學生是信任你的，因此你要對他們表達的情感表現同理心。你希望這對他們個人來說是一次有價值的情商提升體驗，因此你的最初反應很重要。根據雙方所講的故事，如果你認為與你談話的人有明顯的過失，那麼請你告訴他們，聽起來他們對該問題能有更好的處理方式，並鼓勵他們回頭去與對方直接交談以制定雙方都滿意的解決方案。可以向學生建議，討論還必須包括道歉，並且必須以重建的態度進行道歉，以便這個訊息可以被對方聽進去。學生對你的建議的回應決定了下一步該怎麼做。

Based on their responses, we decide how best to proceed. As the teacher, they came to you in trust, so you want to show empathy to their expressed feelings. You also want this to be a valuable EQ sharpening experience for them personally, so your initial response is significant. If, based on the story told, you sense that clear fault rests with the individual you are speaking with, you tell them that it sounds like their contribution to the matter could have been handled better and encourage them to return to the individual with a focus on talking directly to the individual to work out a solution with which they are both satisfied. Suggest to the student that part of the discussion must include an apology and that it has to be given with an attitude of rebuilding so the message can be heard. The student's response to your suggestion determines the next step of the process.

學生嘗試我的建議，或者告訴我，他們認為這樣的面對面在心理上不感到安全的時候，我會用**「學生解決方案」會議**來賦權給他們。學生解決方案會議是由學生召開的會議，參與者是經過預先批准和訓練有素的學生解決方案委員會的成員。當學生向該委員會提請關注時，該學生的同齡人將審理該個案。委員會根據學生的培訓和對問題的理解，討論情況並為學生提供解決方案。關於學生解決方案會議委員會的說明——你可以選擇並確定接受該委員會的標準，但請務必選擇受人高度重視並具有出色情商的學生。你的學生委員會成員必須是那些受到普遍尊重的成員，他們將保持公平、公正並具有較強的社交技巧。績點和高智商倒不一定會在委員會成員的選擇中起很大的作用。對於那些在學術上苦苦掙扎但表現出始終如一的高情商技能的人來說，這個委員會的成立可能是他們理想的領導場所。你可以草擬一套簡單的標準，以選擇該委員會的成員，還可以使用學生提名或徵求意見的方式，說明為什麼有人應該或不應該加入委員會。最終，教師應根據一組規定的標準做出最終選擇。這是領導職務，理應這樣對待。選擇錯誤的學生，該過程就可能會遭遇失敗。選擇正確的解決方案，它就將為健康的衝突解決提供潛在的變革機會以及強大的情商提升機會。

When students have tried my suggestion, or if they tell me that they do not feel such an encounter is psychologically safe for them, I empower them with another plausible path using a STUDENT SOLUTION SESSION. A student solution session is a peer session with pre-approved, and trained classmates who are part of a Student Solution Committee. When a student brings a concern to this committee, the student's peers hear the case. The committee discusses the situation and offers solutions to the student, based on their training and understanding of the problem. A note about the student solution session committee - The criteria for acceptance on to this committee can be selective and determined by you, but be sure to pick students who are highly regarded and have exemplified strong EQ skills. Your Student Session

Committee members must be among those generally respected and who will be impartial, fair, and possess strong social skills. Grade point average and high IQ should not necessarily weigh heavily into committee selection. This committee formation may be the perfect leadership place for someone who is struggling academically, but who demonstrates consistently high EQ skills. You can draft a simple set of criteria to use in selecting members of this committee and you can also use student nominations or solicited opinions as to why someone should or should NOT be on the committee. Ultimately, the teacher should make the final choice based on a prescribed set of criteria. This is a leadership position and should be treated as such. Select the wrong student and the process may fail. Pick the right ones and it will provide a potentially transformational opportunity for change as well as a powerful EQ sharpening opportunity in a healthy conflict resolution process.

以下是關於**學生解決方案會議**工作方式的詳細訊息：感到自己面臨人際衝突的學生可以請求召開學生解決方案會議。該學生將填寫「**學生解決方案會議**」申請表，並提交給委員會考慮。該委員會（我建議五至七名成員，取決於班級人數）開會審議情況。委員會可以批准所請求的會議，或者可以建議先召開會議向委員會進行澄清。

Here are the details about how a STUDENT SOLUTION SESSION works: A student who feels they are struggling with an interpersonal conflict can request a Student Solution Session. That student will fill out the STUDENT SOLUTION SESSION request form and present it to the committee for consideration. The committee (I suggest 5-7 members depending on the class size) meets to consider the situation. The committee may grant the requested session or may suggest a clarification meeting with the committee first.

如果請求被批准，委員會成員將與該學生會面，並告知他／她需要召開會議。在會議開始前,兩名委員會成員可以和需要達成共識的學生會面,或者如果不可行的話,他們可以決定開始澄清情況的細節,並記錄下來。他們應該知道此時並不假設誰有錯、誰清白。他們的首要任務是表示對解決人與人之間的衝突的尊重,並維護所有人的利益。屆時,受要求的學生和提出要求的學生都將被邀請參加**學生解決方案會議**。會話應安排在雙方都同意的時間,但必須在提交請求後的三十六小時內進行。(延遲時間超過三十六小時可能意味著無視提出要求的學生,並且還可能冒著事件改變或問題進一步升級的風險。)因為你將這一過程融入了課堂文化中,所以被要求參加衝突會議的學生無法拒絕該會議。請記住,既不假定誰有錯,也不假定誰清白。會議目的是提高所有人的情商,並使人們更好地理解大家的感受和環境。判斷誰有錯可能是最終的結果,並可能有相應的後果,但尋求真相並尊重流程是至關重要的。

If the request is granted, a committee member will meet with the student and inform him/her that a session may need to take place. Prior to the session, 2 committee members may meet with the student about whom the request was made to try to come to a mutual agreement, or, if that is not possible, they may decide to begin getting the thoughts and details of the situation clarified and documented. They should know that there is no guilt or innocence assumed. Their first priority is to show a respect for resolving an interpersonal conflict for the betterment of all involved. At that point, both the requesting student and the student about whom the request was made are invited to a STUDENT SOLUTION SESSION. The session should be scheduled at a time agreeable to both, but it needs to happen within 36 hours of the request submission. (Delays longer than 36 hours may imply disregard for the requesting student and may also risk the possibility of the story changing, or the problem escalating even further.) Because you build this process into your class culture, a student who is invited to a conflict session cannot refuse the session. Remember, neither guilt nor innocence is assumed. The purpose is to sharpen the EQ of all and to arrive at a better place of human understanding of feelings and circumstances. Guilt may be the eventual result, and consequences may also be included, but seeking the truth and respecting the process is crucial.

學生解決方案會議不應由老師參加,而應由兩名受過訓練的學生委員會成員進行調解。在此計劃中,你作為老師的最大時間投入必須是對學生委員會成員的培訓。如果你沒有充份培訓領導者,則會議過程將遭遇失敗。他們都必須保持公正,在所有事實經過闡明之前,他們不得妄下判斷。成員應始終尋求問題的清晰闡述,並對各方分享和表達的感受表示同情。在這些會議中分享的任何內容都必須保持隱私,如果成員在委員會之外共享相關訊息,則立即將其除名。同樣,調解員應避免在會議期間做出任何判斷或表達自己的感受。這些會議的目的是在委員會成員的情感支持下(希望所有學生都參與提名或選舉),為參與會議的各方創造一個安全的地方,以相互尊重和誠實地分享各自的看法。理想的情況下,要求參加會議的人與被邀請參加會議的人一樣安全。

A STUDENT SOLUTION SESSION should not be attended by the teacher, but should be mediated by 2 trained student committee members. In this program, your biggest time investment as the teacher has to be in the training of the student committee members. If you do not adequately train your leaders, the session process will fail. They all must be impartial, and they cannot pass judgment until all the facts have been illuminated. Members should always seek clarity and show empathy for all feelings shared and expressed. Anything shared in these sessions must be regarded as private, and members would be immediately removed if they shared any of the details outside of the committee. Likewise, peer mediators should refrain from giving any judgments or expressing their feelings during the session. The sessions are to be about creating a safe place for those involved to share respectfully and honestly in front of one another with the emotional support of committee members (that hopefully all students have had a part in nominating or electing).

Ideally, the individual requesting the session feels as safe as the person invited to the session.

會話中的過程無法真正編寫腳本,但應強調某些原則。

1. 所有參與者將致力於表現出對自我、他人以及在整個過程中可能發生的學習的尊重。

2. 雙方有機會與有關各方或彼此之間誠實坦率地分享自己的看法。會議請求者將被賦予首先發言的權利。在請求者說完他／她的所有內容之前,不允許受邀者講話。

The process in the session cannot really be scripted, but certain principles should be stressed.

1. All involved will commit to demonstrating respect for self, others, and the learning that can happen through the process.

2. Both sides will have the opportunity to share honestly and directly with or between those involved. The session requester will be given the privilege to speak first. The one invited will not be permitted to speak until the requester has said all he/she needs to say.

由於「個人感受」可能已經受到傷害,因此必須建立基本規則。以下是一些基本規則的建議:

Because "feelings" may already be hurt, establishing ground rules is necessary. Here are some suggested ground rules:

1. 會話請求者將被授予第一個發言的機會。

1. The session requester will be granted the first opportunity to speak.

2. 「受邀者」應在給予回應之前先傾聽。

2. The "invited guest" shall listen before being given the opportunity to respond.

3. 鼓勵並期許各方使用尊重的話語和以「我」為主的語言（如：我感覺，我注意到，我希望，我感覺，我意識到）。不以這種方式參與進來則會破壞整個過程，並可能損害學生解決衝突的能力。

3. Respectful discourse and "I" language (I feel, I noticed, I hope, I sense, I perceived) will be encouraged and expected from all parties involved. Failure to engage in this manner will damage the process and may compromise the ability of the students to resolve the conflict.

4. 我們強調同理心的定義——無論內心是否同意他們的感受，能夠感受他人感受的能力。他們表達的感情構成了**他們的事實**，但那不一定是**事實本身**。

4. We stress the definition of empathy - the ability to feel what the other person may feel, regardless of whether you agree or disagree. Their expressed feelings make up THEIR reality, not necessarily THE reality.

5. 在給每個參與者公平的分享時間之後，委員會成員將發問以進行澄清。重要的是，委員會成員的問題不得打斷或干擾雙方的分享。委員會成員在聆聽時應寫下問題，並在分享停止後向他們發問。

5. Committee members will ask clarifying questions after each participant has been given fair time to share. It is important that committee member questions do not interrupt or interfere with the sharing. Committee members should write down questions while they are listening and ask them after the sharing has stopped.

6. 控制會議請求者和受邀者的情緒是必不可少的，但並不總是那麼容易做到。通常，情緒可能以哭泣或憤怒的形式表現出來。委員會應設法避免任何極端的情緒表現，並在必要時進行管理。眼淚並不總是表明另一方做錯了事，因此，認為哭泣的人確實承受別人對他們造成的「傷害」是不正確的。許多學生可以用眼淚獲得同情，或出於其他許多原因而這樣做。憤怒、對後果的恐懼和其他情緒都容易讓雙方不勝負荷。委員會成員必須讓會議保持訊息和細節的清晰，而非指責是誰的過錯。

6. Controlling the emotions of both the session requester and the one invited is essential, but not always easy. Frequently, emotions may pour out in the form of tears or even anger. The committee should try to avoid and manage any extreme displays of emotions. Tears do not always indicate a wrong has been done and, therefore, it would be incorrect to assume that the person crying is so distraught over the "harm" done to them. Many students can turn on and off the flow of tears to gain sympathy, or for a host of other reasons. Anger, fear of consequences, and other emotions can easily overwhelm both parties. Committee members must keep the session about clarity of information and details, and not about assigning fault or blame.

7. 一旦會議請求者和受邀者同意不再發言，會議應以委員會一名成員的閉幕詞結束。結束語聽起來大致是：「**我們謹代表學生解決方案委員會，感謝你們每個人今天同意來到這裡。我們相信，有機會聚在一起表達和分享感受，交流互動是健康的事情，並且有助於個人成長和我們團隊（班級）的成功。重要的是，這次會議應作為最後的場所，以便對相關情況進行考慮和決定。本委員會的目標是，請求者和受邀者都認為他們的聲音和經歷很重要。我們將作為委員會開會討論雙方分享的事實和感受，然後在三十六小時內（如果時間和計劃允許的話）與雙方重新開會。我們認為至關重要的是，兩者之間的任何互動和個人交流都應積極而有益。如果隨後的個人互動是報復性的，或試圖讓對方感到尷尬或暴露對方，則委員會可以決定在此問題上採取其他相關步驟。應積極維護學生解決方案會議，以保持不滿情緒處於安全範圍，以期達到個人理解和雙方關係的恢復。與此相反的任何互動將不利於和解的達成和問題的解決。當我們所有人都離開這個地方時，讓我們同意不與別人分享此次會議的內容或情感，除非我們彼此之間直接互相分享。任何其他做法**

都將被視為對流程及其預期結果的違反。」

7. Once the session requestor and the invited person agree that they have no more to say, the session should conclude with a closing statement by one of the committee members. The closing statement should sound something like: *"On behalf of the Student Solution Committee we want to thank each of you for agreeing to be here today. We believe the opportunity to come together to express and share feelings, and exchange mediated interaction is healthy and helpful to the personal growth and the success of our group (class). It is important that this meeting serve as a final place to allow the situation to be considered and decided upon. It is the goal of this committee that both the requestor and the invited guest feel that their voice and experience matters. We will meet as a committee and discuss the facts and feelings shared, then reconvene with both of you within 36 hours (if timing and schedule permits). We believe it is crucial that any interaction and personal exchange between both be positive and helpful to the cause. Should subsequent personal interaction be vindictive or seek to embarrass or expose the other amongst peers, the committee may decide to take additional steps in the matter. The Student Solution Session shall be actively preserved as a safe place to air grievances and feelings, in hopes of reaching personal understanding and the restoring of relationships. Any interaction to the contrary will be detrimental to the cause of reconciliation and resolve. As we all leave from this place, let us agree to not share the content or emotions expressed unless we do so directly with one another. Anything else will be considered a breach of respect for the process and its intended result."*

8. 說完之後，會議可以休會，直到另行通知。

8. With that, the meeting can be adjourned until further notice.

9. 然後，委員會**在老師在場的情況下**召集會議，討論調查結果和雙方表達的訊息。委員會不得與非委員會成員討論任何會議的任何細節。

9. The Committee will then convene in the presence of the teacher to discuss the findings and information expressed. The committee may not discuss any details of any meeting with non-committee members.

10. 委員會將決定他們如何應對請求者和受邀者，以幫助解決人際衝突。陳述的事實必須經過仔細考慮。當務之急是會議請求者發現他／她的聲音和感受得到了證實和仔細考慮。同樣，受邀學生也必須感到被認可和傾聽，這樣他們才能認為該過程是公平的。

10. The committee will decide how they will respond to both the requestor and the invited person with the intent of helping to heal the personal conflict. Careful consideration must be given to the facts as they were presented. It is imperative that the session requestor finds that his/her voice and feelings were validated and carefully considered. Likewise, the student invited to the session also must feel validated and heard for the process to be considered fair.

11. 對結果的判斷應在下次會議上提出。聽起來大致是這樣的：「**學生解決方案委員會的成員要感謝每個人為解決人際矛盾所做的貢獻表現出的興趣。成立該委員會的目的是讓我們所有人都學會如何更好地處理和嘗試解決人際衝突。私下處理個人之間的分歧也是可以的，但有時候當這類分歧被帶到委員會時，可以達到更好的清晰度。委員會在此為所有學生提供服務，透過這種做法，我們大家都將學習並從中受益。我們為請求者和受邀者提供服務。我們對調查結果的決定對我們擁有的任何個人友誼都是公正的，在本次會議中，每個人都應對此保持尊重。本委員會的目的僅僅是為了促進在這種情況下的公正判斷，從而使兩個人都能實現個人關係的恢復。我們並不是要尋求錯誤或清白的判決，而是要在這種情況下尋求澄清事件。因為透過澄清，我們便獲得了同理心、知識以及對他人感受和感知的尊重。在聽完雙方意見，並仔細考慮和討論**

了所陳述的所有事實之後，學生解決方案委員會希望對我們在這種情況下發生的事情進行評估。（領導委員會成員根據與會人員給出和聽取的事實清楚地陳述調查結果。）我們認為可以在以下過程中實現解決和恢復。」（「以下過程」是一個措詞正面的和解聲明，其中每個人的感受都得到證實和表述，但同時又以尊重的方式清楚而小心地澄清了誰「有錯」。如果做出了相應後果的建議，請在此處一併說明。）

A judgment of findings shall be presented in the next meeting. It may sound something like this: *"The members of the Student Solution Committee want to thank each individual for his/her contribution and interest in resolving the personal conflict. The committee is established with the intent that we all learn how to better handle and try to resolve inevitable interpersonal conflicts. Handling such disagreements privately between individuals is ideal, but sometimes better clarity can be achieved when brought before the committee. The Committee is here to serve all students and, in doing so, we all can learn and benefit. We serve both the requestor and the invited. Our decision on the findings is impartial to any personal friendships we have and should be respected by each person in this meeting. The intent of this committee is simply to facilitate impartial judgment in the situation so that both individuals can achieve personal restoration of the relationship as a result. It is not that we seek to find guilt or innocence, as much as it is for us to find clarity in the circumstances. For through clarity, we gain empathy, knowledge, and the respect for the feelings and perceptions of others. After having listened to both individuals, and after careful consideration and discussion of all facts as they were presented, the Student Solution Committee would like to give our assessment of what we think happened in the situation. (A lead committee member states the findings clearly, based on the facts as they were given and heard by those in attendance). We think resolution and restoration can be achieved in the following process."* (The "following process" is a positively worded reconciliation statement where each person's feelings are validated and re-stated, but also where aspects of "guilt" are clearly and delicately stated in a respectful manner. If consequences are recommended, they are delineated here, and at this time, as well.)

12. 積極和解——該聲明應大聲朗讀（並以書面形式提供給所有相關人員）。「生活中充滿了分歧和衝突。它是人類社會所不可避免的一部份。人類受到情感的影響，情感即是我們的情緒。它們可以控制我們的生活和應對方式。因為我們感受，所以我們在意。因為我們在意，所以我們的分歧可以被深刻地感受，因此必須謹慎，並以尊重的態度加以處理。情況就是這樣。一個人深受他／她的情緒影響，並尋求解決人際衝突的方法。雙方都在意自己的感受，因為他們在意，所以他們尋求解決衝突的幫助。這是令人欽佩並且可取的做法。在人為事件中，如果有分歧的人找不到健康的方法來解決問題，他們就可能會轉向不利的方法，從而破壞人際關係並導致進一步的衝突。」

12. POSITIVE RECONCILLIATION - This statement should be read aloud (and given in writing) to each person involved. *"Life is full of disagreements and conflicts. It is an inevitable part of human society. Humans are affected by feelings and feelings are our emotions. They can control our lives and responses. Because we feel, we care. Because we care, our disagreements can be felt deeply and therefore must be carefully and respectfully managed. That was the case here. One individual was deeply affected by his/her emotions and sought resolution for the interpersonal conflict. Both parties cared about their feelings and because they cared they sought assistance in solving the conflict. This is admirable and desirable. In the course of human events, if people who disagree cannot find healthy ways to resolve problems, they may turn to less favorable methods, which destroy relationships and lead to further conflict."*

「當然，大多數人不喜歡衝突解決會議。但是，參與其中是發展一項必要且有價值的生活技能。我們希望該解決過程擺脫任何先入為主的想法,並提供對關係和人類尊重的簡單恢復。進行的過程使每個人的感受都得到傾聽和考慮,並根據其所分享的事實做出決定。兩個人都向其提交了自己的陳述,因此,每個人都應該尊重所執行的過程。現在,我們要求成熟和寬恕,以便進行實現療愈和恢復的目的。」

"Granted, most people do not enjoy conflict resolution sessions. However, participation in them is a necessary and valuable life skill to develop. We wanted this resolution process to be free from preconceived ideas and to provide simple restoration of the relationship and human respect. The process undertaken allowed each person's feelings to be heard and considered, and a determination was made based on the facts shared. Both individuals submitted to it and, as a result, each should respect the process that was carried out. We now ask for maturity and forgiveness to allow healing and restoration to take place."

「我們不要求你們奇蹟般地成為最好的朋友,而只是要求你們尊重各自所表達的感受和在恢復關係的過程中進行投資的願望。恢復的很大一部份是回到一個相互理解和相互尊重的位置。為了向前邁進,衝突中的個人感到被傾聽、重視和理解是很重要的。在理想情況下,感到「冤枉」的一方現在可以感受到寬容,並本著寬恕的精神向前邁進。受邀者同樣可以承擔一些衝突責任,更能理解請求者的感受,並向前邁進。」

"We do not ask that you magically become best friends, but that you simply respect the feelings expressed and the desire to invest in the process of relationship restoration. A big part of restoration is getting back to a place of understanding and mutual respect. It is important that, in order to move forward, individuals in conflict feel heard, valued, and understood. Ideally, he/she who felt 'wronged' can now feel validated and move forward in the spirit of forgiveness. In the same way, the person who was invited into the resolution session can accept some responsibility for the conflict, better *understand the feelings expressed by the requester and move forward as well."*

接下來的步驟：「我們希望大家尊重現在所進行的過程。我們希望每個人都可以從中學到東西，並在學習如何更好地應對未來的人際衝突中提高自己的情感成熟度。希望所有參與者都同意不詆毀或貶低參與該解決會議的任何其他人員。不將解決方案的內容向朋友或其他人分享。會議應保持私密性，其唯一目的是恢復人際關係。如果學生解決方案委員會得知某人將討論的內容與他人進行分享，則可以對該人採取進一步的紀律處份。分享此處所說的話只會阻礙關係的恢復，並損害那些將來需要此類幫助的人。維護本委員會的誠信和聲譽對我們來說至關重要，因此，參與其中的每個人也應如此。」

Next steps: *"It is our desire that the process undertaken be respected. We hope that everyone can learn from it and grow in their emotional maturity, having learned how to better deal with future personal conflicts. It is expected that all participants agree to not slander or disparage any other person involved this resolution session. The details of what was said or decided will not be shared with friends or others. The sessions should remain private and for the sole purpose of restoring personal relationships. If the Student Solutions Committee were to hear one person sharing about what was discussed, then further discipline action could be taken against that individual. To share what was said would only serve to hinder any relationship restoration and damage this process for those who need such help in the future. Preserving the integrity and the reputation of this committee is of the utmost importance to us and so it should also be to everyone who has been part of it."*

繼續前行
Moving Forward

學生解決方案委員會是「耐心計劃」的一部份。作為領導者，你正在嘗試創建和培育一種社群內部相互尊重的文化。這種尊重有助於訓練他們的情商，並為他們提供實用的構建基礎。建立個人尊重的文化並不能消除人際衝突，但確實為解決出現的問題提供了一個明智而有價值的過程。這也是學習過程的一部份。進行構建需要時間和投資，但是正確完成構建會為個人和整個班級帶來巨大的好處。

The Student Solutions Committee is part of the Patience Plan. As the leader, you are trying to create and foster a culture of community respect for one another. This respect helps train their EQ and gives them practical building blocks for the future. Building a culture of individual respect does not eliminate personal conflict, but it does provide a sensible and worthwhile process for resolving issues that arise. This, too, is part of the learning process. It takes time and investment to build, but there are great individual and class-wide benefits when it is done correctly.

我發現，當我精心構建期望的社會模型，清晰地傳達、執行和公開討論時，違紀情況和人際衝突會大大減少。如果一切順利，學生解決方案委員會就不需經常開會，因為尊重的文化已牢固地植根於你的課堂。

I find that when I carefully construct the social model of expectations, clearly communicate it, enforce it, and openly discuss it, discipline situations and interpersonal conflicts are significantly reduced. If all goes well, the Student Solutions Committee doesn't meet that often, because the culture of respect is firmly rooted in your classroom.

這種類型的課堂文化並不是奇蹟般發生的，但是當它完全根植於你的身份以及你作為老師的領導方式時，它看起來就很神奇。最終，班級的學生會在已經了解你的課堂文化和聲譽的情況下開始。隨著時間的流逝，你需要做的越來越少，因為學生會談論並傳播有關你作為領導者所傳達的訊息。即將開設的新班級已經聽說過你領導的文化和過程。它確實需要大量的早期投資，但是一旦奠定了基礎，你的管理就將變得越來越容易。

This type of classroom culture does not happen magically, but when it is fully entrenched in the fabric of who you are and how you lead as a teacher, it is magical to observe. Eventually, you will have students starting in your class already knowing your classroom culture and reputation. With each year that passes, you will do less and less because students will talk and spread the word about you as a leader. New classes coming in will already have heard about the culture and process of your leadership. It does require heavy early investment, but when the foundation is set, it becomes easier and easier for you to manage.

經驗沒有捷徑。經驗就像是教育——你可以汲取經驗教訓，並將其應用於你所面臨的各種情況。作為一名教師和領導者，你將評估你正在建立和投資的文化過程，以便在遇到新情況時，可以利用自己的經驗來解決新問題。「耐心計劃」是一個有用的工具，不僅可以用於管理你的課堂，還可以指導你的學生發展更高的情商，並以更好的尊重和理解來解決難以避免的人際衝突。

There is no shortcut for experience. Experience is a lot like education - you draw upon lessons learned and apply them to situations faced. As a teacher leader, you will evaluate the culture process you are establishing and investing in, so that as new situations are encountered, you will draw on your experience to solve new problems. A Patience Plan is a helpful tool, used not only to manage your classroom, but also to mentor your students into developing a stronger EQ and certainly a greater respect for, and understanding of, the resolution process for those inevitable times of interpersonal conflict.

協作的藝術 The Art of Facilitation

www.ingramcontent.com/pod-product-compliance
Lightning Source LLC
Chambersburg PA
CBHW052205090526
44583CB00017BA/2138